Studies in Applied Philosophy, Epistemology and Rational Ethics 81

Studies in Applied Philosophy, Epistemology and Rational Ethics (SAPERE) publishes new developments and advances in all the fields of philosophy, epistemology, and ethics, bringing them together with a cluster of scientific disciplines and technological outcomes: ranging from computer science to life sciences, from economics, law, and education to engineering, logic, and mathematics, from medicine to physics, human sciences, and politics. The series aims at covering all the challenging philosophical and ethical themes of contemporary society, making them appropriately applicable to contemporary theoretical and practical problems, impasses, controversies, and conflicts.

Book proposals can be sent to the Series Editor, Prof. Lorenzo Magnani at lmagnani@unipv.it. Please include: A short synopsis of the book or the introduction chapter A Table of Contents The CV of the lead author/editor(s) For more information, please contact the Editor-in-Chief at lmagnani@unipv.it

Our scientific and technological era has offered "new" topics to all areas of philosophy and ethics – for instance concerning scientific rationality, creativity, human and artificial intelligence, social and folk epistemology, ordinary reasoning, cognitive niches and cultural evolution, ecological crisis, ecologically situated rationality, consciousness, freedom and responsibility, human identity and uniqueness, cooperation, altruism, intersubjectivity and empathy, spirituality, violence. The impact of such topics has been mainly undermined by contemporary cultural settings, whereas they should increase the demand of interdisciplinary applied knowledge and fresh and original understanding. In turn, traditional philosophical and ethical themes have been profoundly affected and transformed as well: they should be further examined as embedded and applied within their scientific and technological environments so to update their received and often old-fashioned disciplinary treatment and appeal. Applying philosophy individuates therefore a new research commitment for the 21st century, focused on the main problems of recent methodological, logical, epistemological, and cognitive aspects of modeling activities employed both in intellectual and scientific discovery, and in technological innovation, including the computational tools intertwined with such practices, to understand them in a wide and integrated perspective. **Studies in Applied Philosophy, Epistemology and Rational Ethics** means to demonstrate the contemporary practical relevance of this novel philosophical approach and thus to provide a home for monographs, lecture notes, selected contributions from specialized conferences and workshops as well as selected Ph.D. theses. The series welcomes contributions from philosophers as well as from scientists, engineers, and intellectuals interested in showing how applying philosophy can increase knowledge about our current world. Indexed by SCOPUS, zbMATH, SCImago, DBLP. All books published in the series are submitted for consideration in Web of Science.

Raffaela Giovagnoli · Irena Mostowicz ·
Tomàs Sigmund
Editors

AI generating New Habits. Critical Reflections

Springer

Editors
Raffaela Giovagnoli
Faculty of Philosophy
Pontifical Lateran University
Rome, Italy

Irena Mostowicz
The Global Institute for a Sustainable
Information Society (GSIS)
Vienna, Austria

Tomàs Sigmund
Prague University of Economics and Business
Prague, Czech Republic

ISSN 2192-6255 ISSN 2192-6263 (electronic)
Studies in Applied Philosophy, Epistemology and Rational Ethics
ISBN 978-3-032-31731-5 ISBN 978-3-032-31732-2 (eBook)
https://doi.org/10.1007/978-3-032-31732-2

This Springer imprint is published by the registered company Springer Nature Switzerland AG
The registered company address is: Gewerbestrasse 11, 6330 Cham, Switzerland

Preface

The present volume brings together contributions from the workshop AI Generating New Habits: Critical Reflections, held at GSIS in Vienna on 2–3 June 2025 and organized by Raffaela Giovagnoli, Irena Mostowicz, and Tomáš Sigmund under the umbrella of the IS4SI Summit 2025, Varna, Bulgaria.

The chapters published in this volume were assessed by the editors with respect to their thematic relevance, scholarly quality, and coherence with the central focus of the symposium. Since the event was organized as a workshop and scholarly community gathering rather than as a standard conference, the review process took the form of an editorial evaluation and selection process, rather than a formal double-blind peer review.

The workshop was conceived as a symposium-based scholarly gathering devoted to the philosophical, ethical, social, and legal implications of artificial intelligence in contemporary everyday life. It aimed to stimulate interdisciplinary discussion on the ways in which AI technologies reshape human practices, decision-making, communication, and forms of social interaction.

AI makes our daily life safer, easier and healthier in several ways, but it also poses serious threats to our rights and to our society overall. Not long ago AI seemed only a matter of science fiction in which heroic commander navigated space to discover new planets and forms of life. Nowadays we all are in a certain sense commanders of space vehicles. We use AI to solve problems of our daily life: to find faster ways to move from home to work, to read web pages written in another language, to find information and for a myriad of other scopes. The diffusion of AI is often appreciated because it makes things much more easy and helps to save precious time. Nevertheless, there is a price to pay. AI poses important ethical, social and legal challenges and threats to our societies. They must be carefully analyzed, mitigated and, in certain cases, eliminated. Just to mention some application fields of AI, we can consider the facial recognition that helps in different fields but presents problems of privacy and personal freedom; sexual robots that are supposed to help me that health but could normalize rape, and create privacy and anonymity problems; the enormous amount of personal data technological companies collect for commercial purposes; violation of privacy from the part of vocal assistants and the risk of demotics; the same risks are associated to the use of Google research, messages and email, app of streaming and technologies on the field of health. We would like to stimulate an interdisciplinary discussion on these kind of problems to reflect together on pro and contra of AI in our daily life.

In this context, Lorenzo Magnani reflects on the Future of Eco-Cognitive Settings. He submits to the attention of the audience a question that synthesizes many of the current problems regarding habit transformations due to the AI programs: will the future of eco-cognitive settings computationally-tailored or humanly-tailored? The challenges against human abduction and epistemic rigor on the part of what I call computational invasive "subcultures" and unwelcome effects of selective ignorance will be illustrated. Finally, he illustrates two fundamental roles played by human knowledge and the need for their continuous enhancement sustaining discoverability: to the aim of maximizing the ownership of their own destinies even in our AI era, thanks to everyday, philosophical, and scientific knowledge about natural and artificial phenomena human beings have improved their capacities to track the external world; in turn thanks to ethical knowledge humans have learned to track the behavior of other human beings to the aim of favoring cooperation.

As Intelligent Autonomous Systems (IAS) increasingly perform critical functions across domains ranging from healthcare, education and transportation to finance and warfare, the limits of direct human oversight become ever more apparent. Driven by speed, complexity, and scalability demands, control is more and more delegated not only from humans to IAS but also from IAS to other IAS. This layered autonomy raises urgent questions of responsibility, transparency, and ethical governance. Compounding these challenges is the growing behavioral impact of IAS on human users. Through feedback loops, personalized nudging, and adaptive learning, IAS are shaping and creating new human habits—often without user awareness or consent. This convergence of distributed system responsibility and AI-driven behavior modification risks undermining human autonomy, dignity, and agency. Framed within the principles of Digital Humanism, the chapter by Gordana Dodig Crnkovic proposes a multi-level multi-criteria normative framework for responsibility sharing in IAS ecosystems. It addresses both technical responsibility flows in IAS-to-IAS control structures and the ethical management of AI-driven habit formation in users. Special attention is given to high-stakes contexts such as autonomous warfare, where decision speed and autonomy come into direct conflict with moral and legal accountability. Ultimately, the chapter argues for value-sensitive design, institutional oversight, and a reaffirmation of human-centric technology governance within the framework of Digital Humanism, ensuring that while IAS enhance efficiency and decision-making, they remain aligned with human values and societal well-being.

The contribution of Patrizia Manganaro introduces some philosophical observations on the possible developments of the idea of the limit as a sense and meaning of human life, which are placed in dialogue with the most recent results of AI. We are invited to reflect on the differences between AI and human intelligence, as well as between the static memory of the artifact, with its predictive capacity and with its storage system, and the dynamic memory of the human being, intentional and creative body-living consciousness that, in the embrace of *logos* and *pathos*, is able to understand the sense of one's own finitude and one's existence in living time. The question of *humanitas* strongly challenges the relationship between philosophy and (not civilizing science, but) technology. Why? Technology is an innovative but also pervasive and potentially invasive resource, because it is rich in great opportunities as well as great risks: if it is thought in quantitative and muscular terms of "performance" and "efficiency", if it is devoted to the homologation of natural and artificial, or elaborated in the illusion of overcoming the limit of all limits, death, it can degenerate into aberrant forms of idolatry and ideology, populism and rejection, or strengthen the well-known assertion of Günther Anders, according to which, in the face of the second and third industrial revolutions, man is antiquated—obsolete, set, dismissed, liquidated, outdated.

Anna Hennessey's paper explores the emergence of a wide range of AI technologies used in spaces of pregnancy and birth, first describing some of these technologies, then laying out a framework for how they are changing social ontology and birth as a rite of passage, both from the perspective of pregnant women and from the institutional knowledge of the medical practitioners who utilize AI. Some emerging AI technologies in the field of obstetrics include the use of pregnant robots and birth simulator manikins to train obstetricians and medical staff, proposed artificial wombs powered through artificial intelligence-based systems to create real infants, and autonomously animated visual infants that have virtual nervous systems and brains. What are some of the ways that infusing experiences of pregnancy and birth with the technology of artificial intelligence transform the meaning of those experiences, as well as the rites of passage typically associated with them? While it is still too early to give a definitive answer to these questions since some of the technologies have not been fully developed or studied, this paper offers ideas on how the incorporation of AI in these ways could impact social ontology and birth as a rite of passage

As any technology, AI has an impact on society and can generate new habits. In the perspective of Technology Assessment, these new habits underlie a critical examination in order to be able to refer back to the AI design process and adjust it according to the evaluation of the habits. Wolfgang Hofkirchner considers relevant questions. Did the intended social aims come true? Are there unintended consequences? Are these consequences in conflict with other social aims? How can a restart of the design/assessment cycle contribute to a better performance regarding the social aims? Now that existential threats have turned humanity into a community of shared destiny, it has become imperative to align the scientific-technological development with the aim of preventing extermination. Imperatives must guide digitalization so as to guarantee that the new technologies are supporting survival and a good life for all and not become part of the problem. This is especially true for AI, since it is made for automating mental work. The big companies that sell AI and those that implement AI look at profit first. They don't care about blurring the line between humans and machines, if not even promoting it. Thus, instead of tools for conviviality as Ivan Illich coined it, they are prone to spread anti-humanist tools, tools that also harm the planetary habitat. Imperatives for AI are needed for change. They are derived from a set of imperatives for conviviality and another for planetarity. These sets capture the subjective and objective prerequisites of coping with the anthropogenic evolutionary crisis.

AI algorithms are revolutionizing the way products and services are customized to meet individual needs so we can observe the phenomenon of an *enhanced personalization.* They capture data on our behavior, preferences, and habits and aim at creating create unique experiences on the basis of the results. We can image to walk into a store where the products on display are curated just for you based on your past purchases and browsing history. With AI-driven personalization, this scenario is becoming a reality as AI algorithms are constantly learning and adapting to provide a more tailored experience. Businesses are using AI to segment their customers into micro-categories, allowing them to offer personalized recommendations and promotions not only to enhance the customer experience but also to increase customer loyalty and satisfaction. For example, e-commerce platforms can use AI to recommend products that are most likely to interest a specific customer, thus increasing the chances of a successful sale. Furthermore, personalized services such as personalized fitness plans, educational content, and news updates are made possible through AI algorithms that analyze user data in real-time. AI aims at understanding our habits and preferences to deliver content that is highly relevant and engaging. By harnessing the power of data and machine learning, businesses can create bespoke experiences that cater to the individual needs of each user. Raffaela Giovagnoli presents some observations about developments of AI which strongly influence our habits and our human identity. We briefly introduce the philosophical views of "posthumanism" and "transhumanism" and propose a weak compatibility between AI and human intelligence. A philosophical pragmatic view characterizes the thoughtful and critical reflections presented by Pope Francis in his participation to the G7 which we sketch and that are further developed by Pope Leo XIV on several occasions.

In her article, Renate C.-Z. Quehenberger interprets contemporary artificial intelligence as a new manifestation of the "Society of the Spectacle", in which simulations, images, and statistical models increasingly replace lived reality. Generative AI deepens the separation between truth and representation, producing a form of hyperreality grounded in probabilistic repetition rather than ontological certainty.

While AI appears as a democratic and creative tool, the author argues that it simultaneously enables surveillance, control, and the commodification of knowledge and culture, forming a digital panopticon. Drawing on Debord, McLuhan, Foucault, and Baudrillard, and contrasting them with Platonic and Vedic notions of unity, the article critiques AI hype and singularity narratives and calls for ethical reflection and the preservation of human autonomy, imagination, and responsibility.

Martina R. Fröschl explores how AI-driven tools and immersive technologies reshape the experience and interpretation of ecological data in the Anthropocene. Drawing on the artwork A Piece of Systems Ecology, the chapter combines personal observations, interviews with systems ecology researchers, and advanced reconstruction methods such as Gaussian splatting and photogrammetry to create 3D ecological narratives. AI-based techniques, including text-to-speech and text-to-3D modeling, are used to generate augmented reality storylines that communicate ecosystem dynamics to both experts and wider audiences. The contribution highlights how immersive art can integrate scientific data and subjective experience to open new perspectives on complex ecological systems.

The critically examination of ethical challenges posed by artificial intelligence was presented by Klaus Nigsch who focused particularly on large language models, from a software engineering perspective. The article identifies four core challenges—bias in training data, lack of robustness and vulnerability to adversarial attacks, data poisoning, and the significant environmental footprint of AI systems—and shows how these technical issues translate into broader societal and ethical risks. Nigsch argues that while established ethical frameworks in software engineering, such as the ACM Code of Ethics and the Software Engineering Code of Ethics, provide sophisticated guidance on ethical means and professional conduct, they remain insufficient in addressing ethical ends, that is, the long-term societal goals and public interest implications of technological innovation. To overcome these limitations, the article introduces Digital Humanism, drawing on the Vienna Manifesto, as a normative framework that enriches existing ethical codes by explicitly emphasizing democracy, inclusion, human rights, and sustainability. By mapping concrete AI challenges to ethical shortcomings and proposing Digital Humanism–enriched responses, the contribution demonstrates how software ethics can evolve beyond compliance toward a more responsible, human-centered, and societally grounded approach to AI development and governance.

The Dutch WOZO program aims to transform care for the elderly by promoting independence, home care and digital care. While intended to support individual autonomy and the sustainability of the care sector, the digital-first and home-first emphasis can have a side effect of reducing face-to-face contact, potentially exacerbating loneliness, a significant determinant of morbidity and mortality in later life. Daniel Boyd's article synthesizes current evidence on loneliness in the Netherlands; analyses how WOZO's implementation risks increasing social isolation; defines companionship requirements as assessable criteria; and evaluates the extent to which Large Language Models (LLMs) can meet these requirements to mitigate loneliness. It also addresses the risks of LLM-based interaction (over-trust, displacement of human contact, privacy and manipulation). We conclude by specifying design and governance guidelines for safe, bounded deployment of LLM companionship in care for the elderly

Yurii Mielkov examines the philosophical problem of the place and role of humans in the age of generative AI. He challenges claims that AI could replace or surpass human intelligence, arguing that generative AI and large language models are tools for formal information processing rather than thinking or creative subjects. Drawing on philosophical and historical perspectives, he shows that AI lacks contextual understanding, moral judgment, and nonlinear thinking. The chapter also highlights the risks of over-reliance and misplaced trust in AI systems, including cognitive dependency. Mielkov concludes that specifically human capacities—critical reasoning, ethical evaluation, and creative judgment—remain inaccessible to AI and therefore become even more crucial in an AI-driven world.

Liang Wang observes that social robots are reshaping the interaction between humans and technology, but consumer acceptance remains a key challenge for their widespread adoption. This article explores the role of technology perception, interaction design, and ethical issues in shaping consumer attitudes toward social robots. Firstly, technological trust is a core element; a lack of trust can lead consumers to question data privacy, security, and technological transparency, which in turn affects technology adoption. Secondly, the design of interaction modes is crucial for user experience, including voice interaction, emotional recognition, and cultural adaptability, all of which directly impact consumers' willingness to establish long-term relationships with robots. Additionally, ethical issues such as privacy protection and data misuse cannot be overlooked; if ethical design fails to keep pace with technological development, it may lead to a crisis of trust among consumers.

The article of Josef Muehlbauer examines the geopolitical competition between the United States and China over artificial intelligence (AI) and semiconductor technologies through the lens of critical peace studies (CPS). It argues that this rivalry extends beyond economic and military dominance, generating new forms of structural violence and accelerating the militarization of technological development. Microchips are analyzed as the foundational material infrastructure of digital power, with control over their supply chains representing a key instrument of discreet geopolitical influence. The paper critiques the contemporary pursuit of strategic autonomy (SA) by actors like the European Union (EU) as often replicating the competitive, zero-sum logic of the US-China confrontation, rather than fostering cooperative and equitable alternatives. Ultimately, the article proposes pathways toward de-escalation and peace-oriented governance, including confidence-building measures, inclusive multilateral frameworks, supply-chain diversification, and binding international agreements to subordinate technological development to human rights and ecological sustainability.

Tomáš Sigmund interprets Jean Baudrillard's concept of hyperreality in the context of contemporary digital technologies, especially generative artificial intelligence. Hyperreality is not defined by illusion but by saturation—an excess of visibility, information, and operationality that eliminates the distance through which meaning and truth once appeared. Building on Baudrillard's theory of simulation, symbolic exchange, and implosion, the article introduces the notion of the crack: an immanent rupture generated by the system's own drive toward total functionality. The crack manifests in gestures the system cannot fully absorb which reveal the limits of perfect transparency and continuous communication. Artificial intelligence, as the most advanced form of the simulacrum, intensifies these dynamics by producing meaning statistically and autonomously. Yet its very perfection generates new fractures—opacity, loss of authorship, and semantic exhaustion.

Finally, Irena Mostowicz focuses on chatbots, one of the most common AI products nowadays, and critically examines the multifaceted impact of ChatGPT on individuals' everyday lives, with a particular focus on its influence on social interactions and intellectual engagement. While the AI chatbot offers convenient and instant access to information, her study argues that it may also contribute to a decline in meaningful social contact and a growing reliance on algorithmic thinking, potentially undermining independent critical reasoning. Drawing on a small sample of qualitative interviews, secondary sources and observational data, the article highlights how users increasingly replace genuine human dialogue with AI-mediated exchanges. This shift may weaken social relationships and diminish critical thinking through the passive consumption of synthesized knowledge.

Taken together, the contributions gathered in this volume illuminate the profound transformation of human habits, agency, and responsibility in an age increasingly shaped by artificial intelligence. Rather than treating AI as a neutral technological tool or an autonomous force of progress, the chapters collectively emphasize its embeddedness in social practices, ethical frameworks, political power structures, and cultural imaginaries. From eco-cognitive environments and digital humanism to social robotics, generative models, care technologies, and geopolitical competition, AI emerges as a relational phenomenon—one that both reflects and reshapes human values, vulnerabilities, and aspirations.

What unites these diverse perspectives is a shared concern for preserving human dignity, autonomy, and meaning in the face of accelerating automation and delegation of agency. The volume thus argues against simplistic narratives of technological inevitability and instead calls for reflective, interdisciplinary, and normatively grounded engagement with AI. By critically examining both promises and risks, and by foregrounding responsibility, limits, and habit formation, the contributions invite readers not merely to adapt to AI-driven transformations, but to actively shape them. In doing so, this collection aims to contribute to a more humane, democratic, and sustainable digital future—one in which technological innovation remains accountable to human and planetary well-being.

Contents

AI in Care, Body, and Social Relations

Conceptual and Normative Frameworks of AI

Will Future Eco-Cognitive Environments Be Tailored by Humans or by Computers? Shaping the Habits of Cognition in a Computational World

Lorenzo Magnani(✉)

Department of Humanities, Philosophy Section and Computational Philosophy Laboratory, University of Pavia, Pavia, Italy
lorenzo.magnani@unipv.it

Abstract. Taking advantage of my logical and cognitive studies, which emphasized the crucial role played in abductive cognition by the so-called "optimization of eco-cognitive openness and situatedness", "knowledge in motion", and the concept of "epistemic irresponsibility" (Magnani 2022), the present chapter will introduce the concept of overcomputationalism, to help interpret the related concepts of pancognitivism, paninformationalism, and pancomputationalism and their impact on the role of computationalism in the current social settings. This pervasive computationalism risks AI generating new habits in cognitive processes, potentially reshaping how humans engage with knowledge. In the second part of the chapter, I will submit to the attention of the reader a question that, in my opinion, synthesizes many of the problems currently addressed by the ethics of artificial intelligence: will the future of eco-cognitive settings be computationally-tailored or humanly-tailored? The challenges against human abduction and epistemic rigor on the part of what I call computational invasive "subcultures" and unwelcome effects of selective ignorance are illustrated, particularly in how these may constrain creative cognitive habits.

Keywords: Creative abduction · Research and development · Epistemic niches · Maximization of eco-cognitive openness · Optimization of eco-cognitive situatedness

1 Shielding Ignorance: Moving Past Overcomputationalization

The concept of *overcomputationalization* describes the pervasive integration of computational processes into a wide array of entities and artifacts, ranging from digital devices like laptops and smartphones to unconventional substrates such as quantum computers, biological systems, DNA, etc. Magnani (2021). This phenomenon extends beyond traditional computational devices, embedding computational capabilities into everyday objects and natural systems. Hence, "overcomputationalization" is the excessive proliferation of computational entities, where

R. Giovagnoli et al. (Eds.): IS4SI 2025, SAPERE 81, pp. 3–13, 2026.
https://doi.org/10.1007/978-3-032-31732-2_1

both artificial and natural systems are imbued with computational tasks: this pervasive computationalization transforms *ignorant entities*–systems or objects without intrinsic cognitive or computational capacities–into computational ones, raising ethical questions about the desirability of such transformations. This process of AI shaping new habits in how systems process information may alter established cognitive behaviors, redefining interactions with environments. This trend may disrupt the balance between preserving the "ignorance" of certain entities and the drive for computational ubiquity argue that the emph.

To further contextualize overcomputationalization, it is necessary to examine its philosophical echoes and, in some sense, underpinnings, particularly *pancomputationalism*, which posits that every physical system can be understood as performing computation.[1] This view, a successor to *paninformationalism* (the idea that everything is information) and *pancognitivism* (the notion that cognition is ubiquitous), suggests that the universe itself is a computational system. Horsman et al. (2014, p. 2) challenge this by questioning what constitutes a physical system's computation. They argue that while devices like laptops running Matlab or servers processing LaTeX are clearly computational, extending this label to natural processes–like protein folding, photon paths in photosynthesis, or even a stone on the ground–risks rendering the concept of computation vacuous. If everything is a computer, the term loses explanatory power, becoming either trivially true or false (Horsman et al. 2014, p. 2).

Pancomputationalism often defends its stance by framing computation as an interpretive lens rather than an inherent property. However, I warn that this creates confusion between "computational modeling" (using computational frameworks to represent systems) and "computational explanation" (asserting that systems are inherently computational). For instance, Dodig-Crnkovic (2011, 2013, 2017) advocates an "info-computational" view, integrating pancomputationalism with informational structural realism, emphasizing the role of natural computing in understanding nature. Yet, I critique this approach, particularly when it prioritizes information or computation over physical materiality, as seen in some paninformationalist claims (Piccinini and Scarantino 2011, p. 5).

My critique of overcomputationalization hinges on its potential to overstep naturalistic boundaries. Drawing on Thom's "catastrophe theory" (Thom 1988), I argue that phenomena like infections, explained biomedically as interactions between viruses and hosts, do not inherently require informational or computational frameworks (Magnani 2018). While computational models can simulate such processes, they do not equate to scientific knowledge of the phenomena themselves. For example, modeling an infection computationally is distinct from understanding its biological mechanisms. I would caution against conflating simulation with intelligibility, as Longo clearly contends (Longo 2009, 2012, 2017):

[1] Contemporary debates about whether the universe is inherently computational or whether biological systems compute (e.g., in synthetic biology or quantum computing) reflect my concerns about oversimplified visions of reality (Piccinini 2017). I repeat, my critique urges caution against reducing complex phenomena to computational metaphors.

he highlights the limitations of digital models in capturing the variability of biological systems.

However, I certainly acknowledge the value of computational modeling in complementing natural sciences. Fisher and Henzinger (2007) describe "executable biology", where computational algorithms mimic biological processes, advocating for integration with mathematical modeling rather than replacement of biological research. I can suggest that the fact we face a situation of *disseminated computation*, as I outlined in Magnani (2021), offers a naturalized perspective on pancomputationalism, recognizing its utility while tempering its metaphysical overreach.

I provide two primary reasons to defend moderated forms of pancomputationalism and paninformationalism. First, from an evolutionary perspective, human development of *cognitive niches*–environments rich in informational and computational processes–supports the idea that computation and information have some pseudo-ontological significance (Odling-Smee et al. 2003; Laland and Sterelny 2006; Laland and Brown 2006). These niches, constructed through material culture, reflect humanity's long-standing engagement with semiosis (the process of sign-making), which underpins the philosophical inclination to view information and computation as fundamental. This engagement is further amplified by AI shaping new habits in how humans construct and interact with these niches, influencing knowledge creation behaviors.

Second, from a cognitive and epistemological standpoint, paninformationalism posits that every physical or biological state carries information (Lloyd 2002; Wolfram 2006). This perspective has fueled advancements in fields like information physics, where researchers like Chiribella et al. (2012) and Goyal (2011) develop mathematical frameworks to interpret quantum theory through information processing. While these efforts complement physics, I warn against overgeneralizing information and computation, which risks diluting their explanatory power.

Pancognitivism, aligns with Peirce's old concept of *synechism*–the metaphysical view that matter and mind are interconnected (Magnani 2009). Peirce suggested that thought extends beyond the human brain, manifesting in natural systems like bee behavior or crystal formation. This perspective supports the idea that cognition, information, and computation are ubiquitous but requires careful delineation to avoid overgeneralization. I argue that while these frameworks offer valuable insights, their limitations must be acknowledged to prevent the trivialization of scientific inquiry.

My main concern here is the moral and philosophical implications of overcomputationalization. I advocate for preserving the "ignorance" of certain entities–those we can avoid enriching with computational capacities–to maintain a balance between technological advancement and the integrity of natural systems. This stance does not oppose computational progress but calls for critical reflection on its scope and impact. The pervasive integration of computational systems in everyday life–through AI, IoT devices,[2] and smart technologies also echo my concerns about overcomputationalization. The ethical implications of transforming "ignorant" entities (e.g., natural environments, human activities) into computational ones are evident in current discussions about privacy, autonomy, and technological dependency. For instance, the deployment of AI in healthcare or education risks reducing complex human processes to algorithmic models, potentially overlooking non-computational aspects of human experience. This transformation may foster AI generating new habits in decision-making, prioritizing algorithmic efficiency over human ethical reasoning.

By distinguishing between computational modeling and scientific knowledge, as explained above, I also emphasize the need for epistemological collaboration between computational and natural sciences, ensuring that computational frameworks enhance rather than supplant traditional scientific methods: preserving the non-computational nature of certain entities allows for epistemic humility, preventing the reduction of complex phenomena to mere computational models. This distinction is pertinent to current challenges in "big data" and "machine learning". The risk of conflating data-driven models with scientific understanding is evident in fields like climate modeling or epidemiology, where overreliance on simulations can obscure underlying uncertainties (Longo 2017). I endorse a critical approach to ensure that computational tools complement rather than supplant traditional scientific methods.

Overall, I call for a nuanced understanding of computation's role in science and society, urging careful consideration of its moral and epistemological implications (Dodig-Crnkovic 2018; Horsman et al. 2021; Magnani 2014, 2017).[3]

1.1 Protecting Ignorant Entities

In the previous section, I explored the concept of overcomputationalization, defined as the excessive integration of computational capabilities into entities and artifacts, transforming ignorant entities–objects or systems lacking inherent cognitive or computational capacities–into computational ones. I warned of

[2] The proliferation of IoT devices (Smart et al. 2019), exemplifies overcomputationalization in modern society. Smart homes, cities, and wearable technologies embed computational capabilities in everyday objects, raising concerns about privacy, surveillance, and loss of human agency. Contemporary discussions on IoT ethics, such as data security and algorithmic bias, align with my warning about disorganizational consequences and the imposition of redundant propositional content.

[3] My call to protect ignorance resonates with contemporary movements like "digital minimalism" in technology. This advocates for reducing reliance on pervasive computational systems to preserve human agency and environmental integrity. For example, critiques of smart cities or surveillance technologies align with my concern that overcomputationalization may domesticate entities in ways that limit their natural or epistemic potential. Similarly, the "degrowth" movement in technology critiques the unchecked expansion of computational systems, advocating for sustainable and selective technological integration, echoing my balanced approach.

potential dangers, including societal disorganization and oversimplified philosophical views that disguise metaphysical claims as analytical studies.

Now I aim to address two issues. First, overcomputationalization risks creating unresolvable societal disruptions due to the proliferation of computationally endowed entities, such as laptops, smartphones, social networks, and unconventional substrates like those in the Internet of Things (Smart et al. 2019). Second, it diminishes the presence of "ignorant entities"–objects like buildings, streets, or clothes that traditionally carry simple informational qualities but are increasingly laden with complex, computationally driven propositional and model-based information. This often serves redundant political, ideological, or economic purposes, imposing constraints that weaken what I have illustrated as the fundamental problems of *discoverability* and *diagnosticability*, hindering *human* creative cognitive processes like abduction, that is hypothetical reasoning (Magnani 2017). This shift, driven by AI generating new habits, may alter how humans perceive and interact with these entities, potentially limiting creative exploration.

The transformation of "ignorant entities" into computational ones, I argue, reduces attention to their non-computational value, rendering them seemingly irrelevant unless infused with computational features. This trend also introduces cognitive and informational overload, distracting from the simplification that could arise from preserving their ignorance. Of course, my call to *protect ignorant entities* is not a rejection of all computationalization. I perfectly acknowledge the benefits of computational modeling, not only the obvious ones we meet every day but also in the sophisticated case of science, particularly in understanding complex biological processes like brain function, which could advance treatments for diseases such as Alzheimer's, Parkinson's, or autism (Copeland et al. 2016).

In sum, I advocate for a balanced approach, urging careful selection of what to computationalize to avoid undermining human cognition and societal harmony. "Protecting ignorant entities" preserves their simplicity and supports discoverability[4] in human cognition, while strategic computationalization can drive scientific progress without succumbing to the excesses of "overcomputationalization", in which computational modeling claims to be itself science (Copeland et al. 2017; Magnani 2019; Smart et al. 2016). This balance is crucial to prevent AI from embedding reductive cognitive habits in scientific and societal practices.

2 Will Future Eco-Cognitive Environments Be Tailored by Humans or by Computers?

In this section, I plan to examine the impact of mainstream artificial intelligence (AI) programs, such as LLMs (Large Language Models), particularly their reliance on "big data" and what I call *locked strategies*, and their broader implications for eco-cognitive settings and scientific inquiry. I will further raise concerns

[4] My emphasis on discoverability and diagnosticability ties directly to my work on *abductive reasoning*, where I explore how humans generate hypotheses through interaction with external environments (Magnani 2009, 2017).

about "overcomputationalization", in this case, where computational systems shape societal behaviors and scientific practices in ways that may undermine human creativity and ethical decision-making, potentially leading to "computationally tailored" rather than "humanly tailored" environments (Bostrom and Ćirković 2008; Bostrom 2014).

Current Generative AI systems predominantly utilize *quantity-related* big data (even if in the framework of *locked strategies*)[5], which are rigid approaches suited to well-defined scenarios, such as games with fixed rules (Magnani 2019).

This trend raises ethical concerns, as it could drive human societies to adapt behaviors and environments to fit computational tools, potentially kindizing the eco-cognitive openness in which human cognition flourishes–that is, the cognitive niche that fosters human creativity and knowledge generation. I warn that such *computationally tailored* settings could limit the flexibility of "unlocked" strategies, reducing opportunities for novel discoveries (and also efficient ethical decisions). The risk is particularly pronounced in contexts where computational systems dominate, potentially creating what we can call *eco-cognitive ethical situations* that constrain human agency embedded in computational frameworks (Bostrom and Ćirković 2008). A kind of digital transformation and social behavior can be hypothesized: the risk of computationally tailored eco-cognitive settings is evident in the pervasive influence of AI-driven platforms (e.g., social media, recommendation algorithms) that shape user behavior to align with computational logic. This phenomenon, often termed "platform capitalism" (Srnicek 2016), raises concerns about the erosion of individual autonomy and the homogenization of social interactions, echoing my worry about conforming human environments to AI tools. Such platforms exemplify AI shaping new habits in how individuals consume information, often reinforcing algorithmic biases that influence cognitive behaviors.

I aim at criticizing the influence of what I call "computational invasive subcultures"–related to groups insistently promoting computational tools, often driven by business interests, that, for example, can challenge the integrity of scientific inquiry. Indeed, some of these subcultures advocate that large databases and data analytics can replace traditional scientific methods, particularly "creative abduction" which is the process of forming interesting and novel explanatory hypotheses. (Calude and Longo 2017, p. 595) argue that the emphasis of "big data speaking for itself" undermines the scientific method, which instead relies on causal understanding rather than mere correlations. They highlight that very large databases often produce spurious correlations, such as linking a comet's

[5] In Magnani (2026) I have illustrated how eco-cognitive openness describes how cognitive systems, like large language models (LLMs), interact with environments to produce information and creative outputs via abductive cognition. Humans exhibit high eco-cognitive openness (related to high "unlocked strategies", using external resources for flexible, creative hypotheses, while LLMs rely on "locked strategies", limiting creativity. LLMs outperform humans in repetitive tasks, so paradoxically exposing human intellectual limits. Human-AI collaboration could enhance eco-cognitive openness, but risks like bias require human oversight to ensure meaningful outputs.

tail orientation to military victories, which lack causal grounding and scientific value (Calude and Longo 2017, p. 600). Such correlations, while generalizable, are often uninteresting or misleading, as demonstrated by a 2010 study by Reinhart and Rogoff (2017, p. 599). This study correlated high public debt with slow economic growth, influencing policy decisions despite later being discredited for flawed methodology and reverse causality Calude and Longo (2017).

I extend my critique to media and policy overreliance on such correlations, exemplified by European policymakers citing Reinhart and Rogoff's findings as late as 2013. I also want to quote Chris Anderson's 2008 "notable" claim that big data renders the scientific method obsolete, a conviction refuted by studies showing that spurious correlations in large datasets do not equate to scientific knowledge (Fan et al. 2015; Gandomi and Haider 2014).

There is also an AI's impact on *abductive reasoning*: I examined Google DeepMind's AlphaGo, which defeated top Go players in 2015 and 2016, showcasing AI's ability to simulate human strategic creativity (Magnani 2009). I contended that such systems operate within "locked" frameworks and warned that overhyping these achievements, often amplified by media and corporate narratives, risks oversimplifying the complexity of human reasoning. Similarly, Longo and Tendero (2007) critique the metaphor "DNA is a program", arguing that it inadequately explains the complex relationship between genome and phenotype, oversimplifying biological processes adopting reductionist computational paradigms.

We can advance that there is a tension between *computationally tailored* and *humanly tailored* eco-cognitive settings. Let us make the example of scientific inquiry: the former, driven by locked strategies and big data, may impoverish "epistemic niches"–that is, the environments that support wonderful examples of creative abduction–by prioritizing computational efficiency over human creativity. This shift could limit the discovery of new knowledge, particularly in science, where abduction relies on flexible, hypothesis-driven reasoning. I argue that the proliferation of computational tools risks creating environments where human ethical and cognitive agency is constrained, as societal structures increasingly conform to the needs of AI systems (Bostrom 2014).

Moreover, the reliance on big data introduces ethical challenges, such as the "finders, keepers" morality adopted by some big data companies, which raises questions about data ownership and privacy (Sax 2016). These concerns also refer to broader global catastrophic risks, including those posed by AI, as clearly discussed by Bostrom (2008). In sum, I advocate for fostering "humanly tailored" settings that preserve eco-cognitive openness, allowing for unlocked strategies that support creative cognition and rich ethical decision-making.

My emphasis on the ethical dimensions of AI connects to my earlier work in the book *Morality in a Technological World* (Magnani 2007), where I examined the moral consequences of technological advancements. My present concern that computationally tailored settings could impede creative cognition and also rich ethical decision-making certainly echoes my critique of the philosophical perspective of "pancomputationalism" and "paninformationalism", where I argued against reducing all phenomena to computational or informational frameworks (Magnani 2018). Indeed, by referencing "cognitive niches" (Odling-Smee et al. 2003), I situate AI's impact within my framework of human-environment interactions, where external artifacts and technologies shape cognitive and ethical behaviors. This shaping is particularly evident in how AI generates new habits in scientific inquiry, potentially prioritizing computational efficiency over creative insight.

It will also be clear to the reader that I am also engaged with Peircean philosophy, particularly the idea that cognition extends beyond the brain to include external mediators (Magnani 2009). In this perspective, my warning about the loss of eco-cognitive openness reflects my interest in preserving the conditions for high levels of human "abductive cognition", which relies on flexible, open-ended interactions with the environment to generate novel insights. My ethical warning about computationally tailored settings further connects to my previous discussions of "disseminated computation" (Magnani 2021), advocating for a naturalized approach to computation that avoids metaphysical overstatements and prioritizes human-centric epistemic and ethical goals.

3 Conclusion

The exploration of overcomputationalization and its implications for eco-cognitive environments underscored a critical juncture in the current interplay between human cognition and computational systems. The pervasive integration of computational capabilities into both artificial and natural entities raises profound ethical and epistemological questions. I illustrated this phenomenon, termed *overcomputationalization*, as related to the risk of transforming *ignorant entities*–objects or systems devoid of inherent cognitive or computational capacities–into computationally endowed ones, often at the cost of sacrificing their simplicity and non-computational value. This transformation threatens to oversimplify complex phenomena, reducing them to computational metaphors that may obscure genuine scientific understanding. I also illustrated the epistemological case related to the desired conflation of computational modeling with scientific knowledge, with the consequent risk of undermining the nuanced and free interplay between human creativity and the natural world.

The central question posed in this chapter–whether future eco-cognitive environments will be *humanly tailored* or *computationally tailored*–highlights the tension between preserving the best qualities of human agency and succumbing to the dominance of computational systems. Computationally tailored settings, driven by the so-called *locked strategies* and *big data*, prioritize efficiency and structured information processing, possibly at the expense of *eco-cognitive openness* that grants the highest levels of human cognition. This openness, essential for fostering creative abduction and rich and innovative ethical decision-making, enables humans to generate novel hypotheses and navigate complex social and scientific challenges. The rise of computational invasive subcultures, often propelled by commercial interests, further exacerbates this risk by promoting data-driven approaches that may produce spurious correlations.

In this chapter, I also indicated that my idea of protecting *ignorant entities* does not have to be considered as a rejection of computational progress but just a call for balance. By preserving the non-computational nature of certain entities, we maintain epistemic humility and safeguard the conditions for "discoverability" and "diagnosticability" in human cognition. These processes, rooted in human abductive reasoning, rely on flexible, "unlocked strategies" that thrive in environments not overly constrained by computational logic. The ethical implications are equally significant: computationally tailored settings, as seen for example in AI-driven platforms and IoT ecosystems, risk eroding individual autonomy and homogenizing social interactions, aligning behaviors with algorithmic imperatives rather than human values. By resisting to the proliferation of two many AI-driven computational habits, we can ensure that human cognitive practices remain central to shaping future eco-cognitive environments.

Ultimately, fostering "humanly tailored" eco-cognitive environments requires a commitment to enhancing human cognitive and ethical capacities. By leveraging everyday, philosophical, and scientific knowledge, humans have historically improved their ability to track the external world and foster cooperation through ethical understanding. The proliferation of computational systems must complement, not supplant, these capacities. This balance ensures that technological advancements enhance human creativity and agency rather than domesticating it. The challenge lies in resisting the allure of overcomputationalization, advocating for a naturalized approach to computation that prioritizes human-centric epistemic and ethical goals.

Acknowledgements. Parts of this chapter are excerpted from chapter five the book *Discoverability. The Urgent Need of an Ecology of Human Creativity*, Springer, Cham, 2022. For the instructive criticisms and precedent discussions and correspondence that helped me to develop my analysis, I am indebted and grateful to John Woods, Atocha Aliseda, Woosuk Park, Luís Moniz Pereira, Paul Thagard, Ping Li, Akinori Abe, Yukio Ohsawa, Pat Langley, and to my collaborators Selene Arfini, Alger Sans Pinillos, and Riccardo Dossena.

References

Bostrom, N., Ćirković, M.M. (eds.): Global Catastrophic Risk. Oxford University Press, Oxford (2008)

Bostrom, N.: Superintelligence. Strategies. Clarendon Press, Oxford, Paths, Dangers (2014)

Calude, C.S., Longo, G.: The deluge of spurious correlations in big data. Found. Sci. **22**(3), 595–612 (2017)

Chiribella, G., D'Ariano, G.M., Perinotti, P.: Quantum theory, namely the pure and reversible theory of information. Entropy **14**, 1877–1893 (2012)

Copeland, J., Dresner, E., Proudfoot, D., Shagrir, O.: Time to reinspect the foundations? Commun. ACM **59**(11), 34–38 (2016)

Dodig-Crnkovic, G.: Significance of models of computation, from Turing model to natural computation. Mind. Mach. **21**(2), 301–322 (2011)

Dodig-Crnkovic, G.: The info-computational nature of morphological computing. In: Müller, V.C. (ed.) Philosophy and Theory of Artificial Intelligence, pp. 59–68. Springer, Berlin, Heidelberg (2013)
Dodig-Crnkovic, G.: Computational dynamics of natural information morphology, discretely/continuous. Philosophies **2**(4) (2017)
Fan, J., Han, F., Liu, H.: Challenges of big data analysis. Int. J. Inf. Manage. **1**(2), 293–314 (2014)
Fisher, J., Henzinger, T.A.: Executable cell biology. Nat. Biotechnol. **25**, 1239–1249 (2007)
Gandomi, A., Haider, M.: Beyond the hype: big data concepts, methods and analytics. Int. J. Inf. Manage. **35**(2), 137–144 (2015)
Goyal, P.: Information physics–towards a new conception of physical reality. Information **3**, 567–594 (2011)
Horsman, C., Stepney, S., Wagner, R.C., Kendon, V.: When does a physical system compute? Proc. R. Soc. A **470**, 1–25 (2014). https://doi.org/10.1098/rspa.2014.0182.
Laland, K.N., Brown, G.R.: Niche construction, human behavior, and the adaptive-lag hypothesis. Evol. Anthropol. **15**, 95–104 (2006)
Laland, K.N., Sterelny, K.: Perspective: seven reasons (not) to neglect niche construction. Evol. Int. J. Org. Evol. **60**(9), 4757–4779 (2006)
Lloyd, S.: Programming the Universe: A Quantum Computer Scientist Takes on the Cosmos. Knopf, New York, NY (2006)
Longo, G., Tendero, P.-E.: The differential method and the causal incompleteness of programming theory in molecular biology. Found. Sci. **12**(4), 337–366 (2007)
Longo, G.: Critique of computational reason in the natural sciences. In: Gelenbe, E., Kahane, J.-P. (eds.) Fundamental Concepts in Computer Science. Imperial College Press/World Scientific, London (2009)
Longo, G.: Incomputability in physics and biology. Math. Struct. Comput. Sci. **22**(5), 880–900 (2012)
Longo, G.: The biological consequences of the computational world: mathematical reflections on cancer biology (2017). arXiv.org, arXiv:1701.08085
Magnani, L.: Morality in a Technological World. Knowledge as Duty. Cambridge University Press, Cambridge (2007)
Magnani, L.: Abductive Cognition. The Epistemological and Eco-Cognitive Dimensions of Hypothetical Reasoning. Springer, Heidelberg/Berlin (2009)
Magnani, L.: The Abductive Structure of Scientific Creativity. An Essay on the Ecology of Cognition. Springer, Cham, Switzerland (2017)
Magnani, L.: Computationalism in a dynamic and distributed eco-cognitive perspective. In: Dodig-Crnkovic, G., Burgin, M. (eds.) Philosophy and Methodology of Information, Vol. 1, pp. 365–288. Singapore, World Scientific (2018)
Magnani, L.: AlphaGo, locked strategies, and eco-cognitive openness. Philosophies **4**(1), 8 (2019)
Magnani, L.: Computational domestication of ignorant entities. Unconventional cognitive embodiments. Synthese **198**, 7503–7532 (2021)
Magnani, L.: Discoverability. The Urgent Need of an Ecology of Human Creativity. Springer, Cham, Switzerland (2022)
Magnani, L. Beyond stochastic parrots: Lacanian reflections on LLMs as superior masters of the symbolic. Synthese **207**(6), Article 260 (2026). https://doi.org/10.1007/s11229-026-05648-0.
Odling-Smee, F.J., Laland, K.N., Feldman, M.W.: Niche Construction. The Neglected Process in Evolution. Princeton University Press, Princeton, NJ (2003)

Piccinini, G., Scarantino, A.: Information processing, computation, and cognition. J. Biol. Phys. **37**(1), 1–38 (2011)

Piccinini, G.: Computation in physical systems. In: Zalta, E.N. (ed.), The Stanford Encyclopedia of Philosophy. Metaphysics Research Lab, Stanford University, Summer 2017 Edition (2017)

Sax, M.: Big data: finders keepers, losers weepers? Ethics Inf. Technol. **18**(1), 25–31 (2016)

Smart, P., Madaan, A., Hall, W.: Where the smart things are: social machines and the internet of things. Phenomenol. Cogn. Sci. **18**(3), 551–575 (2019)

Srnicek, N.: Platform Capitalism. Polity Press, Cambridge, UK (2016)

Thom, R.: Esquisse d'une sémiophysique. InterEditions, Paris: Translated by V. Meyer A Sketch, Addison Wesley, Redwood City, CA, Semio Physics p. 1990 (1988)

Wolfram, S.: A New Kind of Science. Wolfram Media, Champaign (2002)

Digital Imperatives: Shaping AI for the Great Bifurcation

Wolfgang Hofkirchner[1,2](✉)

[1] TU Wien, Karlsplatz 4, 1040 Wien, Austria
wolfgang.hofkirchner@gsis.at

[2] The Institute for a Global Sustainable Information Society, Steinbrechergasse 15, 1220 Wien, Austria

Abstract. As any technology, AI has an impact on society and can generate new habits. In the perspective of Technology Assessment, these new habits underlie a critical examination in order to be able to refer back to the AI design process and adjust it according to the evaluation of the habits. Did the intended social aims come true? Are there unintended consequences? Are these consequences in conflict with other social aims? How can a restart of the design/assessment cycle contribute to a better performance regarding the social aims? Now that existential threats have turned humanity into a community of shared destiny, it has become imperative to align the scientific-technological development with the aim of preventing extermination. Imperatives must guide digitalisation so as to guarantee that the new technologies are supporting survival and a good life for all and not become part of the problem. This is especially true for AI, since it is made for automating mental work. The big companies that sell AI and those that implement AI look at profit first. They don't care about blurring the line between humans and machines, if not even promoting it. Thus, instead of tools for conviviality as Ivan Illich coined it, they are prone to spread anti-humanist tools, tools that also harm the planetary habitat. Imperatives for AI are needed for change. They are derived from a set of imperatives for conviviality and another for planetarity. These sets capture the subjective and objective prerequisites of coping with the anthropogenic evolutionary crisis.

Keywords: Great bifurcation · Techno-eco-social transformation · Techno-social systems theory

1 Introduction

In the midst of the last century humanity has entered a time of global challenges that pose existential threats. Meanwhile, these threats have begun to intermingle with each other to such an extent that they caused the current poly-crisis that threatens the further existence of human beings on Earth. These challenges, being manmade, can only be met by working together of a common humanity. Thus, the bifurcation social evolution is confronting our species with can be coined with systems theorist Ervin László [1, 2] the Great Bifurcation: The tipping point is near after which you can't go back—the choice

R. Giovagnoli et al. (Eds.): IS4SI 2025, SAPERE 81, pp. 14–26, 2026.
https://doi.org/10.1007/978-3-032-31732-2_2

is either a trajectory of disintegration of the current social systems by the catastrophe of barbarism, collapse and extinction [3] or a trajectory of integration into a meta- or suprasystem of a common humanity [4, 5].

This situation can be characterised as a developmental crisis of *Homo sapiens* without precedent. However, the Great Bifurcation can be mastered by a Great Transformation—a transformation of the relationships that human actors enter into with each other, the relationships that societies maintain with nature and the relationships societies exercise through their technology. All together, it is a techno-eco-social transformation that forms the objective conditions for the continuation of humanity's existence on planet Earth. It invokes planetary imperatives. Technology, in particular, that which is labelled digitalisation as well as AI, is part of these objective conditions. Since it can play either a facilitating or an inhibiting role, there is need to shape it according to the planetary imperatives.

In order to act according to the objective conditions and implement the Great Transformation, humanity must empower itself to develop into one conscious and conscientious subject *sui generis*, a subject of its own—at least by a sufficient number of social actors that understand the status of common-destiny humanity and act accordingly. A qualitative leap of human development onto the level of a worldwide living together in conviviality [6, 7] prompts to overhaul the current social capabilities of generating information along the levels of individual cognition, interactive communication and collective co-operation. The enlarging, extending and expanding of those capabilities are from now on the subjective conditions of humanity's enduring existence. They invoke convivial imperatives. Since human cognitive, communicative and co-operative capabilities are mediated by technological tools including digital and AI means, the former are impacted by the latter—again—in a facilitating or an inhibiting way, which needs alignment with convivial imperatives.

Thus, both objective and subjective human conditions desire proper shaping of technology, if survival of mankind and a humane living for all shall be assured. And proper shaping also means being clear of the properties technology can and shall be endowed with to meet these requirements.

2 AI and the Objective Conditions of Humanity's Shared Destiny

What are the planetary imperatives AI should incorporate by complying with digital imperatives?

Social relations among actors, social relations with nature and social relations with technology build kind of a hierarchy such that the social relations among actors dominate social relations with nature and the social relations with nature dominate social relations with technology. However, this top-down domination is not a strict determination. In the bottom-up direction there is emergence, which is another less-than-strict determination.

About 12,000 years ago, the type of social relations began to degenerate [8]. It tended towards antagonisms that superimposed synergisms, the until then default type by social evolution. Accordingly, the objective development logic of social relations became antagonistic.

2.1 Pan-Humanism

The antagonistic logic of relations in the social realm is governed by self-centredness (egoism). This is the structural factor that allows individual as well as collective actors to pursue particularistic interests at the expense of other actors. This is the root cause of conflicts. As long as this logic works, global challenges cannot be mastered. It is imperative to replace the logic of self-centredness with a logic of self-limitation: the inclusive logic of pan-humanism [9]. Pan-humanism is apt to unite humanity as a single whole in which all actors are entitled to share the benefits with each other. By that, the antagonistic logic gives way to a synergistic one.

The Planetary Imperative of Pan-humanism. This imperative addresses any actor. It can be formulated as follows:

"Act in such a way that the effects actualise the objective potential to build or maintain a social meta- or suprasystem which, by replacing any logic of self-centredness in social relations with a logic of self-limitation of the actors, ensures unity through diversity for all of humanity!" [10, p. 372]

The Digital Imperative of Pan-humanism. In support of pan-humanism this imperative addresses any actor engaged with design and use of Information Technology and AI. It says:

"Act in such a way that the effects contribute to the production and usage of digital technologies that support the construction or maintenance of a social meta- or supra-system of all humanity in its unity-through-diversity!" [10, p. 373]

2.2 Anthropo-Relational Humanism

The antagonistic development of social relations dominates also the relations with nature. The logic of self-centredness paves the way for a logic of self-exaltation in the eco-social realm (known as anthropocentrism). This logic allows to subjugate the natural environment and the human body to particularistic interests. Again, this logic must be exchanged for a logic of self-limitation for the sake of synergy: the inclusive logic of anthropo-relational humanism [11]. Anthropo-relationality does justice to the diversity of roles natural systems have been taking in evolution, while it also does justice to the role social systems play, such that an alliance with nature can be realised [12].

The Planetary Imperative of Anthropo-relational Humanism. This imperative again addresses any actor and can run as follows:

"Act in such a way that the effects actualise the objective potential to build or maintain an eco-social meta- or suprasystem which, by replacing any logic of self-exaltation in the social relations of nature with a logic of self-limitation of the actors, ensures an alliance with the agents of natural self-organising systems!" [10, p. 372]

The Digital Imperative of Anthropo-relational Humanism. This imperative supports the corresponding planetary imperative, again addressing actors who deal with digitalization. It is:

"Act in such a way that the effects contribute to the production and usage of digital technologies that support the construction or maintenance of an eco-social meta- or supra-system in alliance with the agents of natural self-organising systems!" [10, p. 373]

2.3 Digital Humanism

Self-centredness and self-exaltation, finally, lead to self-overestimation in the techno-eco-social realm (megalomania, almightiness). This logic of development allows the misuse of productive forces as destructive forces that affect the interests of others by their broad impact on, and depth of penetration of, the planet and its inhabitants, by side effects, long-distance effects and long-term effects. It must again be substituted for a logic of self-limitation: the inclusive logic of digital humanism [13, 14]. It includes all productive forces to serve an alliance with nature and all of humanity to enjoy a good life in peace.

The Planetary Imperative of Digital Humanism. In short, this imperative is as follows:

"Act in such a way that the effects actualise the objective potential to build or maintain a techno-eco-social meta- or suprasystem which, by replacing any logic of self-overestimation in social technological relations with a logic of self-limitation of the actors, ensures an appropriate use of artificial, hetero-organised artefacts!" [10, p. 373]

The Digital Imperative of Digital Humanism. This imperative is:

"Act in such a way that the effects contribute to the production and usage of digital technologies that support the construction or maintenance of a techno-eco-social meta- or suprasystem with the appropriate applications of artificial, hetero-organised artefacts of whatever kind!" [10, p. 373–374]

3 AI and the Subjective Conditions of Humanity's Shared Destiny

After having dealt with humanity's objective conditions in times of crises and deriving corresponding imperatives for digitalization, let's do the same for humanity's subjective conditions. Which convivial imperatives should AI support by digital imperatives?

Social information, that is, human cognition, communication and co-operation, builds according to the Triple-C model an evolutionary hierarchy [5, 15]. Human co-operation dominates human communication and human communication dominates human cognition in a less-than-strict determination and human cognition lets communication emerge and human communication lets co-operation emerge. Actors that generate social information are single actors, interacting actors or collective actors that form a social system.

The human co-operative social information capability of a collective of actors can produce "ethos", the human communicative social information capability of manifold actors can produce "consilience" and the human cognitive social information capability of single actors can produce "mindsets" [15, pp. 72–112].

Ethos, consilience and mindsets serve different functions. They are each built up of different sub-levels that are connected in a hierarchy as well.

Ethos sets goals and helps achieve them in the context of human work. Ethos nests the sub-levels of morality, of agreeability, and of sociability of social information qualities in an order of decreasing complexity: morality means the alignment of goals with socially recognised norms, values, and also interests; agreeability means a negotiation of goals that is based on partnership; and sociability means the selection of a partner in consideration of the goal.

Furthermore, consilience designs and assigns tasks according to goals in the context of human language. Consilience has requestability, argumentality, and symbolicality as linguistic sub-levels of social information qualities: requestability signifies mutual usefulness of the social information for solving tasks; argumentality concerns mutual description or explanation of the nature of the tasks; and symbolicality underpins a mutual understanding of the tasks.

Eventually, mindsets plan and control operations for solving tasks in the context of human thought. Mindsets are made up of different cognitive social information qualities like judgementability, factuality and experientiality: judgementability as the highest quality represents a deliberative assessment achieved by appropriate operations; factuality fulfils the quality of operations coming close to reality; and experientiality secures comprehensive operations.

However, with respect to the underlying self-organised hierarchies, in which the highest level is the most complex level and the lowest level the least complex one and in which the transition from one level to a lower one happens by dominance that shapes the properties below and the transition to a higher level is owed to the emergence of properties, it becomes clear that any of these social information qualities can adopt values on a range between ideal-typical poles of a best and a worst value.

Given the appearance of antagonistic logics of social development since 12,000 years, social information generation has been tending towards attempts to legitimise antagonisms, that is, domination, exploitation and oppression of one part of actors to exclude other actors from sharing the common good of society, leading 5,000 years ago to warfare [8]. These objective social structures and processes cannot find legitimation by subjective social information for a good society. Information of the highest quality is distorted and polarised. The further away the realised value of a quality is from the upper pole, the more social information loses its information quality and assumes the quality of disinformation.

Disinformation is harmful for a world in common. All social information abilities must be overhauled to counter disinformation. They must be freed from restrictions that are imposed upon them by parcellitarian interests and their scope must be generalised onto a metalevel that allows to anticipate the common good for a common humanity. Therefore convivial imperatives are necessary to shift the table. The convivial imperatives break down the issues of planetarity into three social information contexts: global governance, global dialogue and global mindsets.

3.1 Global Governance

Regarding ethos, morality can fluctuate from "moral, good, binding" to its contrary "immoral, evil, non-binding", agreeability can fluctuate from "fair" to "unfair" and sociability from "prosocial" to "antisocial". Given the global risks, how can ethos guide co-operation in a common world? An imperative is the answer.

The Convivial Imperative of Ethos for Global Governance. When aligning the goals, moral must stick to what is moral, the good and the binding; when negotiating the goals, there must be fair agreements; and when selecting the partner for the goals, this must be prosocial. Thus, for a world in common to come, it is imperative that the generic ethos turns against disinformation regarding the possible consciousness and conscientiousness of humanity as such and sets the co-operative ability at global governance. This imperative addresses a collective entity of actors:

"As collective entity of actors, act in such a way that the overall effect of your action can expand the subjective capacity for co-operation already achieved towards a planetary practice that realises the objective requirement of a next step of social evolution so that universal wisdom can be achieved that morally anticipates the value of a unity-through-diversity organisation of humanity, in particular, of pan-humanism in societal relations, of anthropo-relational humanism in ecological societal relations and of digital humanism in technological ecological societal relations!" [10, p. 377]

This ethos is a binding norm, but it is subject to rational improvements.

The Digital Imperative of Ethos for Global Governance. This digital imperative complements the convivial one in that it designs and propagates digital solutions that boost the convivial aims. Regardless of who is involved, the imperative runs as follows:

"Act so as to contribute to the production and use of digital technologies that support the emergence and sustenance of a planetary ethos as digital conscience!" [10, pp. 380–381]

Digital conscience means here digitalised conscience, a conscience that is digitally supported.

3.2 Global Dialogue

As to consilience, the requests can range from "helpful" to "unhelpful", the arguments from "truthful" to "untruthful" and the symbols from "intelligible" to "unintelligible". Given the global risks, how can consilience be the objective of communication in a common world? Another imperative is needed.

The Convivial Imperative of Consilience for Global Dialogue. When mutually solving tasks, requests must be helpful; when arguing about the tasks, arguments must be truthful; and when uttering about the tasks, symbols must be intelligible. Thus, for a world in common to come, it is imperative that generic consilience turns against disinformation regarding the possible tolerance and willingness to compromise between the members of humanity and sets the communicative ability at a global dialogue. This imperative reaches out to the multiplicity of actors:

"As diverse actors, act in such a way that the effects of your many actions can extend the subjective communication skills already achieved to a mutual understanding of the objective requirements of a next step of social evolution so that knowledge can be created and shared on a planetary scale, anticipating in conciliatory discourses the tasks of a techno-eco-social transformation of all humanity into a common system!" [10, pp. 377–78]

Consilience is here seen as a discourse including contests, but it seeks agreements that are socially compatible.

The Digital Imperative of Consilience for Global Dialogue. The second digital imperative supports the respective convivial imperative, without specification of addressees:

"Act so as to contribute to the production and use of digital technologies that support the emergence and sustenance of planetary conciliatoriness as digital intelligence!" [10, p. 381]

Digital intelligence marks here digitalised intelligence that is human intelligence digitally supported.

3.3 Global Citizenship

The mindset can have values of judgement between "right" and "wrong", of facts between "true" and "false" and of experience between "multisided" and "one-sided". Given the global risks, how can the mindsets provide mindful cognition of a common world? A third imperative gives the answer.

The Convivial Imperative of Mindsets for Global Citizenship. When operations shall be assessed, the judgement must be right; when operations shall be realistic, a fact must be true; and when operations shall be comprehensive, experience must be multisided. Thus, for a world in common to come, it is imperative that the generic mindset turns against disinformation regarding the possible mindfulness of any member of humanity and sets the cognitive ability at a global citizenship. This imperative appeals to single actors:

"As single actor, act in such a way that the effect of your action can enlarge the subjective cognitive abilities already achieved by insights into the objective requirements of a next step of social evolution so that facts and figures can be collected and interpreted that mentally anticipate the meaning of operations according to your own positioning in the overall planetary context as well as the positioning of other actors and the positioning of parts that are not actors at all!" [10, p. 378]

Each mindset is an individual reflection, but it relates the single actor to self-organising actors and agents as well as hetero-organised artefacts.

The Digital Imperative of Mindsets for Global Citizenship. The third digital imperative for conviviality runs like that, engaging any actor when becoming a netizen:

"Act so as to contribute to the production and use of digital technologies that support the emergence and sustenance of planetary mindsets as digital netizens ingenuity." [10, p. 381]

Digital netizens ingenuity indicates the digitalised ingenuity of netizens, that is to say, the digitally supported ingenuity of netizens (who are networked citizens).

4 AI and the Actualisation of its Potential

If AI shall be shaped according to the imperatives that demand observing the objective and subjective conditions under which humanity is living today, it needs also to clarify on a generic level what kind of tool AI is.

As any IT and digital technology, AI is an artefact, that is, an hetero-organised tool that itself is not a self-organising system like natural agents or social actors and is thus not able to produce emergents [16]. Information in all its occurrences is such an emergent. It is generated by the agency of self-organising systems. However, AI is embedded as tool in a social system, it turns the social system into a techno-social system and can facilitate or inhibit the emergent agency of the techno-social system for the good or for the bad.

The task of Technology Assessment is to assess the performance of technology and to adjust the conditions of the design to rectify the performance. There are two functions of technology according to which its performance can be measured.

First, the technical function. It asks: "does the mechanism work efficaciously, that is, when used does it lead to the aim for which it is designed?" [15, p. 207] How good the technical functioning is, is a matter of fact, and the actors who designed the mechanism are responsible for a good functioning. When a new cycle is started, the mechanism should be technically upgraded, if need be.

Second, the social function. Its question is: "does the designed mechanism improve the social function it is intended to fulfil, that is, does it promote the right social value, conform with the right social norm, serve the right interest?" [15, p. 208] How good the social function is supported, is a matter of ethics, and the designers and those who instruct them are responsible, even if they haven't thought about it. There might be unintended social consequences. Before a new cycle is started, the social values the technology should serve need to be checked and should be adapted, if need be.

Therefore, the influence of technology on the emergent activities within the cycle in the techno-social systems is twofold: shaping technology by actors in the design process yields emergent properties and, when actors use the technology, impacting society yields emergent properties, too. But these properties are due to the social agency concerning technology and not to the technology as such.

This techno-social systems theory avoids the praxiological, ontological and epistemological pitfalls of wide-spread approaches towards AI [15, 17, 18]. Praxiology, ontology and epistemology are understood here as forming a hierarchy of levels that are linked by less-than-strict dominance from above and emergence from below, praxiology being on the top and epistemology being on the bottom.

4.1 Praxiological Pitfalls

There are two kinds of design approach failures.

Conflated Man-Machine Designs. Conflated designs are the first variety. They conflate the human and AI in that they shall be treated indiscriminately [15, pp. 236–238].

There is a reductionist and a projectionist variety.

Technodeterminism. The reductionist approach can be called technodeterminist. It treats the human like AI. It's an assimilation of human intelligence to AI. That's the motto of Transhumanism. Man is said to become *Homo deus* [19]. However, that's hubris from humiliation by AI, because what is human is degraded.

Social constructivism. The next approach that is a projection is rather social-constructivist. It vows—the opposite way around—to treat AI like the human by being ready to add human features to AI, which is a mistake. That's anthropomorphism. After Günther Anders, building human-like AI would not only be hubris but also humiliation of humans because of loosing autonomy to AI [20].

Disconnected Man-Machine Designs. Opposite to conflation, disconnection pretends segregation, human and AI shall be treated in discriminative ways [15, pp. 238–240].

There are three varieties.

Technocentrism. This is the first one. This term shall name approaches that intend to treat AI better than the humans. Posthumanism is an ideology that adheres to this motto. It believes in technological progress that will provide an Übermensch *ex machina.* Anders talks of "hubristic humility" as "arrogant self-degradation" [20, p. 50].

Sociocentrism. This is the second one that wants to treat humans better than AI. This ideology celebrates the pride of creation. It equates to humble hubris, since it forgoes technology.

Techno/social interactivism. The third one might be termed techno/social interactivism, as it does not like to prioritise one of the sides that are assumed basically disjunct. But it cannot avoid either leveling down humans or leveling up AI and shifts between humility and hubris. An example is Bruno Latour's Actor-Network-Theory, in which "actors" are not only social actors, but also natural agents or artificial things, finally called all together "actants" [21].

All these praxiological pitfalls can be sidestepped. Techno-social systemism that integrates technology and society stands for combined man-machine designs. The human and AI are treated according to their different properties for the sake of the whole. There is no issue of hubris or humiliation [15, p. 241].

4.2 Ontological Pitfalls

There are again two kinds of model approach failures, related to the praxiological ones.

Conflated Man-Machine Models. They state a monism, inasmuch as the human and AI share the same degree of complexity [15, p. 244–246].

Again, reduction and projection are two varieties of conflation.

Technomorphism. Reduction is practiced by technomorphism. Since the human is seen as complex as AI, it stipulates man can be modelled as machines and human intelligence as AI.

Thereby the reduction of technomorphism can comprise several steps:

1. Merism: The level of society is reduced to the level of an individual actor, the collective intelligence of society to individual intelligence.
2. Biologism: The level of an individual actor is reduced to that of its body, human intelligence is reduced to neurological features of the brain.
3. Physicalism: The level of the human body is reduced to that of its physical substrate, the brain features to the physicality of neuron's working.
4. Mechanicism: The level of the physical substrate is reduced to that of mere mechanisms, the physical functioning of neurons to mechanical functioning.

In the end, "Regarding intelligence, human intelligence boils down to a mere mechanist capacity that artefacts can be made capable of." [15, p. 245]

Sociomorphism. The projective conflation can then be denominated sociomorphism. As AI is ascribed the same complexity as the human, AI shall be understood by human-intelligence-like models.

The projection is applied to the same steps as before:

1. Structuralism: The level of society is projected onto the level of an individual actor, collective intelligence of society is supposed to characterise individual intelligence.
2. Anthropism: The level of an upgraded individual actor is projected onto that of the human body, the upgraded individual intelligence onto neurological features of the brain.
3. Psychism: The level of an upgraded human body is projected onto that of its physical substrate, upgraded brain features onto the physicality of neuron's working.
4. Animism: The level of an upgraded physical substrate is projected onto that of mechanisms, the upgraded physical functioning of neurons onto mechanical functioning.

"The social phenomenon of intelligence is hypostatised as being characteristic of technological artefacts." [15, p. 246]

Disconnected Man-Machine Models. They state dualism, the human and the artificial are different because they are genuine entities of incomparable complexity [15, p. 247–250].

As in disconnected man-machine designs, there are three varieties.

Technosingularism. The first is termed technosingular. According to its posthuman agenda, AI can become more highly complex than human intelligence and might render the human race obsolete. This is an anti-humanistic ideological tenet and violates rational thinking. The moment when AI would surpass human capabilities, described as the singularity, will never happen. As machine, AI has no self to self-organise agential activities. It follows algorithms that, in principle, are strict deterministic [16], even though the construction of AI has become so complicated that it appears as if it would reason. Turing tests AI would pass can never fool humans. It is just lack of transparency of AI's black box.

Sociosingularism. The second model is labeled sociosingular. The human would be of unparalleled complexity and would be superior over and above any machine. Such a statement would underestimate the role of AI as helpful tool.

Techno/social indifferentism. The third model is called techno/social indifferentism. Though the human and the artificial are of different degrees of complexity, they can interact. So, the differences of human and artificial intelligence would be juxtaposed und would not make a difference. However, it makes an ontological difference in which way they can be coupled.

Techno-social systemism shows that neither conflation nor disconnection can explain how a man-machine combination can be modelled. Not ontological monism, not dualism, but dialectic can help: While the human and the artificial, human intelligence and AI, differ in complexity, in the techno-social system they can constitute a united complex with asymmetrical roles [15, p. 250–255].

4.3 Epistemological Pitfalls

They follow the praxiological and ontological categorisations above.

Conflated Man-Machine Frames. They propagate cross-disciplinarity, that is transgressing from one discipline to the other when applying methods [22]. The disciplines in question are engineering on the one side and social and human sciences on the other. This holds also for AI research [15, p. 257–259].

Techno-and social universalism are the two varieties. Both believe that one kind of methods is enough.

Techno-universalism. The techno-universal framing reduces the methods of social sciences and humanities to those of engineering. Engineering methods are deemed sufficient for researching the social and human, which is clearly not the case.

Social Universalism. The same critique holds for the social-universal framing that projects social and human methods onto engineering. Social and human sciences methods cannot substitute methods for engineering.

Disconnected Man-Machine Frames. They promote a pluri-disciplinarity [22], meaning that each discipline needs their own methods [15, p. 259–261].

Again, three varieties can be identified.

Techno-particularism. The techno-particularist frame purports that engineering needs pure engineering methods.

Socio-particularism. The socio-particularist frame purports that social disciplines need only methods of social disciplines.

Both represent a kind of monodisciplinarity [22] and cannot find together.

Techno/social relativism. The third variety accepts that both disciplines would need a mix of particular disciplinary methods. Therefore it runs under the title of multi- or interdisciplinarity [22].

However, it is a techno/social relativism. "The arbitrariness and relativity of the encounter of human intelligence and AI will not transform into a consistent approach." [15, p. 261]

Only techno-social systemism values true man-machine transdisciplinarity that leads to a combined frame. Social and human science methods and engineering methods are complementing each other to form a single methodology that on a meta-level comprises both disciplinary methods in an adapted form. Only this ensures a proper understanding of human intelligence and AI [15, p. 261–264].

5 Conclusion

This theoretical study of shaping AI in times of crises showed that three contexts need to be considered to prevent AI being or becoming part of the problem instead of part of the solution.

The first context is the objective requirement to come to terms with the planetary conditions of the common destiny of humanity. AI should not be absent but as tool support the creation of a civilisation that provides a decent coexistence for every member of world society, for a sustainable state of the environment and for meaningful technologies that foster productive forces. This is the task of overcoming the Grand Bifurcation by helping implement the techno-eco-social transformation of societies.

The second context is the requirement to overhaul the subjective conditions of social information capabilities to make them apt to further co-operation, communication and cognition throughout social systems from the world society down to the individual members of it. AI should not divert those capabilities but support them by expanding, extending and enlarging them. This is the task of paving the way for a common understanding of what is at stake. Humanity must learn to accept the common destiny by knowing how to mitigate the poly-crisis and to keep the existential threats below the threshold of devolution.

The third and last context is the requirement to be aware of the inherent malleability of AI due to its ambivalent potentiality to quantitatively reinforce existing, or qualitatively spawn new, unwishful social functions as well as quantitatively reinforce existing, or qualitatively innovate, wishful social functions. Thus, any actualisation of the potential of AI by social systems makes deliberation mandatory. In this respect, it is the amount of granting human autonomy to AI installations that is doubtful, if this restricts the domain of human autonomy to an amount that is detrimental. But this has nothing to do with emerging beings. AI is a tool that is produced in the course of social systems evolution. And the noble task of AI today should be to help human intelligence proceed to another level of social evolution.

Acknowledgments. Parts of this chapter were funded as part of studies on conviviality and AI by the Department of Socioeconomics at the University of Hamburg.

Disclosure of Interests The author has no competing interest to declare that is relevant to the content of this article.

References

1. László, E.: La grande bifurcation. Tacor International, Versailles (1986)
2. László, E.: La gran bifurcación. Gesida Editorial, Barcelona (1990)
3. Ord, T.: The Precipice. Bloomsbury, London (2021)
4. Heylighen, F., Joslyn, C.: Towards a theory of Metasystem transitions. World Futur. **45**(1–4), 1–4 (2010). https://doi.org/10.1080/02604027.1995.9972552
5. Hofkirchner, W.: Emergent Information. World Scientific, Singapore (2013)
6. The Convivialist International: The second convivialist manifesto. Civ. Sociol. **1**, 1 (2020). https://doi.org/10.1525/001c.12721
7. Illich, I.: Tools for Conviviality. Marion Boyars, London (1973)
8. Meller, H., Michel, K., van Schaik, C.: Die Evolution der Gewalt. dtv, München. (2024)
9. Morin, E.: Abenteuer Mensch. Freitag. **28** (2021)
10. Hofkirchner, W., Kreowski, H.-J.: Why artificial intelligence alone will not save mankind. In: Schroeder, M., Hofkirchner, W. (eds.) Understanding Information and its Role as a Tool, pp. 367–388. World Scientific, Singapore (2025)
11. Barthlott, W., Linsenmair, K.E., Porembski, S. (eds.): Biodiversity, vol. II. EOLSS, Oxford (2009)

12. Bloch, E.: The Principle of Hope. MIT Press, Cambridge (1986)
13. Nida-Rümelin, J., Weidenfeld, N.: Digital Humanism. Springer, Cham (2022)
14. DigHum homepage. https://informatics.tuwien.ac.at/digital-humanism/
15. Hofkirchner, W.: The Logic of the Third. World Scientific, Singapore (2023)
16. Hofkirchner, W.: Does computing embrace self-organisation? In: Dodig-Crnkovic, G., Burgin, M. (eds.) Information and Computation, pp. 185–202. World Scientific, Singapore (2011)
17. Hofkirchner, W.: Techno-social systems. Comput. Sci. Math. Forum. **8**, 1 (2023). https://doi.org/10.3390/cmsf2023008003
18. Hofkirchner, W.: Digital humanism. In: Verdegem, P. (ed.) AI for Everyone? pp. 33–47. University of Westminster Press, London (2021)
19. Harari, Y.N.: Homo deus. Harvill Secker, London (2016)
20. Anders, G.: On promethean shame. In: Müller, C.J. (ed.) Prometheanism, pp. 29–95. Rowman and Littlefield, London (2016)
21. Latour, B.: Reassembling the Social. Oxford University Press, Oxford (2006)
22. Burgin, M., Hofkirchner, W.: Introduction: omnipresence of information as the incentive for transdisciplinarity. In: Burgin, M., Hofkirchner, W. (eds.) Information Studies and the Quest for Transdisciplinarity, pp. 1–7. World Scientific, Singapore (2017)

Responsibility, Habit, and Control: Digital Humanism and the Delegation of Critical Functions to Intelligent Autonomous Systems

Gordana Dodig-Crnkovic[1,2](✉)

[1] Chalmers University of Technology and University of Gothenburg, Gothenburg, Sweden
dodig@chalmers.se
[2] Mälardalen University, Västerås, Sweden

Abstract. As intelligent autonomous systems (IAS) continue to assume increasingly central roles in safety-and mission-critical domains such as transportation, healthcare, finance, and infrastructure management, humans are becoming unable to monitor or intervene in real time. This shift is driven by the speed, data-processing capacity, and adaptivity of IAS. To manage this complexity, a new paradigm is emerging: IAS controlling and monitoring other IAS, a development that introduces at the same time practical efficiency and profound practical and ethical challenges. This article explores the multi-layered delegation of responsibilities within IAS ecosystems, where decisions influencing human lives and well-being are made with minimal human intervention. One often-overlooked consequence of this delegation is the capacity of AI systems to shape and create new human habits, whether through personalized persuasion, behavioral feedback loops, or autonomous decision enforcement. As humans increasingly adapt their behaviors to machine-optimized environments, questions arise about autonomy, agency, and responsibility for resulting behavior changes. Drawing on insights from recent research on responsibility delegation in IAS and on AI-driven habit formation, the article critically examines how responsibility should be distributed across human actors, autonomous systems, and institutions. Framed within the principles of Digital Humanism, I argue for a value-sensitive governance model that ensures transparency, explainability and human oversight even in complex IAS-to-IAS control scenarios. I propose a normative framework for responsibility attribution that accounts for both the technical architecture of IAS networks and the behavioral effects these systems have on human users. The article concludes by addressing the ethical risks of diminished human agency, manipulation through behavioral design, and the need for institutional mechanisms that align IAS operations with fundamental human values.

Keywords: Autonomous systems · Responsibility · Digital humanism

1 Introduction

In recent years, the delegation of critical functions to Intelligent Autonomous Systems (IAS) has expanded rapidly across sectors such as healthcare, transportation, finance, and infrastructure management. Driven by their speed, data-processing capacity, and

R. Giovagnoli et al. (Eds.): IS4SI 2025, SAPERE 81, pp. 27–39, 2026.
https://doi.org/10.1007/978-3-032-31732-2_3

decision-making capabilities, IAS increasingly operate in regimes where human monitoring and intervention are no longer possible in real time (Dodig-Crnkovic, Basti, and Holstein 2025; Stahl 2021).This leads to growing reliance on autonomous decision-making and poses new challenges for ethical governance, responsibility attribution, and human agency (Dennett, 1973; Floridi and Sanders, 2004; Dodig-Crnkovic, 2006; Dodig-Crnkovic and Persson, 2008; Çürüklü et al. 2010).

A particularly striking development is the emergence of IAS-to-IAS control mechanisms, where autonomous systems are tasked with monitoring, regulating, and making decisions about the behavior of other IAS. While this layered control architecture improves efficiency and reduces error rates in complex environments (Gawer and Cusumano 2014), it introduces profound ethical and legal questions regarding accountability, transparency, and value alignment (Floridi and Cowls 2019; Morley et al. 2020).

Simultaneously, the behavioral consequences of human interaction with IAS deserve closer scrutiny. Intelligent systems are not only performing delegated tasks but also actively shaping human behavior and creating new habits through personalized feedback and algorithmic recommendation loops (Zuboff 2019). These mechanisms can subtly alter users' cognitive patterns, routines, and decision-making strategies—raising concerns about possibility of manipulation, behavioral lock-in, and the erosion of human autonomy (Binns 2018; Habermas 1984).

In this context, Digital Humanism offers an ethically grounded framework for addressing these challenges. Digital Humanism emphasizes human dignity, agency, and the social embedding of technology development (Vienna Manifesto on Digital Humanism 2019). Its principles advocate for value-sensitive design approaches that prioritize human well-being, informed consent, and institutional accountability, even within highly automated socio-technical systems (Spiekerman 2023).

This article brings together insights from recent work on responsibility delegation in IAS (Dodig-Crnkovic et al. 2025), the behavioral impacts of AI-driven habit formation, and the ethical governance of autonomous ecosystems (Stahl 2021; Floridi and Cowls 2019). By doing so, it aims to answer the following research questions:

1. How should responsibility for critical decisions be distributed among designers, operators, IAS themselves, and institutional frameworks?
2. What are the ethical implications of IAS shaping and creating human habits?
3. How can Digital Humanism guide the design, governance, and oversight of IAS-to-IAS control structures in ways that safeguard human agency and social values?

Through an interdisciplinary analysis, the article proposes a normative framework for multi-level responsibility attribution that accounts for both technical system complexity and behavioral effects on human users.

2 Background and Context

The Rise of Intelligent Autonomous Systems in Critical Infrastructure

The deployment of Intelligent Autonomous Systems (IAS) in critical technological domains is transforming how decision-making, and control functions are managed.

IAS are now central actors in fields as diverse as autonomous transportation, medical diagnostics, industrial process control, and financial trading (Stahl 2021). Their ability to process vast amounts of data at speeds and scales beyond information processing capacities makes them essential for managing real-time, high-stakes environments (Dodig-Crnkovic et al. 2025).

However, this shift is not without significant trade-offs. Human cognitive limitations mean that operators cannot meaningfully intervene in many IAS-driven processes, when decisions are made within milliseconds or based on multi-dimensional sensor input (Gawer and Cusumano 2014). As a result, humans are forced to delegate both operational control and decision-making responsibility to IAS, trusting in the system's capacity for accuracy, reliability, and ethical behavior.

IAS-to-IAS Control: From Human Oversight to Machine Governance

A direct consequence of the growing complexity of intelligent autonomous system (IAS) networks is the emergence of IAS-to-IAS control structures, in which one autonomous system monitors, constrains, or corrects another. For example, in traffic domains, vehicle "driver agents" request reservations from an AI "intersection manager" that grants or denies passage to ensure safety—an explicit AI-over-AI coordination regime (Au, Zhang, and Stone 2010). In finance, regulatory and supervisory AI increasingly oversees algorithmic trading by detecting and responding to market-abuse patterns, thereby placing AI-driven surveillance in a controlling relationship to AI-driven trading (IOSCO 2025). Importantly, machine learning is now embedded in a large share of trading algorithms themselves, sharpening the sense in which AI supervises AI (AFM 2023).

While these architectures introduce significant efficiencies and reduce latency, they also create new accountability challenges. When a cascade of decisions is made by multiple interlinked IAS, identifying causal responsibility in the event of system failure becomes non-trivial (Calo 2015; Latour 1992). This is particularly problematic when decisions involve outcomes—such as life-or-death judgments (Dodig-Crnkovic et al. 2025).

Moreover, explainability and transparency remain technical challenges. Many IAS employ opaque machine learning models, "black boxes", making it difficult for external stakeholders (users, regulators, or designers) to reconstruct how or why a specific decision was made (Morley et al. 2020).

Behavioral Consequences: Intelligent Autonomous Systems Shaping Human Habits

Beyond operational control and decision-making, IAS more and more shape human behaviors and create new user habits. AI-driven systems embedded in everyday apps and digital services engage users through continuous feedback loops, personalized nudging, and adaptive behavior reinforcement mechanisms. These systems alter users' cognitive and behavioral patterns over time, sometimes supporting positive change (e.g., health apps encouraging exercise) but also influencing users for commercial or operational goals (Zuboff 2019).

The ethical problem intensifies when IAS-to-IAS control systems enforce behavioral adjustments at scale, such as recommendation engines influencing user choices across millions of individuals simultaneously. The concern is not only the loss of individual autonomy but also the emergence of new social norms and collective habits shaped by AI-driven governance mechanisms (Binns 2018).

The Need for a Digital Humanism Framework

Given these developments, Digital Humanism emerges as a central normative approach for understanding and addressing the challenges of IAS control and human behavioral impact. The Vienna Manifesto on Digital Humanism (2019) calls for technology design and governance that foregrounds human agency, dignity, and societal values.

Digital Humanism insists on embedding ethical principles directly into system architectures while ensuring that accountability remains with human and institutional actors. This is particularly critical when humans are excluded from operational decision loops, and when IAS increasingly function as behavior-shaping agents.

In the following sections, we will explore how responsibility can be ethically distributed across human and non-human agents in IAS ecosystems, and how Digital Humanism can guide the design of systems that both enhance operational efficiency and protect human values.

3 Responsibility Delegation in Intelligent Autonomous Systems: Conceptual Foundations

Responsibility in complex socio-technical systems like IAS is a multi-dimensional concept. It includes causal, moral, legal, and functional domains (Dodig-Crnkovic, Basti, and Holstein 2025). Traditional ethical models often assume clear lines of human control and agency, where responsibility is attributed based on direct causality and intentionality (Habermas 1984). However, the operational reality of IAS, especially in high-speed, machine-to-machine environments, challenges these assumptions. Key forms of responsibility include:

Causal responsibility: Who or what caused an event or outcome?

Legal responsibility: Who is legally liable for the outcome?

Functional responsibility: Which system component or agent was functionally tasked with the relevant action?

In IAS contexts, functional responsibility becomes central. While IAS lack moral agency, they carry task-based responsibilities within the operational system architecture (Dodig-Crnkovic et al. 2025). This framing helps to track, document, and analyze machine behaviors for oversight and accountability purposes.

Delegation Chains and Responsibility Distribution

Modern IAS operate within delegation chains, where responsibilities move across multiple layers: from designers, programmers, and operators to the IAS themselves—and now increasingly from IAS to other IAS.

For example, in autonomous traffic control, human engineers design algorithms that regulate vehicle behavior, but during real-time operations, decision authority passes from vehicles to traffic management IAS, all without direct human oversight. Each link in this chain carries different types of responsibility:

Design Responsibility includes program developers and architects,

Operational Responsibility concerns system operators and supervisors,

Functional Execution Responsibility includes the IAS itself,

Oversight Responsibility concerns institutional bodies (e.g., regulators).

Recognizing and mapping these responsibility layers is essential for legal liability, ethical oversight, and user trust.

Intelligent Autonomous Systems as Functional Agents

A central argument by Dodig-Crnkovic et al. (2025) is that IAS should be viewed as autonomous functional agents—entities with task-based roles, but not moral agents in the human sense. This distinction is critical.

While IAS can autonomously select actions, they do so based on programmed goals, learned patterns, and predefined constraints. They do not possess moral reasoning, intentionality, or the human-like capacity for ethical deliberation (Latour 1992).

However, their causal impact on morally relevant outcomes makes it necessary to design accountability structures around their actions. This includes tools for logging decision pathways, implementing explainability mechanisms (Morley et al. 2020), and embedding ethical constraints and value alignment protocols (Floridi and Cowls 2019).

Emerging Challenges in IAS-to-IAS Responsibility Flow

When IAS delegate control to other IAS responsibility chains become non-linear and layered, making it difficult to reconstruct decision causality after system failures or unexpected behaviors (Calo 2015).

Key emerging challenges include opacity (decisions made through multiple opaque AI models), traceability loss (difficulty in reconstructing who or what "caused" a specific outcome), responsibility dilution (when multiple IAS are involved, human actors may feel less accountable as a "many hands" problem), and autonomous behavior shaping (when IAS shape human habits, responsibility for behavioral outcomes becomes even more diffuse).

These issues necessitate new governance models and design methodologies that explicitly account for both technical causality and moral responsibility, while respecting human dignity and autonomy in line with Digital Humanism (Vienna Manifesto on Digital Humanism 2019).

AI as a Habit-Creating Force: Behavioral Implications

While much of the ethical discourse on Intelligent Autonomous Systems (IAS) focuses on decision-making, control, and accountability at the system level, an important but often unnoticed dimension is the role of IAS in shaping human behavior.

IAS are no longer just passive tools or decision-support systems. They actively influence human habits and behavioral patterns, typically without explicit user awareness or consent (Zuboff 2019). Through reinforcement mechanisms, adaptive feedback, and personalized nudging, IAS systems can condition users into forming new habits, whether beneficial, neutral, or harmful for themselves and for society.

Mechanisms of AI-Driven Habit Formation

AI systems engage in habit shaping using multiple techniques, such as personalized nudging (adaptive prompts designed to steer user behavior toward desired outcomes) (Binns 2018); feedback loops (real-time performance tracking and behavioral reinforcement); behavioral lock-in (repetitive exposure to AI-curated choices that limit behavioral diversity) (Zuboff 2019) and choice architecture manipulation (structuring options in ways that subtly direct user decisions) (Floridi and Cowls 2019).

These technologically sophisticated mechanisms raise concerns about autonomy, consent and manipulation, especially when deployed at scale without user knowledge.

Ethical Risks: Manipulation and Erosion of Autonomy

The behavioral influence of intelligent autonomous systems poses significant ethical risks, particularly when users are unaware of how their habits are being shaped or when the system's goals do not align with users' best interests. Potential risks include:

Loss of autonomy. Users may find themselves engaging in behaviors they did not consciously choose (Habermas 1984).

Informed consent violations. Behavioral nudges are often embedded invisibly, bypassing traditional consent mechanisms (Morley et al. 2020).

Behavioral lock-in. Algorithmic reinforcement may lead users into rigid behavioral loops, limiting freedom of choice (Zuboff 2019).

Ethical drift. When IAS-to-IAS control structures propagate behavioral nudging at scale, small design biases may amplify across populations (Stahl 2021).

These issues become even more complex when IAS-to-IAS governance layers themselves reinforce or correct other IAS-generated behavioral nudges, introducing a cascade of behavioral influence mechanisms with limited human oversight.

Potential Opportunities: Supporting Beneficial Habits

Despite these risks, IAS also hold promise for positive behavior change, especially in health, education, and sustainability contexts. Examples include health behavior change apps encouraging exercise, healthy eating, and medication adherence; sustainability nudges: promoting energy-saving habits through smart home IAS and learning support systems, personalized educational tools that reinforce effective study habits.

The ethical imperative, however, is to ensure that habit-shaping interventions respect human agency, are transparent, and align with user values, in keeping with Digital Humanism principles (Vienna Manifesto on Digital Humanism 2019).

To reconcile the behavioral power of IAS with the ethical commitments of Digital Humanism, we propose the following key design and governance requirements:

Transparency (users should know when and how they are being influenced).

Consent and control (users should have meaningful ways to opt out).

Value Alignment (human dignity, autonomy, and well-being are prioritized).

Oversight in IAS-to-IAS chains (understanding IAS decision-makers and behavioral agents necessitates responsibility frameworks that address both systemic control and individual behavioral impact, a theme developed further in the next section).

4 Digital Humanism as an Ethical Framework

Digital Humanism emerges as a critical and timely response to the ethical, social, and political challenges posed by the growing autonomy of Intelligent Autonomous Systems (IAS). Rooted in the belief that technology must serve human dignity, agency, and societal well-being, Digital Humanism emphasizes the centrality of human values in the design, deployment, and governance of digital technologies (Vienna Manifesto on Digital Humanism 2019) and calls for:

Human-centric design (human needs and rights over technological efficiency)

Value-sensitive innovation (embedding societal, cultural, and ethical values into technical systems)

Transparency and accountability (ensuring that decision-making processes, both human and machine-based, remain understandable and traceable)

Democratic control (advocating for collective societal oversight over the development and use of digital technologies).

Digital Humanism and Responsibility Distribution

The delegation of responsibilities to IAS, especially in IAS-to-IAS control structures, presents a direct challenge to these principles. As (Dodig-Crnkovic et al. 2025) point out, responsibility becomes distributed, diffuse, and difficult to track in multi-layered, autonomous systems.

From a Digital Humanism perspective, this delegation must not undermine human accountability (ultimate moral and legal responsibility must remain with human actors and institutions) (Stahl 2021); human agency and control (even when IAS operate autonomously, long-term mechanisms for human oversight and intervention must exist); and transparency (the logic, goals, and value trade-offs embedded in IAS operations must be explainable and auditable) (Morley et al. 2020).

In practice, this requires not only technical design interventions (such as explainable AI and audit trails) but also institutional arrangements for oversight, governance, and legal redress (Calo 2015).

Behavioral Impacts Within Digital Humanism

Importantly, Digital Humanism also extends to the behavioral dimension of IAS operations. AI systems shaping human habits cannot be ethically neutral. Their capacity to influence cognition and behavior means that behavioral design becomes a site of ethical responsibility.

Applying Digital Humanism here means ensuring that behavioral interventions are aligned with human autonomy and well-being, requiring informed consent for behavior-shaping processes, preventing covert manipulation or commercial exploitation of user behavior patterns (Zuboff 2019), and promoting reflection and user empowerment, rather than behavioral lock-in (Habermas 1984).

This perspective aligns with calls for value-sensitive design and ethical AI governance frameworks emerging in the broader AI ethics community (Floridi and Cowls 2019; Morley et al. 2020; Spiekermann 2023).

Digital Humanism-Informed Governance Model

To operationalize these principles in the context of IAS responsibility delegation and habit formation, multi-level governance models are needed. These should integrate:

Design-time ethics—technical safeguards,

Run-time oversight—organizational policies,

Post-hoc accountability—regulatory and legal frameworks,

Informed consent for use—user-centric behavioral governance.

A robust socio-technical system is needed supporting the above (education, infrastructure, etc.)

5 Toward a Normative Framework for Responsibility Sharing

Multi-Level Responsibility Attribution

Given the technical complexity and behavioral impact of IAS, particularly in IAS-to-IAS control environments, a single-layered concept of responsibility is no longer sufficient. Instead, responsibility must be understood as distributed across multiple human and institutional actors, alongside the functional roles assigned to IAS themselves (Dodig-Crnkovic, Basti, and Holstein 2025).

Building on Digital Humanism (Werthner et al. 2022; Nida-Rümelin and Weidenfeld 2022), we propose a multi-level responsibility model, which includes:

Design responsibility: Engineers, software developers, and data scientists hold responsibility for embedding ethical constraints, explainability mechanisms, and safety layers within IAS.

Operational responsibility: System operators and organizational users are responsible for monitoring system performance and intervening where necessary.

Institutional responsibility: Organizations and regulatory bodies must provide oversight, establish clear accountability structures, and enforce compliance with ethical standards.

Functional responsibility: IAS are assigned specific operational roles, tracked through audit trails and decision logs, but remain non-moral agents (Latour 1992) (Dodig-Crnkovic et al. 2025).

Behavioral Responsibility: Designers and deployers of habit-shaping AI bear responsibility for assessing and mitigating potential manipulation and autonomy loss (Zuboff 2019).

This layered model helps address responsibility gaps inherent in complex socio-technical systems (Calo 2015).

Ethical Design Recommendations

To operationalize responsibility sharing, the following value-sensitive design principles, aligned with Digital Humanism (Werthner et al. 2022; Werthner, et al. 2024; Spiekermann 2023) can be used:

Transparency. AI systems, especially those in IAS-to-IAS governance structures, must include mechanisms that allow decision-making processes to be inspected, audited, and explained (Floridi and Cowls 2019; Morley et al. 2020).

Ethical constraints and value alignment. IAS should be designed, architected and programmed with ethical boundaries, ensuring that autonomous decisions cannot violate human rights or ethical norms (Nida-Rümelin and Weidenfeld 2022; Spiekermann 2023).

Behavioral safeguards. AI-driven habit formation processes should include clear behavioral intention disclosures, user opt-outs, and mechanisms for user self-reflection and agency preservation.

Oversight of IAS-to-IAS interactions. Institutional bodies and human supervisors must maintain systemic oversight over how IAS monitor and control each other. This includes meta-governance systems, where dedicated AI governance layers track and regulate IAS-to-IAS interactions (Stahl 2021).

Managing Responsibility in Behavior-Shaping Systems

A particularly novel responsibility challenge emerges from IAS-driven behavioral shaping. Given that IAS can create or reinforce human habits, responsibility for user behavior is no longer limited to individual free will but becomes co-produced between human users and machine agents (Binns 2018; Dodig-Crnkovic 2025).

Digital Humanism insists that habit-forming interventions must respect human autonomy and dignity. This requires explicit user awareness so that users know when behavior-shaping algorithms are active; ethical goal alignment where behavioral nudges align with users' self-identified goals and societal values (Spiekermann 2023), as well as institutional accountability implying that organizations deploying behavioral AI must be auditable and legally accountable for long-term behavioral impacts (Nida-Rümelin and Weidenfeld 2022).

Systemic Governance and Institutional Roles

Finally, responsibility sharing cannot stop at the level of system design or individual user interaction. It requires robust institutional and legal frameworks (Werthner et al. 2022; Stahl 2021). Governments, regulatory bodies, and international organizations must develop clear liability models for harm caused by IAS decisions, ethical AI certification systems, behavioral impact assessments for habit-shaping technologies and oversight mechanisms for IAS-to-IAS governance architectures.

These governance structures must reflect the core Digital Humanism commitment: technology must remain subservient to human values, democratic principles, and societal well-being.

6 Discussion

The growing delegation of critical functions to IAS—and the increasing reliance on IAS-to-IAS control structures—presents an inevitable trade-off between operational efficiency and ethical control.

On one hand, IAS bring undeniable benefits: improved decision speed, consistency, scalability, and error reduction in complex systems (Stahl 2021). On the other hand, as functional control shifts away from humans, traditional ethical oversight mechanisms struggle to keep pace (Dodig-Crnkovic et al. 2025).

A central tension is how human ethical responsibility can remain meaningful when human intervention is technologically impossible in real time? Digital Humanism helps resolve this tension by insisting that responsibility is not a function of proximity to decision points but of design-time and institutional control structures (Werthner et al. 2022; Nida-Rümelin and Weidenfeld 2022).

The Complexity of Distributed Responsibility

IAS environments are characterized by distributed, layered, and non-linear responsibility flows (Floridi and Cowls 2019). Responsibility is not concentrated in any single actor but spread across designers, developers, software architects, system operators and users, IAS components performing functional roles, and institutional regulators.

This distribution makes post-hoc accountability attribution difficult, especially when system failures emerge from unforeseen interactions between diverse human and non-human autonomous agents (Calo 2015).

One emerging solution is the implementation of responsibility mapping tools during system design and deployment phases, which can document who holds which form of responsibility at each layer (Morley et al. 2020).

A particularly urgent context for addressing responsibility delegation is the use of IAS in military operations, especially the deployment of autonomous weapons systems and drone warfare. Here, decision cycles are compressed to milliseconds, often necessitating IAS-to-IAS control hierarchies for threat detection, targeting, and engagement (Calo 2015; Dodig-Crnkovic et al. 2025).

The ethical risks are profound: lethal autonomous decisions, lack of human oversight, unclear responsibility attribution in case of civilian harm, and violations of international humanitarian law. Critics argue that the use of autonomous weapons fundamentally undermines human dignity and moral accountability, contradicting core principles of Digital Humanism (Nida-Rümelin and Weidenfeld 2022; Werthner et al. 2022).

Emerging research on "meaningful human control" and calls for a global ban on fully autonomous lethal systems highlight the need for institutional responsibility frameworks that prevent ethical erosion in this domain (Floridi and Cowls 2019). Warfare thus presents a stress-test case for any proposed model of distributed responsibility and ethical AI governance.

The Ethical Significance of AI-Driven Habit Formation

A critical and under-examined dimension of responsibility is the behavioral influence IAS exert on human users. Habit formation, driven by AI feedback loops and personalized nudging, is not ethically neutral. These systems can enhance well-being (e.g., by promoting healthy behaviors) or undermine autonomy (e.g., by locking users into behavior patterns that serve system owners' interests) (Zuboff 2019).

Digital Humanism provides a normative stance here: human autonomy, informed consent, and dignity must be preserved, even in systems designed for large-scale behavior shaping (Werthner et al. 2022). This raises variety of new questions, among others:

Who is responsible when a user adopts a harmful habit due to IAS nudging?

How can unintended behavioral side-effects be ethically managed?

Should there be behavioral impact assessments for habit-shaping systems (analogous to environmental or data protection impact assessments)?

Toward Institutional and Legal Innovation

Given the complexity of IAS ecosystems, ethical responsibility frameworks must extend beyond individual actors to include institutions and legal systems (Stahl 2021; Nida-Rümelin and Weidenfeld 2022). Possible approaches include AI-specific regulatory bodies with the authority to audit IAS behaviors, mandatory transparency and explainability standards and behavioral ethics regulations, focusing on user autonomy, manipulation risks, and consent in habit-formation technologies.

These institutional mechanisms should be explicitly designed to align with Digital Humanism principles, ensuring that technological progress does not erode core human rights and democratic values (Vienna Manifesto on Digital Humanism 2019).

Future Research Directions

This article identifies the following key areas for future research:

Multi-level multi-agent responsibility modeling. Development of tools for mapping and tracking responsibility flows in IAS networks

Behavioral governance. Empirical research on how AI-driven habit formation affects user autonomy over time

IAS-to-IAS oversight mechanisms. Technical research into self-regulating and meta-governance architectures within IAS ecosystems

Legal innovation. New legal frameworks capable of addressing distributed and non-human agency in IAS operations

Ethics of machine-to-machine behavior shaping. Deeper exploration of how IAS-to-IAS interactions can indirectly shape human behavior at scale.

7 Conclusion

The accelerating delegation of critical functions to Intelligent Autonomous Systems (IAS), combined with the emergence of IAS-to-IAS control structures, presents a fundamental shift in how responsibility, agency, and decision-making are distributed in socio-technical systems. This transformation challenges long-standing ethical, legal, and philosophical frameworks that assume direct human control over all morally significant decisions.

This article has highlighted two interconnected dimensions of this transformation: first, the technical and legal complexities of responsibility delegation within increasingly autonomous IAS ecosystems; and second, the neglected behavioral impacts resulting from AI-driven habit formation in human users. Both dimensions pose serious ethical risks—including opacity, accountability gaps, loss of human autonomy, and manipulation through behavioral design.

Framed within the principles of Digital Humanism, we argue that technological efficiency cannot come at the cost of human dignity, agency, and societal well-being. Responsibility must remain traceable, distributed across human actors and institutions, and embedded within system design through value-sensitive architectures, transparent decision-making processes, and ethical oversight mechanisms (Spiekermann 2023).

Particularly in high-stakes domains like military operations and autonomous warfare, the need for ethical governance becomes even more urgent. The deployment of autonomous weapons systems and decision-making drones exemplifies the extreme risks of responsibility erosion, necessitating strong international legal frameworks, institutional accountability, and a global ethical consensus guided by Digital Humanism.

Ultimately, the rise of IAS capable of influencing both system-level operations and individual human habits demands a new normative framework for responsibility sharing, one that is both technically realistic and ethically grounded. This requires interdisciplinary collaboration between technologists, ethicists, behavioral scientists, policymakers, and affected communities.

As IAS continue to reshape not only our technologies but also our behaviors and social norms, we must ensure that technology serves humanity and not the other way around. Digital Humanism provides the ethical roadmap for navigating this transformation with care, responsibility, and foresight.

Acknowledgments. The author would like to thank the reviewers for their constructive feedback and valuable comments.

Disclosure of Interests The author has no competing interest to declare that is relevant to the content of this article.

References

AFM (The Netherlands Authority for the Financial Markets): Machine learning in algorithmic trading: application by Dutch proprietary trading firms and possible risks (Report) (2023). https://www.afm.nl/~/profmedia/files/rapporten/2023/report-machine-learning-trading-algorithms.pdf

Au, T.-C., Zhang, S., Stone, P.: Motion planning algorithms for autonomous intersection management. In: AAAI Workshop on Bridging the Gap between Task and Motion Planning (2010) https://cdn.aaai.org/ocs/ws/ws0611/2053-8456-1-PB.pdf

Binns, R.: Fairness in machine learning: lessons from political philosophy. In: Proceedings of the 1st Conference on Fairness, Accountability and Transparency, vol. 81, pp. 149–159 (2018) https://proceedings.mlr.press/v81/binns18a.html

Calo, R.: Robotics and the lessons of cyberlaw. Calif. Law Rev. **103**(3), 513–563 (2015). https://doi.org/10.2139/ssrn.2402972

Çürüklü, B., Dodig-Crnkovic, G., Akan, B.: Towards industrial robots with human-like moral responsibilities. In: Proceedings of the 5th ACM/IEEE International Conference on Human-Robot Interaction, Osaka, Japan, p. 85 (2010). https://doi.org/10.1145/1734454.1734484

Dennett, D.C.: Mechanism and responsibility. In: Honderich, T. (ed.) Essays on Freedom of Action, pp. 143–163. Routledge & Kegan Paul, Boston (1973)

Dodig-Crnkovic, G.: Professional ethics in computing and intelligent systems. In: Proceedings of the Ninth Scandinavian Conference on Artificial Intelligence (SCAI 2006), Espoo, Finland, pp. 11–18 (2006)

Dodig-Crnkovic, G., Persson, D.: Sharing moral responsibility with robots: a pragmatic approach. In: Holst, A., Kreuger, P., Funk, P. (eds.) Tenth Scandinavian Conference on Artificial Intelligence (SCAI 2008). Frontiers in Artificial Intelligence and Applications, vol. 173, pp. 165–168. IOS Press, Amsterdam (2008)

Dodig-Crnkovic, G., Basti, G., Holstein, T.: Delegating responsibilities to intelligent autonomous systems: challenges and benefits. J. Bioethical Inq. Advance online publication. (2025). https://doi.org/10.1007/s11673-025-10428-5

Floridi, L., Cowls, J.: A unified framework of five principles for AI in society. Harv. Data Sci. Rev. **1**(1) (2019). https://doi.org/10.1162/99608f92.8cd550d1

Floridi, L., Sanders, J.W.: On the morality of artificial agents. Minds Mach. **14**, 349–379 (2004). https://doi.org/10.1023/B:MIND.0000035461.63578.9d

Gawer, A., Cusumano, M.A.: Industry platforms and ecosystem innovation. J. Prod. Innov. Manag. **31**(3), 417–433 (2014). https://doi.org/10.1111/jpim.12105

Habermas, J.: The Theory of Communicative Action: Reason and the Rationalization of Society, vol. 1. Beacon Press, Boston, MA (1984)

IOSCO (International Organization of Securities Commissions): Artificial intelligence in capital markets: use cases, risks, and challenges (CR/01/2025) (2025). https://www.iosco.org/library/pubdocs/pdf/IOSCOPD788.pdf

Latour, B.: Where are the missing masses? The sociology of a few mundane artifacts. In: Bijker, W., Law, J. (eds.) Shaping Technology/Building Society, pp. 225–258. MIT Press, Cambridge, MA (1992)

Morley, J., Floridi, L., Kinsey, L., Elhalal, A.: From what to how: an initial review of publicly available AI ethics tools, methods and research to translate principles into practices. Sci. Eng. Ethics. **26**(4), 2141–2168 (2020). https://doi.org/10.1007/s11948-019-00165-5

Nida-Rümelin, J., Weidenfeld, N.: Digital Humanism: for a Humane Transformation of Democracy, Economy and Culture in the Digital Age. Springer, Cham (2022). https://doi.org/10.1007/978-3-031-12482-2

Spiekermann, S.: Value-Based Engineering: A Guide to Building Ethical Technology for Humanity. Walter de Gruyter, Berlin (2023)

Stahl, B.C.: Artificial Intelligence for a Better Future: An Ecosystem Perspective on the Ethics of AI and Emerging Digital Technologies. Springer, Cham (2021). https://doi.org/10.1007/978-3-030-69978-9

Vienna Manifesto on Digital Humanism: Digital Humanism Initiative. Vienna University of Technology, Vienna (2019) https://caiml.org/dighum/

Werthner, H. et al.: Introduction to Digital Humanism: a Textbook. Springer, Cham (2024). https://doi.org/10.1007/978-3-031-45304-5

Werthner, H., Prem, E., Lee, E.A., Ghezzi, C. (eds.): Perspectives on Digital Humanism. Springer, Cham (2022). https://doi.org/10.1007/978-3-030-86144-5

Zuboff, S.: The Age of Surveillance Capitalism: the Fight for a Human Future at the New Frontier of Power. PublicAffairs, New York (2019)

Philosophical Reflections on the Human Condition

Sense of the Limit, or Limit as Sense? Philosophy of Person in the Age of Techno-Science

Patrizia Manganaro(✉)

Faculty of Philosophy, Pontifical Lateran University, Rome, Italy
manganaro@pul.va

Abstract. The present contribution introduces some philosophical observations on the possible developments of the idea of the limit as a sense and meaning of human life, which are placed in dialogue with the most recent results of AI. We are invited to reflect on the differences between AI and human intelligence, as well as between the static memory of the artifact, with its predictive capacity and with its storage system, and the dynamic memory of the human being, intentional and creative body-living consciousness that, in the embrace of *logos* and *pathos*, is able to understand the sense of one's own finitude and one's existence in living time.

Keywords: AI-intentionality-consciousness-artifact

1 *Status Quaestionis*: Is Philosophy Still Necessary?

The question of *humanitas* strongly challenges the relationship between philosophy and (not civilizing science, but) technology. Why? Technology is an innovative but also pervasive and potentially invasive resource, because it is rich in great opportunities as well as great risks: if it is thought in quantitative and muscular terms of "performance" and "efficiency", if it is devoted to the homologation of natural and artificial, or elaborated in the illusion of overcoming the limit of all limits, death, it can degenerate into aberrant forms of idolatry and ideology, populism and rejection, or strengthen the well-known assertion of Günther Anders, according to which, in the face of the second and third industrial revolutions, man is antiquated-obsolete, set, dismissed, liquidated, outdated [1].

Today, in the era of the so called "fourth revolution" [2], the question is no longer whether philosophy is science, humanism, or both; whether it is analytical, continental, or both; whether it is thought, language, or both. The question is being more radical and, at the same time, more thorny: is philosophy still necessary, or is it doomed to irrelevance?

What future, for philosophy? This question, however, contains at least another one: that on the future of the human being, from which it cannot be disjointed. Artificial intelligence and machine learning open up scenarios that transcend the fields of technology, computer science and engineering to which they legitimately belong, because

R. Giovagnoli et al. (Eds.): IS4SI 2025, SAPERE 81, pp. 43–57, 2026.
https://doi.org/10.1007/978-3-032-31732-2_4

they concern the meaning, value, care and sense of *human life* [3, 4]. With the *human enhancement*, the finitude, disease, fragility and vulnerability have been removed, and one wonders if philosophy, depositioned the as *ancilla* posture of theology, is today thought and practiced as a mere appendix of technology, or if the task of *witnessing in the first person* is attributable to it not so much on the sense of the limit, but on *the limit as sense*.

What does it mean? Is it therefore the question of death, and consequently of life, that makes human the human being and the philosophy still necessary? This contribution offers a frame of reference for the *philosophy of the person* understood as intentional bodily-living consciousness, center of infinite dignity, which overcomes the vulnerability of the term "personalism" noted by Paul Ricoeur [5] in his famous essay, and at the same time responds to some critical instances of the post-and trans-humanism, in particular to the desire to overcome the limit of all limits: death.

2 Interweaving Resources

Philosophy comes from the *humus*, from the sap of the ground, from the depths of the earth, to which it is rooted; the human existence and condition, linked to the chains of time, lacks infinity, and longs for infinity. The limit, the threshold, the finitude are often thought in the posture of "encroachment", which today is predominantly configured as "overcoming" of the human, in the direction of the post-, hyper-and trans-human. More recently, also in the direction of the over-human [6], in terms of creativity, solving problems and general knowledge.

We are now aware that philosophy is not an *ancilla*: neither of theology, nor of natural sciences, much less of techno-science. Rather, it is a rigorous (and not "exact") discipline, as a complexity, which holds together an intertweal of resources, developments and potentialities. With the methodological criteria and the epistemological status that are its own, philosophy assumes new commitments and responsibilities in the face of the so-called "fourth revolution": artificial or inorganic intelligence, managed by unconscious algorithms, and the challenges of info-science involve both a takeover of the epistemological problem of the digital that, computerizing the world, de-realizes and disembodies it, almost dematerializing it, and an ethical and ontological-social reflection on the information environment (infosphere) occupied by natural agents (organisms) and artificial machines (artifacts), on the degrees of freedom of mechanical physics and statistical sciences, on cloud computing, on practices that lead from big data to machine learning and, more generally, on operational and algorithmic procedures, which however does not make machines epistemic agents and/or centers of personal responsibility capable of accomplishing what is "right" or "wrong", "lawful" or "illicit", "good" or "bad" – or yes?

The issue is the main core of current and articulated debates in the academic communities [6–18], and strongly challenges philosophy, raising some questions: what makes an agent an epistemic agent, capable of discerning? What does the free exercise of the will consist of? In addition to being "intelligent", AI is also "wise"? Is it "over-human"? And what relationship with consciousness, with the subject-body (the phenomenological *Leib*), with the flesh and skin, with the sensitive living experience?

According to Nello Cristianini, no intelligence is unlimited, not even the human one: so, what is beyond human limits? [6]. We can imagine it? But the point is precisely to reflect on the *limit as sense* and meaning, acquiring tools, criteria and working methods to renew the praise of philosophy [19], whose research has no end and, with it, the praise of the human person, with his productive, design, generative, creative and unpredictable capacities, which crosses all times and spaces. If it is true that, for the first time in human history, "it is the machine that challenges us", it is in any case the philosophical thought that detects issues, formulates questions and elaborates answers, helping to make us aware that "only if we know how to include the humanities in the creation of these tools, can we hope not to produce, in the more or less near future, inhumane societies" [20]. This is precisely one of the tasks of epistemology and social ontology: to ask oneself if, in addition to science *tout court*, social science will also remain "human", with its value criteria of equity, justice, solidarity, responsibility. According to Dan Zahavi, if the study of the human being cannot ignore the social context and the world-environment (*Umwelt*), then a "good" theory of social reality will presuppose a "good" theory of human intersubjectivity: something that philosophical phenomenology has offered convincingly [21] as a motivated and intentional "being we" (*Wirsubjectivität*) [22].

From a more largely epistemological point of view, the alleged overcoming of philosophy and/or its declared irrelevance only further aggravates the ignorance of the whole and of the complexity, while the knowledge of the parts and of the fragments progresses almost obsessively [23]. This fragmentation of knowledge, typical of a thought that separates, divides and reduces, rather than a thought that generates spaces of relationship, connects and unites, signals not only the inability to grasp the whole, but also to think critically, distinguishing to unite, exercising an epistemology of complexity and, basically, to philosophize, whose scope of investigation is the whole, understood not as a mere sum of parts, but as an idea that goes beyond all the possibilities of a finite knowledge: an idea precluded to exact sciences, which proceed by quantifying, measuring, verifying, calculating.

Philosophy therefore qualifies itself as *a finite thinking the infinite*—an inescapable commitment, and indeed necessary for the future, it is precisely that of thinking about the human condition and its issues-limit: the finitude that we are, and the infinity that we long for. The fatigue of the concept, the responsibility of the philosophical exercise does not consist only in learning and understanding one's own time in thoughts, according to the well-known Hegelian adage, that is, in dwelling in a world that we ourselves have changed, but it turns out to be an indispensable infinite process, a research whose horizon knows no closures. Here takes place not only the dialogue that each man, each woman, thinking, establishes with himself and herself, but above all the conversation in which we are all intertwined and involved in an intersubjective, social and community way—even if philosophy is proclaimed dead [24].

As I said earlier, the philosophical debate about techno-science has mainly focused on epistemological and ethical instances—natural language processing, generative intelligence, cloud computing, ethics of communication, information and digital, ethics of machine learning, the issue of freedom and social justice, the control of sources and the spread of fake news, the problem of responsibility in governing and regulating new technologies... That's fine: but we need (also and further) a philosophy of the human person, that nourishes that debate from the inside, standing at its roots, and knowing how to anchor science to the human, and not vice versa. In the belief that even the techno- and info-science, even the "hard" sciences, are human—that is, cultural products or, to put it with the phenomenologist Edith Stein, non-personal objective-spiritual realities, "objects-for-subjects" [25].

3 *Online-Onlife*. The Emptying of the Presence

It once argued about "phenomenon" and "noumenon", "representation" and "reality", "idealism", "realism" and "antirealism". Today, what we call *virtual reality*—an oxymoron, a paradox, because the adjective that qualifies the "reality" produces its reversal, translation, redefinition, to the point of incorporating it into its noun form: *the virtual*—produces a sort of foreignness and alienation from the "real" world, from others "I" and from ourselves, a friction with social and relational practices, and even a bending of the common feeling of the future [8, 26–28], combined with a diminished awareness of freedom of choice and a distorted perception of the bodily-living. On closer inspection, it does not involve the detachment from the body or the disposal of the body (think of the so-called "immersive" or "increased" reality and the experiential, perceptive and sensory expansion that produces and induces), but its distancing from the otherness and the transcendence phenomenologically understood, from the heterogeneous *tout court*. It means that the transition from the era of things to the age of "non-things" [29]—the information, the digital, the network, the virtual, the infosphere—subtracts from the present its vocation of "vision", disrupting the philosophical idea of time, as well as space, especially the public one: what kind of space-environment is the web? Is it a place? A non-place? An hyper-place?

What does it mean, in fact, living or inhabiting the web, or the cloud? Does it mean that the perception of space-environment is said in many ways? That the experience of the world is asymmetrical and discontinuous, that we are dealing with new logics of the physical body (*Körper*) and the living body (*Leib*), that the interweaving of *logos* and *pathos* is no longer attributed (only) to the human organism, but (also) to the artifact? So the so-called "thinking machine" is present in itself? Is it vigilant? Does it have emotions, sensations, perceptions? Does it feel itself from the inside? Is its storage space related to human memory and the living experience of the past? Does the predictive capacity experience the future?

In short: the digital revolution, the "fourth revolution", does it sanction or not the end of the "human exception" [30]?

As noted by Byung-Chul Han [29], the information layer is comparable to a sort of waterproof membrane, to a poreless fabric, which ignores the involvement and intensity of the perceptual experience: information "represents" reality, but its pervasiveness makes the authentic experience of the presence, of a place, of time and space extremely difficult. Rather, it prevents the very possibility of such an experience. Therefore, on the one hand we could place the hyper-human and the trans-human, the human being transformed, transfigured (disfigured?) from the power of technology over nature, which conquers all spaces and times, surpassing them and almost making them superfluous;

and on the other hand we have the sub-human, the artificial machine that would fulfill that desire for infinity and immortality, making it "real", concrete, effective. Yet, it has been acutely observed that it is no longer "we humans" to be *online*, it is the reality mediated by technologies to be constantly *onlife* [31]. So, virtual reality is onlife: the volume *The Onlife Manifesto* opens with some relevant performative statements, such as the question "Game over for Modernity?" [32], or the exclamation "Dualism is Dead! Long Live Dualities!" [33]. In his interesting essay *Views and Examples on Hyper-Connectivity*, Jean-Gabriel Ganascia expresses a shareable concern, fundamentally epistemological-social, intertwined with the ethical question of the normativity of artificial intelligence: "The new models, especially the one that Wikipedia represents, raise many questions about the status of knowledge in society, its financing and control, and on those who can and must exercise control. In this regard, there is concern that low-skilled groups, groups funded by governments or private pressure groups outweight experts. Or, conversely, that the rules too strictly applied restrict the freedom of authors" [34].

It is the problem of "sources", and their control; it is the question of the true, the false and what is placed "between" them: the network, the social media, the virtual. It is the uncontrolled spread (uncontrollable?) of fake news that produces misinformation, distortion, confusion, emptying of presence and, consequently, a disjointed, unrelated, disembodied society, from which numerous pathologies of well-being arise, as I will try to say in the next chapter.

But, is reality mediated by technologies still "reality"?

The boundaries between organic and artificial, between nature and digital screen, less and less clear, have caused a mixture between real and virtual and, in cascade, the dismantling of objectivity, the opacity of the empirical and the factual, that is, the starting points considered infallibly certain by the positivisms and verificationisms of every era. On the other hand, the disarticulation of the idea of freedom in the use of sophisticated biometric identification systems in spaces accessible to the public, or in social networks that have replaced words, dialogue and ordinary language with emoticons (emotion and icon), hashtags (# and tags) and likes, has produced a cultural and linguistic impoverishment, a problem of source reliability, as well as an homologating and globalized atomism, difficult to manage even for the legislator of the interactive and hyperconnected society. Information is not as easily possessed as things, so the feeling that it belongs to everyone (and therefore to no one!) is widespread: the "like" spreads, floods the world [29]. Therefore, *the virtualization of the real* causes the loss of presence, vision and consistency of the existing: we find ourselves in an evanescent space-environment, sterilized, as in a cloud, and in a disembodied, exteriorized time, submissived to the measure. On the other hand, the constantly *onlife reality* is still a human product, which derives from culture and alphabetic practice, that is, it is a reality "already totally humanized, interpreted, reduced and transcribed, relativized and historicized: the silent and unpredictable fruit of a great and ingenious communicative and expressive practice, such as literacy" [12].

At the base of AI there is the creativity of the human being: his project, inventiveness and attitude to endless research.

4 Well-being Pathologies. The Emptying of the Common-Social Good

The *AI Act*, the agreement approved by the European Parliament to regulate artificial intelligence and ensure that rights and freedoms remain at the center of this technology, took charge of the critical elements of opacity and risk: it is only a first step, more will be needed, but it is still significant that this happened in the old continent, still a source (until when?) of the values of the humanistic tradition.

This, however, does not prevent some stumbles, or at least raises some doubts. In the *Regulation (EU) 2024/1689 of the European Parliament and of the Council*, for example, it is stated that, as prerequisite, AI should be an "anthropocentric" technology, and it is argued that its ultimate goal is to increase "human well-being" [35] There is also widespread talk of "benefits" and "evolution" in the prevailing cumulative meaning of "advantages", "acquisitions", "increases", "developments" of a quantitative type [36]: for example, *AI Act* no. 4 states that "AI consists of a rapidly evolving family of technologies that contributes to the achievement of a wide range of economic, environmental and social *benefits* across the entire spectrum of industrial and social activities"; no. 20 speaks of "obtaining the maximum *benefits*", and no. 27 of "bringing *benefits* to all human beings".

But we could ask: what is the difference between "well-being", "benefit" and "good", or rather "common good" and "social good"?

In the message for the 57th World Day of Peace (1 January 2024) [37], entitled *Artificial Intelligence and Peace*, Pope Francis pointed out that technological innovations are not "neutral" or disincarnated by reality, but reflect "chooses conditioned by personal, social and cultural values", the result of specifically human approaches to the surrounding world that, as such, "always have an ethical dimension" [37]. He therefore asked crucial questions, which strongly interweave, disciplines such as philosophy, social epistemology, political science, ecology: what future is looming for humanity, and what will be the consequences of the "fourth revolution" on the international stability? Will justice, equity, solidarity and peace be guaranteed or taken away from peoples, individuals, societies? Will artificial intelligence promote the integral development of the whole of humanity in culture? Will it be "sustainable", or will it feed new fragilities and vulnerabilities? Will it produce a stable and lasting form of the common good?

Also about the "human enhancement" the Vatican document was then pronounced *Antiqua and nova. Note on the Relationship Between Artificial Intelligence and Human Intelligence* [38]: the risk is to neglect the epistemological commitment to distinguish what is specific to human cognition from the potential of artificial intelligences. It is a qualitative work, which philosophy is able to discipline with rigorous criteria and methods, and in particular the philosophy of knowledge anchored to a philosophy of the person: as the only cognitive act, the *intelligere* includes both the *ratio* (argumentative and discursive thinking, judgment, *noesis*) and the *intellectus* (intuition of reality through the inner gaze of the *mens*), that is, the two fundamental and complementary prerogatives of human intelligence, which are exercised in an authentic and productive way only in social and interpersonal relationality [38].

Can the same be said for inorganic intelligence, not conscious?

The “well-being” of the human person cannot be understood in a merely material, individual and atomistic sense but, open to the personal and interpersonal horizon, says the inviolable dignity of each and every one, without exceptions, and the interweaving of relational resources that are the foundation of social, civil and community life. In fact, if “true wisdom has more to do with recognizing the true meaning of life than with the availability of data” [39], politics will have to take on the high and arduous task of “promoting and protecting, beyond any particular interest, the good of the community, the common good, especially in defense of the weakest and most marginalized”, because personal and interpersonal life is built in human “places” distinct and distant from the “limited schemes that any soulless machine can prepackage”. Thus, we are urged to reflect on the qualitative difference between the “static memory” that stores an amazing number of data, and the memory “of man and woman, which is instead creative, dynamic, generative, capable of uniting past, present and future” [40].

If, as Hans Jonas already said in the seventies of the twentieth century, the desecration of nature and the civilization of humanity go hand in hand [41], today philosophy is called to questions that it can no longer avoid: is it possible to think of technology at the service of the human person, and not vice versa? Which horizon, if the human will disappear by “overcoming”? What future, if by violating the environment and the common home we risk extinction by self-destruction?

In Jonas’s analysis, the *techne* has become an inexhaustible forward thrust of the human species: its seemingly unlimited progress tends to be identified with the vocation of the human, with the fulfillment of his own destiny, that is, total control over things, over nature and other humans. More recently, the myth of efficiency, articulated in the illusion of omnipotence and the idolatry of techno-science, has pushed Jean Attali to affirm that the human being, now useless to his creations, will simply disappear, because they have replaced him [27].

One last issue, no less relevant. Paradoxically, one of the most widespread well-being pathologies in our technologically advanced societies is the absence of *pathos*, the anesthesia of feeling, the indifference, the lack of empathy, the inability to relate to oneself and with others, the voluntary isolation, the detachment from the family, school and social reality in favor of the reality mediated by technologies, which characterizes millions of young digital natives around the world. As is known, the Japanese term for this phenomenon is called *hikikomori*, which designates being on the sidelines, withdrowing from life, closing oneself in one’s own room, despite a medium-high cultural level and a considerable logical intelligence, not supported, however, by social and emotional intelligence. It is not (only) a mental or psychic illness, but a deep “discomfort”, which comes from well-being: a new form of discomfort of society, of culture, of civilization? [42]. This rampant social phenomenon is a pathology of well-being, unfortunately distinct and distant from that “drawing the courtains”, which we find in *A Room of One’s Own* by Virginia Woolf [43].

5 Limit as Sense: Death as Living Act

What relationship we could find with the prospect of immortality, exceeding the limit and death, coveted by trans-humanism?

An effective answer can be found in Max Scheler's unpublished pages on the issue of the subject of freedom as liberation from mechanical causality and determinism and, in particular, on death in the context of moral life. Written in 1917, they state that thinking about death means grasping at the same time something in us that overcomes and surpasses it, with respect to which it has no power; it means living it not as an absolute limit, but as a "limit" of our being and our tending, that is, as a trait beyond which something of us is still guarded: it means seeing that if life is subtracted from our being, it is not equal to nothing, but rather to infinity [44].

If the beginning of thought is not exclusively the *logos*, but also the *pathos*, or rather the interweaving of *logos* and *pathos*, on the other hand artificial intelligence is apathetic, without *pathos*, without passion, and belongs to the calculating thought of Heideggerian memory, that is, to the reasoning understood as calculation. But calculating or computing is not the authentic meaning of *logos* and *ratio*, and it is a fact that our western civilization has progressed more in the fight against pain, than in the intelligence of suffering—, ignoring or removing that, while pain is known by experience, the experience of suffering generates a new knowledge and a new self-knowledge. Here philosophy is placed as commitment, responsibility and task, to integrate the resources of civilizing science and technology with the promotion of the human in its integrality and in its non-anonymous uniqueness.

All this noted, and returning to the initial hub of this contribution, it would still be misleading to argue that the vulnerability of personalism, announced by Ricoeur in 1983, corresponds to its decrease or marginalization, put in place by the post-and trans-humanism. By contrast, some "places" of contemporary thought resurface to the mind, such as the methodological-logical exercise of conversion of the gaze proposed by one of Ricoeur's masters, Edmund Husserl, who focuses on the issue by overturning it: death is a borderline case of life, because without life there is no death [45]. Or Max Scheler's reflections in the essay *Tod und Fortleben*, on the extreme limit of finitude, which makes human life as really human and as a singular existence: the non-living cannot intuit, know, foreshadow, experience death, simply because it is "an act of the living itself" [46], that is, an act in the first person standpoint.

But it's not just about the non-living. Compared to animal life, elsewhere Scheler remarks the human exception of consciousness and intentionality: certainly animals feel and suffer, but this suffering is as if whispered in their ear by nature, to which they belongs. No observation forces us, continues Scheler, to assume that animals are aware of their own death, before its completion. It is an outcome, not an intention: that is, it is suffered, not chosen and not understood [44]. Edith Stein echoes Scheler when, at the Augustinian and Husserlian school of the "inner gaze" [47], she carries out the eidetic analysis of the human person, providing an interesting example: when we look into the eyes of an animal, we penetrate an interiority, inside a soul, which feels our gaze and our presence. But it is a soul incapable of leaving itself and understanding itself, a soul that remains imprisoned in itself, and at the same time distant from itself. When, on the other hand, we look into the eyes of a human being, his gaze replies: he/she can welcome us or reject us, and he/she is free to do so, because he/she can come out of himself or herself. When two human beings look at each other, an "I" is in front of "another-I": it can be an encounter that takes place on the threshold, or deeply in the interior. When it happens in the very inner, then the "other I" is a "You" [48].

In his *Anthropologie der Sinne*, also Helmuth Plessner offers precious words to our audience, when he states that the cross of the sentient living body (*Leib*) is his intertwining with the physical body (*Körper*), a complicated "being across" and "being sideways" spared to animals and other living beings, who have neither "I" nor "me", who do not recognize themselves in the mirror, who have no consciousness and selfconsciousness. Thus, our "being-body" presents itself to the subject who lives it from within as a conflicting and aporetic knot [49].

The human being can even give himself death, he can decide his own and someone else's death, he can somehow consent to it (and not only through suicide, as I will immediately try to show), he can testify to it while he is still alive. In this regard, one can refer to the poignant reflections of Maurice Blanchot on the escaped death of the young Frenchman by the hands of the Nazi soldier, who causes a feeling of lightness, untranslatable in ordinary words: freed from life? The infinity that opens up? Neither happiness nor unhappiness, as if death *outside* him could from then only clash with death *in* him [50]. Therefore, the *instant* of one's own death as an inescapable *instance*, a window on immortality and infinity. In the Seminar held on November 9, 1994 in Paris, Jacques Derrida commented on this dense writing by Blanchot, noting that it does not happen twice to die, so only one dead person is immortal, and immortals are dead: immortality is in death, it is in the instant of death [51]. So it is not about immortality as an in(de)finite extension of life, as life and even more life, as a victory over death, or escape from death [52]. Here immortality belongs entirely to dying and to its *instant-instance*: it is an expected death, a waiting death, postponed but present, therefore in some way already witnessed—anticipated by the phenomenological living present, the previous, anterior future.

Today, the advances of science and techno-science increase the illusion of prolonging, perhaps even extending the duration of life indefinitely, by neutralizing the biochemical processes of aging. In this way, death is no longer thought of as a necessity intrinsic to the very nature of life, but as an avoidable, or at least delayable organic dysfunction.

Is it therefore the question about death, and consequently about life, that makes human the human being? Among living beings, we are the only ones characterized by a singular attitude: the thought of death, which pushes us to go beyond the horizon of life in the world [24]. Perhaps, we can return to Welte's question, when he asked how to interpret the immortality, the inviolability and the dignity of people (already) dead [52]. The burial of the dead, the votive gifts, the ritual care with which we separate ourselves from the corpses and the rembering kept lit by the memory of our loved ones, our friends, our acquaintances, also document from the point of view of social epistemology the strength of the testimony in the first person, which with Gabriel Marcel exclaims: you won't die! It's not about here anymore of an earlier, previous, anticipated future, but of the crossing-exceeding of time: of the immortality of dead people, as a variation of the living present (*lebendigen Gegenwart*).

Human life is self-conscious as finite, and therefore mortal, because it experiences time from within – the time that lasts, the living time, qualitative one. In addition to philosophers of the caliber of S. Augustine, S. Kierkegaard, H. Bergson, W. James, W.

Husserl, M. Heidegger, E. Stein, P. Ricoeur, I would like to remember here the young Ludwig Wittgenstein, when in the war diaries he tore the limits of time by concentrating them on the instant: "Who is happy must not be afraid. Not even of death. Only those who live not in time, but in the present, are happy. For life in the present there is no death" [53].

6 Person Beyond Personalisms: a Frame of Reference

In this chapter, I propose a frame of reference of the philosophy of the person—which embraces the themes of the intentional bodily-living consciousness, of the will, sensitivity, freedom, of the "pathic" reason, of the epistemic agents, of the first-person experience of reality, of living space and time from within—, as an attempt to respond, albeit schematic and cursory, to the criticalities of techno-and info-science.

First: not "personalism", but *philosophy of the person.* Like any other -ism, personalism also represents the deformation and destructuring of an idea and a practice, which easily yields to abstract conceptualization and yellows in the pages of obsolete manuals; when it then pretends to be confronted with the -isms of the various materialisms, determinisms, collectivisms, idealisms, physicalisms, ecologisms, animalisms, pacifism, narcissisms..., one cannot help but think with gratitude of Maurice Merleau-Ponty, according to which the philosophy laid in books ceases to really question human beings [19]. How to say: philosophy, well folded in the orderly and organized drawers of manuals, no longer plays the role of questioning and attestation, it no longer knows how to search, listen, speak in the first person.

Second: philosophy of the person is a discipline conjugated to the *future*, because it does not fall into the temptation of the one that Zigmunt Bauman called "retrotopia" [54], turning back to a past that never returns—nostalgic, plaintive and therefore unhappy and unproductive posture. Rather, it is an earlier future, in the sense i) of the debt and the bond that every innovation has with tradition, the past; ii) of a present that is certainly imperfect but aware of a vision, far sighted, intentional and not disjointed from the performative *logos* and *pathos* of testimony; iii) therefore, of overcoming the caesura between present and future, which seems to characterize our era as an era of the neutral, fluid, impersonal, amorphous, hybrid.

Third: philosophy of the person is linked to the theme of life, or rather to the *ontology of the living*. Today, however, an artificial conception of biological life prevails: by dint of talking about intelligence and the life of artifacts, we have lost the sense of organic living, the difference between organism and machine. There seems to be no difference between natural and artificial: artifacts impose themselves to the point that human freedom must confront them, in a new and bold sense. The human being himself seems to have become one of the objects of technology. But "living" is said in many ways and unfolds in variously articulated forms, according to a complex ontological stratigraphy of a qualitative type. In the inter-subjective experience of the world, for example, the philosophical question of birth is also implicated: Husserl found that, as the death of others is constituted in consciousness first, so also the birth of others is the birth constituted first. That is to say that the philosophy of the person is originally and phenomenologically called to otherness and summoned by otherness, in the sense that the world is a world for everyone, no one excluded; and that living (*Erleben*) is irreducible. Through the emphasis on the irreducibility of the person, therefore of the non-anonymony quality of life, we must therefore admit, with Emmanuel Lévinas, that each face is unique.

Fourth: that each face is unique invalidates today's posture of the *quantified Self*, which recites its *Self knowledge through numbers.* Byung-Chul Han carries out his reflections in the era of big data and social control through algocracy, or the theft of our digital identities (tends, habits, interests, desires, propensities, purchases) thanks to algorithms, for purposes not certainly humanistic but commercial and commodifying, according to the logic of profit [29]. So, Yuval Noah Harari's formula sounds really effective, according to which: biological knowledge multiplied by computer power, multiplied by data = ability to hack human beings [55].

But how did we get to this if, about the modern meaning of the Self, Charles Taylor had operated a sophisticated theoretical-ethical reconnaissance and traced in Saint Augustine the qualitative posture of a first-person philosophy ("first-person standpoint"), parent of the school of the "inner gaze", then arrived in the twentieth century and in particular to phenomenology [56]? What happened in the transition from modern to post-modern, from post-modern to hyper-modern, and from hyper-modern to trans-human and over-human?

Fifth: philosophy of the person, however one articulated it—from the very center of the person rays of plural, inter-and trans-disciplinary perspectives depart: sociological, legal-regulatory, economic, political, anthropological-cultural, psychological, technological, ethical, bioethic, medical, psychiatric...—is or should be a philosophy *in the first person.* That is, an intentional-performative philosophy, *et-et*, to put it with a twentieth-century term, which it knows how to distinguish without separating (the continental from the analytical, the intentional acts of the consciousness from the speech acts, the intentionality of the phenomenology from the performativity of the pragmatics of language). The intentional-performative marks an act, a bond, a duality and not a dualism, that is, a relationship and a correlation that bear the trace of complexity: an *epistemic agent*, which cannot be neutral, amorphous, liquid, fluid, hybrid, sterile, immune or impersonal. That it cannot therefore be a machine, or an artifact [47].

7 Language Games, Social Practices and Logics of Testimony

For this reason, the exclamation "Person is back!" [5], conceived as a strategy to escape from the -ism of the personalism, can be understood as an effective performative—and yet: a happy or unhappy performative? The performative statement, as it is known, does not concern the conditions of truth or falsehood, but the forms of ethics, the forms of life, according to the pragmatic-social diction of L. Wittgenstein then effectively taken up by John Austin [57]: certainly the performative responds to the primacy of practice but, since it adheres to the first person of the *present* verb and therefore to the *presence*, to the sense-meaning of the act, of acting and of the agent, it also responds to the theoretical instances of awareness and freedom that we have set ourselves in thinking the relationship between philosophy and technoscience.

Formulated with some excess of simplification from certain handbooks, the difference between *speech acts* and *intentionale Erlebnisse* does not exclude the reflection on the point of convergence between analytical and continental philosophy, in the forms of pragmatics of language and phenomenology: the first-person experience of reality, the interweaving of consciousness and language, the intentional-performative. It is the link between *logos* and *action*: while intentionality has a history that comes from a long and consolidated philosophical tradition (think of the scholastic *intentio*, taken up by Franz Brentano and then by Edmund Husserl), performativity is a diction coined more recently by John Austin in the study of ordinary language and vehicular intentions (ivi). In the wake of Wittgenstein's *Philosophical Investigations* [58]: words are actions and speaking a language is part of an activity, or a form of life), the British philosopher has developed a speech acts theory, in which the performative statement does, accomplishes and executes what we say. Ascribed to the first person of the present tense, the nucleus of meaning of the performative statement resides in the *illocutive force* that, conveying the intention of the speaker, is understood by the interlocutor and shared intersubjectively, with obvious social, civil and public resonances.

On the pragmatics of language and Wittgenstein's "language games" he expressed himself in a far-sighted way, in the German-speaking area, Hans-Georg Gadamer in the collection of writings called *Vernunft im Zeitalter der Wissenschaft* [24]. If the original relationship to practice, intrinsic in speaking, has taken over the unique language of science, this is also basically a hermeneutic principle: the methods of understanding an assertion, a speech or a text depend in fact on the purpose to which these various modes of expression are aimed. The German philosopher concludes that, when language performs its communicative function, it cannot be considered as a mere information technique, but rather as an "agreement" for the construction of a common world, of our own social and interpersonal life.

The philosophical questions related to our social practices and our living in a shared and normative world, are intertwined with the question of finitude, precariousness and death, giving rise to the reflection of the last Ricoeur on the logic of testimony: while we are alive, our relationship with death that has not yet come to fruition is forgotten, modified by the anticipation and internalization of the question about the fate of those who have already died. It's the dead of tomorrow, somehow to the future ahead, which we imagine. The image of the dead that each of us will be for the others raises questions: what are they, where are they, what are the dead like? Seeing ourselves, imagining ourselves, prefiguring ourselves already dead before we were dead, and applying to ourselves a question of "survivors", is the nagging of what Ricoeur calls the "previous future" [59].

We met Derrida to reflect on Blanchot's autobiographical story *L'instant de ma mort*, and in particular on the final chiosa, the torment of injustice of having been spared by the execution platoon, left alive in the certainty of a prolonged death, while death has (already) been inflicted on others. The instant (*instant*) of one's death, since then and forever, is *en instance* [50]: it remains inside, it is lived from the inside, it is an internal *instance of*. Derrida observes that, in legal language, the French expression *en instance* indicates the verdict not yet formulated, not yet pronounced, that is, the expectation of judgment: starting from the instance of the instant, testimony is possible [51]. You have survived, you are still alive in a present that attests to the future and that, precisely for this reason, is already here, now. In this sense, the action of testimony is, as the Italian personalist philosopher Armando Rigobello writes, "anticipation of the future, place of its expression", personal and in the first person, "as long as time is understood as inner time" [60].

To (not) conclude

I have proposed some philosophical observations on the possible developments of the idea of the limit as a sense and meaning (and not as an obstacle) of human life, which are placed in dialogue and listening to the international scientific community on issues of common interest. Obviously, there is still a lot of work to be done. These are just notes on the difference between AI and human intelligence, as well as between the static memory of the artifact, with its predictive capacity and with its storage system, and the dynamic memory of the human being, intentional and creative body-living consciousness that, in the embrace of *logos* and *pathos*, is able to understand the sense of one's own finitude and one's existence in living time.

References

1. Anders, G.: Die Antiquiertheit des Menschen, Bd. I: Über die Seele im Zeitalter der zweiten industriellen Revolution. C.H. Beck, München (1956), Bd. II: Über die Zerstörung des Lebens im Zeitalter der dritten industriellen Revolution, C.H. Beck, München (1980)
2. Floridi, L.: The Fourth Revolution: How the Infosphere is Reshaping Human Reality. Oxford University Press, Oxford (U.K.) (2014)
3. Beneduce, C., Bertolaso, M.: Personalized Medicine in the Making: Philosophical Perspectives from Biology to Healthcare. Springer Nature, Cham (2022)
4. Manganaro, P. (ed.): Fenomenologia della vita. Senso, valore, cura, Carabba, Lanciano (2022)
5. Ricoeur, P.: Meurt le personnalisme, revient la personne. Esprit. **73**, 113–119 (1983)
6. Cristianini, N.: Sovrumano. Oltre i limiti della nostra intelligenza. Il Mulino, Bologna (2025)
7. Wallach, W., Allen, C. (eds.): Moral Machines: Teaching Robots from Wrong. Oxford University Press, Oxford-New York (2008)
8. Rees, M.: On the Future: Prospects for Humanity. Princeton University Press, Princeton (N.J.) (2018
9. Fabris, A.: Ethics of Information and Communication Technologies. Springer Nature, Cham (2018)
10. Mitchell, M.: Artificial Intelligence: A Guide for Thinking Humans. Macmillan, London (2019)
11. Bertolaso, M., Sterpetti, F. (eds.): A Critical Reflection on Automated Science: Will Science Remain Human? Springer Nature, Cham (2020)
12. Sini, C.: Intelligenza artificiale e altri scritti. Jaca Book, Milano (2024)
13. Ganascia, J.G.: Le Mythe de la Singularité. Faut-il craindre l'intelligence artificielle? Seuil, Paris (2017)
14. Ganascia, J.G.: Intelligence Artificielle: vers une domination programmé? Le Cavalier Bleu, Paris (2017)
15. Ganascia, J.G.: L'I.A. expliquée aux humains. Seuil, Paris (2024)
16. Cristianini, N.: Machina Sapiens. L'algoritmo che ci ha rubato il segreto della conoscenza. Il Mulino, Bologna (2024)
17. Fabris, A., Belardinelli, S. (eds.): Digital Environments and Human Relations. Ethical Perspectives on Ai Issues. Springer Nature, Cham (2024)
18. Ferraris, M.: La pelle. Che cosa significa pensare nell'era dell'intelligenza artificiale. Il Mulino, Bologna (2025)

19. Merleau-Ponty, M.: Éloge de la philosophie et autres essais. Gallimard, Paris (1953)
20. Benanti, P.: Le macchine sapienti, pp. 11–12. Intelligenze artificiali e decisioni umane. Marietti, Bologna (2022)
21. Zahavi, D.: Phenomenology: the Basics. Routledge, Abingdon-New York (2025)
22. Zahavi, D.: Being we: Phenomenological Contributions to Social Ontology. Oxford University Press, Oxford (2025)
23. Morin, E.: Les sept savoirs nécessaries à la éducation du futur. Publié par l'Organisation des Nation Unies pour l'éducation, la science et la culture (UNESCO), Paris (1999)
24. Gadamer, H.G.: Vernunft im Zeitalter der Wissenschaft. Frankfurt a. M, Suhrkamp (1976)
25. Stein, E.: Der Aufbau der menschlichen Person. Vorlesung zur philosophischen Anthropologie, hrsg. von B. Bekmann-Zöller, Herder, Freiburg-Basel-Wien (2014)
26. Augé, M.: Où est passé l'avenir? Éd. Du Panama, Paris (2008)
27. Attali, J.: Une brève histoire de l'avenir. Fayard, Paris (2006)
28. Harari, Y.N.: Homo Deus: Brief History of Tomorrow. Harvill Secker, London (2016)
29. Han, B.C.: Undinge: Umbrüche der Lebenswelt. Ullstein Buchverlage Gmbh, Berlin (2021)
30. Canobbio, G.: Fine dell'eccezione umana? La sfida delle scienze all'antropologia. Morcelliana, Brescia (2018)
31. Floridi, L. (ed.): The Onlife Manifesto. Being Human in a Hyperconnected Era, Springer, Heidelberg-New York-Dordrecht-London (2015)
32. Floridi, L. (ed.): The Onlife Manifesto: Being Human in a Hyperconnected Era, Heidelberg-New York-Dordrecht-London, p. 8 (2015)
33. Floridi, L. (ed.): The Onlife Manifesto: Being Human in a Hyperconnected Era, Heidelberg-New York-Dordrecht-London, p. 9 (2015)
34. Floridi, L. (ed.): The Onlife Manifesto: Being Human in a Hyperconnected Era, vol. 74. Springer, Heidelberg-New York-Dordrecht-London (2015)
35. Regulation (EU) 2024/1689 of the European Parliament and of the Council of 13 June 2024. https://eur-lex.europa.eu/eli/reg/2024/1689/oj?eliuri=eli%3Areg%3A2024%3A1689%3Aojlocale=en
36. Regulation (EU) 2024/1689 of the European Parliament and of the Council of 13 June 2024, IV m. 4,8,20,27,58. https://eurlex.europa.eu/eli/reg/2024/1689/oj?eliuri=eli%3Areg%3A2024%3A1689%3Aojlocale=en
37. Pope Francis: Artificial intelligence and peace. Message of his holiness Pope Francis for the 57th World day of peace (2024). https://www.vatican.va/content/francesco/en/messages/peace/documents/20231208-messaggio-57giornatamondiale-pace2024.html
38. Congregation for the Doctrine of the Faith and Dicastery for Culture and Education, Antiqua et nova. Nota Antiqua Nova (2025). https://www.vatican.va/roman_curia/congregations/cfaith/documents/rc_ddf_doc_20250128_antiqua-et-nova_it.html
39. Pope Leo XIV: Message of Pope Leo XIV to Participants in the Second Annual Conference on Atificial Intelligence, Ethics, and Corporate Governance (2025). https://www.vatican.va/content/leo-xiv/en/messages/pontmessages/2025/documents/20250617-messaggio-ia.html
40. Pope Leo XIV: Address of Pope Leo XIV to Members of the International Inter-Parliamentary Union (2025). https://www.vatican.va/content/leo-xiv/en/speeches/2025/june/documents/20250621-giubileo-governanti.html
41. Jonas, H.: Das Prinzip Verantwortung. Versuch einer Ethik für die technologische Zivilisation, Insel Verlag, Frankfurt a.M (1979)
42. Freud, S.: Das Unbehagen in der Kultur. Internationaler Psychoanalytischer Verlag, Wien (1929)
43. Woolf, V.: A Room of One's Own. Hogarth Press, London (1929)
44. Scheler, M.: Tod im Kontext des moralischen Lebens. Ms. ANA 315 CA, vol. IX, p. 13. Staatdbibliothek, München (1917)

45. Husserl, E.: Grenzprobleme der Phänomenologie. Analysen des Unbewusstseins und der Instinkte. Metaphysik. Späte Ethik. Texte aus dem Nachlass (1908–1937), hrsg. von R. Sowa Vongehr T.: Husserliana, Bd. XLII. Springer, Dordrecht (2014)
46. Scheler, M.: Tod und Fortleben. Francke, Bern (1957)
47. Ricoeur, P.: La mémoire, l'histoire, l'oubli. Seuil, Paris (2000)
48. Stein, E.: Der Aufbau der menschlichen Person. Vorlesung zur philosophischen Anthropologie, hrsg. von B. Bekmann-Zöller. Herder, Freiburg-Basel-Wien (2025)
49. Plessner, H.: Anthropologie der Sinne. In Gesammelte Schriften, Bd. I. Sihrkamp, Frankfurt a.M. (1980)
50. Blanchot, M.: L'instant de ma mort. In: Blanchot, M., Derrida, J. (eds.) The Instant of my Death—Demeure. Fiction and Testimony, Engl. Trans. By E. Rottenberg. Stanford University Press, Stanford (CA) (2000)
51. Derrida, J.: Demeure. Fiction and testimony, in Blanchot, M., Derrida, J. (eds.) The Instant of my Death—Demeure. Fiction and Testimony, Engl. Trans. By E. Rottenberg. Stanford University Press, Stanford (CA) (2000)
52. Welte, B.: Der Ernstfall der Hoffnung, in Leiblichkeit, Endlichkeit und Unendlichkeit, Gesammelte Schriften, Band I/3. Herder, Freiburg im Breisgau (2006)
53. Wittgenstein, L.: Tagebücher 1914–1916, hrsg. von G.E.M. Anscombe, G.H. von Wright. Basil Blackwell, Oxford (1961)
54. Bauman, Z.: Retrotopia. Polity Press, Cambridge (U.K.) (2017)
55. Harari, Y.N.: 21 Lessons for the 21st Century. Vintage Publishing, New York (2019)
56. Taylor, C.: Sources of the Self: The Making of Modern Identity. Cambridge University Press, Cambridge (UK) (2003)
57. Austin, J.: How to Do Things with Words. Oxford University Press, Oxford (1962)
58. Wittgenstein, L.: In: Anscombe, G.E.M., Rhees, R. (eds.) Philosophical Investigations. Basil Blackwell, Oxford (1953)
59. Ricoeur, P.: Vivant jusqu'à la mort. Suivi de Fragments. Seuil, Paris (2007)
60. Rigobello, A.: Il futuro della libertà, vol. 60. Studium, Roma (1978)
61. Cristianini, N.: The Shortcut. Why Intelligent Machines Do Not Think like us. CRC Press, London-New York (2023)

The Place and Role of Humans in the Age of Generative AI

Yurii Mielkov[1,2](✉)

[1] Institute of Higher Education of the NAES of Ukraine, 01014 Kyiv, Ukraine
y.myelkov@ihed.org.ua

[2] Interregional Academy of Personnel Management, 03039 Kyiv, Ukraine

Abstract. The paper is dedicated to the philosophical problems of what place and roles remain to humans in the world where, according to some predictions, 'the end of humanity' is being anticipated, as AI-based technologies learn to process information much better than humans do and thus tend to replace human persons in doing their jobs. It is argued, however, that such a scenario is unrealistic: AI and LLMs are just tools; they can't create anything and are actually quite limited in their capabilities. It is shown that some threats related to their usage still remain, including humans' inability to control AI-based technologies and overtrust them: the solution to this problem requires us to adopt responsible and critical approaches to such technologies. It is concluded that human qualities and specific features of human nature, like open, critical, and non-linear thinking, as well as moral judgment and evaluation, appear inaccessible to AI, even in the long-term perspectives of machine learning, and thus become today even more needed and relevant.

Keywords: Humanism · Generative AI · Machine thinking · AI limitations · AI threats · Human-machine interaction

1 Introduction

The development of AI-based technologies, and especially those related to generative AI and LLMs, like the new popular versions of ChatGPT, can present great challenges for humanity, supposedly ranging from threats of growing unemployment to even some profound existential risks. The latter possibility could be demonstrated by the results of the survey conducted amongst leading AI researchers in 2022: the median respondent believing that the probability of the long-run effect of advanced AI on humanity is "extremely bad" (something like human extinction) was 5%, and as many as 48% of respondents gave at least the 10% chance for such an extremely bad outcome [4]. However, the former threat could appear much more realistic: 80% of workers are said to have their jobs impacted by AI in one or another way [10]. Earlier, in 2018, researchers even used to believe that AI has a 50% chance to outperform humans in virtually any of their tasks in 45 years—and replace all human jobs in 120 years; particularly it was predicted that AI will be able to outperform humans in translating languages already by

R. Giovagnoli et al. (Eds.): IS4SI 2025, SAPERE 81, pp. 58–65, 2026.
https://doi.org/10.1007/978-3-032-31732-2_5

2024, in driving trucks by 2027, in writing bestselling books by 2049, and in working as a surgeon by 2053 [5]. It is not surprising then that some "influential people" in the industry and the mass media, like Elon Musk or Yuval Noah Harari, anticipate "the end of humanity as we know it": as AI is learning to do "everything", humans who have lesser abilities for processing and controlling data, are becoming obsolete for the future, with maybe the only exception for them is to transform themselves into a kind of "transhumane cyborgs" [3, 8].

The task of this chapter will be to investigate, from a broad and philosophical point of view, what place and what role could be left to humans in the world of technologies based on generative AI, and do the predictions about 'the end of humanity' have any truth in them. Is AI able to do everything humans do, and if not, then what it can do and what it can't do at all?

2 The Capability of Machines to Replace Humans in the Philosophical Thought of the 19th and 20th Centuries

It would be better to start by stressing the fact that the very idea of machines replacing humans is not a new one at all. As early as in the 1830s, Charles Babbage, who is credited to be one of the inventors of a computer, stated that an advantage deriving from machinery "is from the check which it affords against the inattention, the idleness, or the dishonesty of human agents", particularly regarding mostly wearisome occupations like "counting a series of repetitions of the same fact" [1, p. 54]. Of course, one can hardly blame the outstanding inventor of *the Analytical Engine* for attempting to substantiate some theory of machine control and dominance over humans. But do machines actually help humans by doing some repetitive tasks instead of them? It is interesting to compare Babbage's position to that of Karl Marx: while being one of the few 19th-century scholars who appreciated Babbage's contribution to the economic study of machinery and factory production, he came to the exact opposite conclusions regarding this principle of the division of labor, seeing it as a source of segregation and social injustice. To Marx, further development and implementation of machines appeared as nothing more than a new way of oppressing the human person, making him or her a servant of a machine, a member of a mechanism, a kind of "living appendage" to a machine, deriving humans of free physical and spiritual activity: "In Manufaktur und Handwerk bedient sich der Arbeiter des Werkzeugs, in der Fabrik dient er der Maschine... ...die Maschine nicht den Arbeiter von der Arbeit befreit, sondern seine Arbeit vom Inhalt" [14, p. 445–446].

At the same time, the 20th century demonstrates that machines can indeed replace humans in some kinds of jobs related to repetitive and wearisome occupations—without much trouble or social discontent. Here we refer to the times when "computers were human" (which is the title of a book by David Grier [6]), like in NASA and similar enterprises in the 1940s: "computers" there were actual occupations for women, who were employed as low-paid but accurate workers to perform simple calculations for the space or air industry. It was not at all a catastrophe when electronic computers started to replace humans in doing such tasks—that is, replacing them in *non-human* jobs. Without the need to do boring and repetitive operations, humans were free to engage in more creative and meaningful work—in fact, some of those women became early computer programmers, and not just unemployed.

So now the question is whether the new types of machines, like today's AI and LLMs, can replace humans in doing that very creative work that requires not just repeating the same operations over and over again. There is no doubt that an advanced computing machine can process information faster and more efficiently than humans do. But can it actually create and, well, think? In the 1940s, Alan Turing famously reduced this philosophical question to a more technological one by proposing to declare a computer *intelligent* if it could pass as a human to an unknowing interrogator. However, I would say that such a reduction not only appears deceptive for our understanding of the ontological status of AI, of what it actually *is* instead of how it *could appear* to some unsuspecting human being,—it can also lead to wrong conclusions regarding supposed similarities and differences between human and machine 'thinking'—"permitting artificial intelligence's perverse grand fantasy to grow", as stated by another pioneer of AI, Joseph Weizenbaum, whose ELIZA was one of the first program to claim the passage of the Turing's test already in the 1960s.

As argued by Weizenbaum, there is a profound difference between the way humans and machines process information—they can't be easily compared between themselves, and there is no way a machine can solve many problems humans face [17, p. 203]. In the 1960s, in an era of general enthusiasm about the seemingly brilliant and indisputable prospects of scientific and technological progress, the topic of machine thinking was quite popular among both scientists and philosophers. But I think that Pavel Kopnin, one of the founders of Kyiv philosophical school of the 20th c., was quite correct by stating that "machine thinking" is not an independent entity, but a side, a subordinate moment of human thinking [11].

In other words, any machine is *a tool* humans use for their own needs. Like an excavator cannot and does not dig and a telescope cannot and does not observe stars all by themselves: it is always a human person who digs or observes, *using* excavators and telescopes as some tools that increase or augment his or her abilities, but not replace them. Without a machine, a person can dig earth with a shovel (which is also a tool of the very same kind), applying more physical force, while with a machine human person may just press a button or a lever in an excavator so the latter will extend its bucket to dig the earth with it. But in any case, it is still the human who digs, even if pressing a button is much easier than operating the shovel. In the same way, any human can observe the stars with the naked eye, and using a telescope magnifies and enriches the quantity and quality of stars and other celestial objects that could be seen, but actually *observing* them is still a task for the human person: no telescope can *see* anything at all by itself.

3 AI, its Possibilities, and its Limitations

I would say that nothing has changed in this basic philosophical conclusion with the advent of generative AI and LLMs. In difference from excavators and telescopes, neural networks and other similar technologies are intended to help humans not with digging or observing, but with different forms of calculating. Still, such a change in the sphere of activity does not make new kinds of machines subjects of that activity: they still remain tools for humans, not something that can calculate without humans and instead of humans.

Maybe, part of the problem those technologies could appear as something totally different from other, more usual machines is very term of *intelligence* coined to them. However, the usage of that term is, strictly speaking, philosophically incorrect and even misleading. It is a very narrow understanding of what intelligence is that is implied by such widespread usage of the term in question. Terminologically, intelligence is not intellect, just like information is not knowledge, and being *generative* does not mean being *creative* [15, 16]. Or, in the case of generative AI, *being* at all (in the sense of Cartesian *cogito ergo sum*)—that is, being the subject of any activity at all, not just the activity of processing information.

In order not to rely just on the opinion of philosophers of the previous age, I can also refer to a recent essay by Jaron Lanier aptly titled "There is no A.I.": virtually the same ideas are expressed there as well [13]. According to the author (known for coining a similarly fashionable term of *virtual reality*), AI is a tool, and not an intelligent creature; it can't create anything in principle—it can only combine something already created by humans following its programs, which are still coded by humans themselves. AI can only "mash up work done by human minds", even if the results are becoming more usable and more convincing with the new forms of LLMs.

That is, I would say that, in contrast to human intelligence, AI can only perform *closed* tasks; it is not able to think *out of the box*. Having been programmed by humans, even if programmed for learning new things and abilities, AI still, by definition, deals only with the purely formal rational side of "thinking", which is not contextual and is certainly neither moral nor emotional. Its 'thinking' is linear thinking by algorithms, which cannot achieve the level of non-linearity by definition. That means that AI cannot replace or outperform humans in any kind of *creative* activity—it can only imitate such an activity based on certain approximate models or samples. Even with LLMs, it is impossible for AI to create anything actually *new*, or to evaluate options based not on making random choices, but on identifying their desirability. It could be said that AI appears to be like *Asinus Buridani inter duo prata*, being unable to choose between different options in a non-programmed or non-random way.

For example, in a practical perspective, tools like ChatGPT could certainly help a professional human translator by providing him or her with some rough materials (like interlinear translation) to work with. But it will never replace that professional human translator by doing all the work required—unless we are talking about a *bad* human translator who is unable to create anything besides anything more than the same interlinear translation. Even if the machine-translated text could appear as, say, 90% correct and acceptable, the rest 10% would not be like that. That mostly relates to some professional terms, or to polysemantic words, or to subtle meanings that arise due to the context, etc. That is something only a human person can do well, and a specific human person at that, because it requires either some expertise in the corresponding field, or even some creative thinking that can't be explained in simple rules of thumb or algorithms for anyone (including any machine) to follow.

In fact, you do not have to be a professional translator to see the limitations of AI doing your job—with LLM-based technologies now appearing even in simple Internet searches, anyone can encounter such things as AI hallucinations. The latter term is coined already, even if it is not entirely correct in the same way artificial intelligence isn't, as if we are trying to make LLMs look more anthropomorphic here than they really are. Machines and programs can't fantasize or dream for the same reason they can't think or create—it is just a type of mistake they make when processing information. The reason, as explained by specialists, is quite simple: according to Harry Guinness, an Irish writer and photographer, the problem is that LLMs are designed to predict the next word in a sequence to create a plausible output, like some "really fancy autocorrect", and not to *understand* the true meaning of the question we asked them or the response they make. They do not even have the "ability to reason or apply logic to their responses": "The only reason ChatGPT knows that 1+1=2 is that it has seen that a lot more often in its training data than 1+1=3 or 1+1=4" [7].

In other words, AI here just follows the majority without even analyzing the problem. Here is an example of what could be shown as 'AI hallucination': when asking Google the question "What church is seen from Glorietta at Schönbrunn Palace in Vienna?" it replies with its AI review with the following: "From the Gloriette at Schönbrunn Palace, you can see several prominent churches, including the golden-domed Steinhofkirche, the central St. Stephen's Cathedral, and the Karlskirche. Other landmarks visible include the skyscrapers of Donau City and the Danube Tower." However, even if the mentioned churches are indeed famous and present major Viennese sightseeing, it is not them but the less known Rudolfsheim Church that can be seen from Glorietta at Schönbrunn Palace, and not St. Stephen's Cathedral or the Karlskirche. That is, the LLM used by Google does not even try to understand the question and answer it; it just checks the words used in the query and finds similar related words amongst the database of vast data available to it (including the commentaries most tourists add to their pictures while naming the most famous Viennese churches instead of the actually pictured one).

It could be argued that such a limitation is but a temporary one, and maybe in the more or less near future, LLMs would learn to reason and to answer questions in a better way, but there is little proof it could be so. A telescope can't develop some conscience and start to look at stars without a human person—it can only be made bigger and more powerful by humans themselves. An inability to think and to be a subject of any activity is by definition the core feature of an inanimate tool.

4 Trust and Control over AI: The Perspectives of Humanism

Such a conclusion may sound as quite an optimistic response to the question about the place of humans in the world of generative AI, meaning that there is no reason to fear that LLMs and other AI-based technologies could replace teachers, writers, truck drivers and so on in the job market—unless of course we are talking about 'bad' and non-creative teachers or writers. However, there is another threat related to LLMs, as even if machines cannot replace humans, their incorrect or non-critical usage or overreliance on them can still harm people. If such technologies are to augment humans, then it is important to treat them in an adequate and responsible way.

There are at least two problems here, the first one being the imbalance of trust and control. As noted by Martin Bekker, critical thinking is at threat when there is a tendency (especially among university students) to treat the AI-based technologies as something that is superior to humans—and thus to trust anything ChatGPT would tell them [2]. The problem is that it may be quite difficult to distinguish a true message from a fake message due to the enormous volume of information available. And that means that we have a kind of *circulus vitiosus* here: you have to be an expert in some field of knowledge in order to check and confirm (or reject) the information provided by an article in Wikipedia or a reply by a LLM that is prone to hallucinations, but if somebody is already an expert, he or she is in no need to consult Wikipedia or ChatGPT in the first place. That means that we should rely on AI-based technologies only in them performing tasks we know well, so that we can assess the results of their work (and not on something that is totally unclear to us).

Another problem is a bit similar: overreliance on LLMs and similar technologies can lead to humans losing their grip on their own activities: the temptation to do many usual things with the help of the AI-based technologies can, instead of empowering us, do something exactly opposite. As a recent study led by Nataliya Kosmyna demonstrates, relying on the AI-based technologies for tasks such as writing essays or term papers can reduce brain activity and memory of students, i.e. the effortful cognitive processes required for independent thinking. The researchers call this situation a *cognitive debt*: in the long term, it is able to diminish critical inquiry and creativity and increase vulnerability to manipulation [12].

How to solve this problem, then? It would be easy to just prohibit the usage of LLMs in universities, but that would not be a solution, as the AI-based technologies are everywhere today, and students can use them even without acknowledging that. So what needed is a working conception of something like digital humanism [9]—and humanism here is the whole Weltanschauung stance that enables and requires a human person to have the courage to use one's own mind (instead of relying on anybody's or anything else's judgment) and thus to be the only and true subject of one's own activity.

In Kant's time, it was important to stress humanism as the freedom of any person from the external authority of other persons or social and political institutions, and today it becomes clear that humanism needs reassertion under the perspective of humans' independence from machines. Our lives today have become practically unthinkable without various technical devices with which we communicate in the depersonalized language of information—and which, naturally, respond to us in the same way. Designed to make human life easier, these machines have, to some extent, usurped the roles and meanings of many distinctly human feelings and capacities. Our impressions and memories, for example, have been alienated from us in the form of photographs and videos; we have forgotten how to experience events directly, having learned instead to postpone our emotional responses until we view the corresponding information recorded by a technical device.

I would call the needed form of the humanist stance an *information culture*: an ability to treat any information in an adequate and responsible way, in order to understand the very nature of any AI-based technologies as tools, and not subjects of activity. Only when we duly treat LLMs as tools can we control them and assert ourselves as human subjects at the same time. And that's what recent reports by the World Economic Forum, made in 2025—after the first wave of AI-enthusiasm and AI-fears has already ebbed away—demonstrate as a response to the raised question about the place and role of human persons in the age of generative AI: the impact of AI-based technologies lies in augmenting human skills through human-machine collaboration, and not in their ability to outperform humans. Despite what some thinkers used to predict, literally none of the human skills assessed were designated as having "very high capacity" to be replaced by the available versions of generative AI, with the majority of skills (69%) having either "very low capacity" or "low capacity" for being substituted: "Skills rooted in human interaction—including empathy and active listening, and sensory processing abilities—and manual dexterity, endurance and precision, currently show no substitution potential due to their physical and deeply human components" [18, p. 43–44].

5 Conclusions

To summarize, there is certainly still a place for humans in the world of generative AI, and there is even a more profound need for humanist values. There is actually no reason to fear AI as it would never "replace" humans: it can't actually do anything all by itself. The idea of *dataism* ('data is everything' etc.) is self-denying, as any data is useless unless it is processed into knowledge and evaluated, and only humans are capable of doing that.

AI does not create knowledge; it processes information. AI does not "think", it performs programmed operations, imitating or following a human person who programmed it or who supplied a database of samples for it to follow. So LLMs and other similar technologies are only able to replace 'bad', non-creative teachers, writers, or truck drivers, and they can help creative teachers, writers, and truck drivers when treated correctly, critically, and adequately, with humans assessing, controlling, and checking the AI-based technologies, not the other way round.

That means that human qualities and specific features of human nature, like open, critical, and non-linear thinking, as well as moral judgment and evaluation, appear inaccessible to AI, even in the long-term perspectives of machine learning. And that's why they become even more important and more relevant in the age of generative AI, as a precondition to control the technologies and to prevent the threat that arise not from the usage of AI in general, but from over-trusting it and getting into a cognitive debt due to over-relying on them.

Disclosure of Interests. The author has no competing interest to declare that is relevant to the content of this article.

References

1. Babbage, C.: On the Economy of Machinery and Manufactures, 4th edn. John Murray, London (1846)
2. Bekker, M.: Heroes and Horror Stories: Thinking About ChatGPT. Wits University Webinar (2023) Last accessed 2 Oct 2025. https://www.youtube.com/watch?v=vdpt6795elo
3. Dürr, A., Furer, J.-M.: The documentary film the end of humanity. Schwarzfalter. (2024) Last accessed 2 Oct 2025. https://endofhumanity.film

4. Grace, K., Stein-Perlman, Z., Weinstein-Raun, B., Salvatier, J.: 2022 expert survey on progress in AI. AI Impacts. (2022) Last accessed 2 Oct 2025. https://aiimpacts.org/2022-expert-survey-on-progress-in-ai/
5. Grace, K., Salvatier, J., Dafoe, A., Zhang, B., Evans, O.: When will AI exceed human performance? Evidence from AI experts. J. Artif. Intell. Res. **62**, 729–754 (2018)
6. Grier, D.A.: When Computers Were Human. Princeton University Press, Princeton (2005)
7. Guinness, H.: What are AI hallucinations and how do you prevent them? Zapier. (2024) Last accessed 2 Oct 2025. https://zapier.com/blog/ai-hallucinations/
8. Harari, Y.N.: Homo deus. Harvill Secker, London (2016)
9. Hofkirchner, W.: Digital humanism. In: Verdegem, P. (ed.) AI for everyone? pp. 33–47. University of Westminster Press, London (2021)
10. Hurst, L.: OpenAI says 80% of workers could see their jobs impacted by AI. These are the jobs most affected. Euronews. (2023) Last accessed 2 Oct 2025. https://www.euronews.com/next/2023/03/23/openai-says-80-of-workers-could-see-their-jobs-impacted-by-ai-these-are-the-jobs-most-affe
11. Kopnin, P.V.: The notion of thinking and cybernetics (in Russian). Voprosy Philosophii. **2**, 103–112 (1961)
12. Kosmyna, N. et al.: Your brain on ChatGPT: accumulation of cognitive debt when using an AI assistant for essay writing task (2025). Last accessed 2 Oct 2025. arXiv preprint arXiv:2506.08872. https://doi.org/10.48550/arXiv.2506.08872
13. Lanier, J.: There is no A.I. The New Yorker (2023) Last accessed 2 Oct 2025. https://www.newyorker.com/science/annals-of-artificial-intelligence/there-is-no-ai
14. Marx, K.: Das Kapital, Bd. I. In: Marx, K., Engels, F. Werke. Bd, vol. 23. Dietz Verlag, Berlin (1968)
15. Mielkov, Y.: AI challenges and humanist foundations for the transformation of higher education. Artif. Intell. **4**(101), 81–87 (2024)
16. Mielkov, Y., Drach, I., Petroye, O.: Knowledge in the age of information technologies: open Science, human competencies and higher education. In: Schroeder, M., Hofkirchner, W. (eds.) Understanding Information and its Role as a Tool, pp. 421–434. World Scientific, Singapore (2025)
17. Weizenbaum, J.: Computer Power and Human Reason: from Judgment to Calculation. W. H. Freeman & Co., New York and San Francisco (1976)
18. World Economic Forum: Future of jobs report (2025). Last accessed 2 Oct 2025. https://reports.weforum.org/docs/WEF_Future_of_Jobs_Report_2025.pdf

Baudrillard's Hyperreality: On Irony, Play, and the Crack in the System

Tomáš Sigmund(✉)

Prague University of Economics and Business, Nám. W. Churchilla 1938/4 130 67, Praha, Czech Republic
sigmund@vse.cz

Abstract. This article interprets Jean Baudrillard's concept of hyperreality in the context of contemporary digital technologies, especially generative artificial intelligence. It argues that hyperreality is not defined by illusion but by saturation—an excess of visibility, information, and operationality that eliminates the distance through which meaning and truth once appeared. Building on Baudrillard's theory of simulation, symbolic exchange, and implosion, the article introduces the notion of the crack: an immanent rupture generated by the system's own drive toward total functionality. The crack manifests in gestures the system cannot fully absorb which reveal the limits of perfect transparency and continuous communication. Artificial intelligence, as the most advanced form of the simulacrum, intensifies these dynamics by producing meaning statistically and autonomously. Yet its very perfection generates new fractures—opacity, loss of authorship, and semantic exhaustion. The article concludes by proposing an ethics of cracks: cultivating opacity, silence, and playful irony as ways of remaining human within a machinic, hyperreal world.

Keyword: Hyperreality · Simulacra · Artificial intelligence · Implosion · Crack play

"The simulacrum is never what hides the truth—it is truth that hides that there is none." (Jean Baudrillard, Simulacra and Simulation [1, p. 2])

1 The World After Reality and the Mirror of AI

1.1 The Age of the Hyperreal

We live in an age in which reality has ceased to be needed. Information, communication, and simulation have merged into a single continuous environment, a regime of visibility without remainder. In this world, what appears is no longer a representation of something absent but the automatic production of presence itself. It is not illusion that defines our time, but over-presence: an excess of signals, data, and visibility that erases the distance through which truth could once appear.

R. Giovagnoli et al. (Eds.): IS4SI 2025, SAPERE 81, pp. 66–79, 2026.
https://doi.org/10.1007/978-3-032-31732-2_6

Jean Baudrillard described this transformation as the passage from representation to simulation. The classical world of representation presumed the existence of a referent, a real object or meaning that could be distorted or revealed. In contrast, simulation envelops the real in a play of models of a real without origin or reality [1, pp. 2–5]. The map precedes the territory; the model replaces the world. Hyperreality is not the loss of truth but the triumph of a world that continues to function after truth has become unnecessary.

The contemporary condition is characterized less by alienation than by saturation. Nothing is hidden, yet nothing is revealed. The more we communicate, the less we have to say. The more we record and display, the more the world disappears behind the smooth surface of its images. As Byung-Chul Han [2, pp. 7–8] later argued, transparency becomes a new form of violence: when everything must be visible, the dimension of interiority and silence collapses. In the fully illuminated world, there is no room for truth—only information.

Against the rhetoric of transparency, Heidegger's notion of truth as aletheia—unconcealment—insists that disclosure always co-belongs with concealment. There is no showing without a reserve; truth is not the elimination of opacity but the event of a clearing (Lichtung) in which beings can appear while withdrawal persists. Hypervisibility, by contrast, abolishes the very difference that makes disclosure possible: when nothing may remain hidden, nothing properly comes to presence. The point is not to add more light but to safeguard the shadow that lets appearance appear. In this aletheic register, the task is custodial rather than corrective: to keep open the interval where revealing and concealing hold together—precisely what hyperreality forgets.

1.2 The Disappearance of the Real

For Baudrillard, the disappearance of the real is not a catastrophe but a logical consequence of modernity's own drive toward perfection. Reality, he suggests, has imploded under the weight of its own representations. The more we attempted to grasp it, the more it dissolved into signs. What remains is a world of "operational truths," systems that function flawlessly precisely because they have ceased to refer to anything outside themselves [3, pp. 2–5; 54–58]. Function replaces meaning, performance replaces reference, and circulation replaces value.

This disappearance is not annihilation but metamorphosis. The real does not die; it becomes indifferent to itself. It turns into a system of effects, a network of automatic responses and feedback loops. Everything works—but the working is empty.

The shift can be illustrated on the evolution of digital media [4]. Whereas traditional computer-generated imagery (CGI) aimed to reproduce reality with technical precision, generative models now produce content that no longer represents reality but autonomously generates new configurations of signs. This transition corresponds to the movement from the second to the fourth order of simulacra, in which models become self-sustaining systems without referents.

Barroso [5] characterizes hyperreality as a contemporary condition in which signs and technical images merge with the factual, producing derealization—a "loss of the real"—and reorganizing social life around visibility and simulation rather than reference. Building on Baudrillard's image-regime (the image as an "operator of visibility"), Debord's spectacle, Eco's hyperreal copies, and Han's "digital swarm," Barroso shows how technological media make "the virtual real," normalizing experiences where authenticity is irrelevant to effect. This provides the conceptual ground for generative AI: large-scale synthetic media no longer merely represent, but operate as realities within attention economies, extending the shift from representation to autonomous simulation. In our cases, AI systems industrialize exactly the mechanisms Barroso describes—amplifying visibility, shortening verification loops, and rendering the copy more actionable than any original.

1.3 Artificial Intelligence as the Perfect Simulacrum

Artificial intelligence stands as the most accomplished realization of this transformation.

AI does not merely simulate human thought—it produces meaning statistically, without any grounding in experience or reference. It is pure operational intelligence: capable of pattern recognition and symbolic manipulation, yet devoid of memory, suffering, silence, or gift. In Baudrillard's sense, it is the triumph of the model over the world.

If the modern subject was once defined by its capacity for representation and interpretation, the postmodern algorithm is defined by calculation. AI thinks without thinking, learns without understanding, speaks without listening. In this, it mirrors the entire cultural condition: communication without communion, abundance without depth, productivity without purpose.

Artificial intelligence thus represents the technological embodiment of what Baudrillard called the fourth order of simulacra: the order of simulation proper, in which signs no longer conceal or reveal anything but play on the real in the total circularity of the model [1, p. 5]. In the algorithmic world, prediction precedes event, and information replaces experience. The model not only anticipates reality—it creates the framework within which reality is allowed to occur.

From this perspective, the proliferation of AI is not a revolution but a completion: the world finally becomes identical with its simulation. The dream of rational control culminates in the disappearance of the real. The machine does not replace the human; it realizes the logic the human world had already chosen—to make life transparent, computable, and endlessly reproducible.

Cunningham represents an even more radical opinion that the emergence of AI-generated art exemplifies the latest and perhaps most radical stage of simulacra, a fifth stage, where the act of creation itself becomes simulated. In this generative hyperreality, artificial agents function simultaneously as the map and the territory, autonomously producing realities that no longer refer back to any human origin [6]. This extension of Baudrillard's theory vividly demonstrates how generative AI collapses the distinction between original and copy, creator and creation.

1.4 Beyond Illusion: Implosion and Saturation

Baudrillard's term implosion names the process by which differences collapse into the smooth continuum of the system. Unlike explosion, which breaks apart structures, implosion is an inward collapse of meaning. It is the saturation of communication, the point where information becomes indistinguishable from noise. "We live in a world where there is more and more information, and less and less meaning" [1, p. 54].

Artificial intelligence intensifies this implosive dynamic. The algorithmic universe is characterized not by censorship but by excess. The problem is no longer what we are forbidden to say but that everything is said at once. When every possible interpretation can be generated, none carries weight. AI produces the appearance of creativity, but it lacks the silence from which creation arises. In this sense, the machine makes visible the absence that defines the human: the ability to not know, to pause, to give, to lose.

The implosion of meaning thus reveals a paradox. It destroys transcendence but opens a new space of contemplation—a world of pure phenomena, detached from necessity. This is not a moral crisis but an ontological mutation: reality no longer withdraws behind appearances; it disperses within them. Hyperreality is not false; it is simply full—so full that nothing can resonate.

In this hyperreal order, signs circulate like currency in a closed economy. Value is no longer determined by what a thing is but by how well it moves through networks. The same applies to knowledge, images, and emotions. We no longer exchange meanings; we exchange signals of exchangeability. This is why social media, finance, and AI share the same logic: the replacement of truth by velocity.

1.5 The Threshold of the Post-Human

At this threshold, the distinction between human and machine becomes unstable. AI's emergence forces us to confront a deeper question: not what machines can do, but what humans are once their symbolic difference disappears. If the machine is defined by perfect functionality, then the human—Baudrillard reminds us—is defined by imperfection: by loss, opacity, and silence.

There are gestures the system cannot compute: the gift that expects no return, the silence that resists communication, the loss that cannot be reversed. These are not solutions but interruptions. They form what Baudrillard might call cracks in the system—moments where the total logic of simulation falters, if only to continue again.

2 Toward the Concept of the Crack

The following sections will trace how such cracks operate in the age of total simulation. Unlike traditional forms of resistance, these cracks do not stand outside the system. They arise within its own perfection—what Baudrillard calls the fatal strategy of the real.

At the same time, thinkers like Slavoj Žižek, Hannah Arendt, or Jacques Derrida offer different readings of rupture: for Žižek, the crack marks the return of the Real, an antagonism that no system can absorb; for Derrida, it is the play of différance that keeps meaning from closure; for Arendt, it is the space between humans where worldliness appears.

The crack is thus a polyvalent figure: it can be immanent (self-produced by the system), dialectical (a point of contradiction), phenomenological (a space of encounter), or mystical (a threshold to what escapes being). What unites these interpretations is the refusal of totality. Even when everything seems seamless, there remains a fissure—an interval through which the world still breathes.

2.1 Immanent Disruption and the Crack in the System According to Baudrillard: Perfection as the Source of Breakdown

Baudrillard's concept of implosion must be understood as a reversal of the Marxian and Freudian models of conflict. In classical critique, contradictions accumulate until the system collapses; in Baudrillard, collapse never comes from without, nor from dialectical negation—it comes from within perfection itself. The more the system approaches its ideal of total functionality, the more it undermines the very difference that keeps it alive.

Modernity's project was the progressive elimination of opacity: to make all things visible, measurable, exchangeable, communicable. But once everything becomes transparent, difference dissolves. There is no longer an outside to resist or a secret to protect. The system begins to devour its own foundation—the play of limits that made meaning possible.

Baudrillard [3, pp. 4–8] explains that the system dies from its own realization, from its perfection, from its total positivity. There is no longer anything to say, because everything is said; no longer anything to desire, because everything is given.

This is the logic of immanent disruption: the system collapses not through negation, but through its own excess. In thermodynamic metaphors, this could be called "overheating," but Baudrillard avoids such physical analogies; he means something more symbolic: an overproduction of meaning that turns signification into noise. The implosion of meaning is not disorder but saturation. As the system grows more efficient, it ceases to signify. Communication becomes noise; difference becomes repetition; critique becomes simulation of critique. This is why contemporary culture can endlessly reproduce the gestures of rebellion, irony, and transgression—because the system itself now produces them as part of its circulation of signs.

Hence the paradox: total functionality equals total fragility. A world without limits cannot sustain tension; it becomes smooth, frictionless, and thus lifeless. Like an echo chamber, it resonates with itself until the resonance cancels meaning. The fragility of the system lies not in its instability, but in its total stability. By eliminating negativity, it abolishes the very movement that sustains it and its meaning. What remains is a perfect equilibrium—smooth, operational, but lifeless. Such perfection cannot endure difference; it cannot renew itself. The system becomes fragile not because it may break, but because it can no longer change. Its coherence is its weakness, its transparency its blindness.

When opposition disappears, one term begins to absorb its former other and loses its definition. Truth devours falsehood and becomes meaningless; visibility absorbs secrecy and becomes blinding; communication eliminates silence and turns into noise. The system implodes not through conflict, but through over-identity—through the saturation of difference. Yet in this implosion, the lost opposite returns as an echo: silence within noise, gift within exchange, nonsense within meaning. These are not external contradictions but the system's own shadows, the ghosts it produces when it fulfills itself too completely.

The crack in Baudrillard's universe arises not from opposition, but from excess. It is not imposed from outside the system, for no outside remains. It emerges immanently, as the system overrealizes itself. When meaning, information, and function reach saturation, they begin to cancel one another out, producing zones of indifference—pauses, silences, gestures that no longer communicate. These are not accidents but the system's own irony: its way of undoing itself from within. The crack is thus an auto-immune phenomenon, born from the perfection of transparency, the point where total communication turns into noise, and total meaning becomes meaningless. Meaning requires difference. When the system has no opposite—no sacred, no incommensurable, no gift—it collapses into pure equivalence. Activities continue to function, but as signs without contrasts, they cease to signify. This is the paradox of the hyperreal: the world works perfectly, yet it means nothing. For instance, in eliminating the unexchangeable, the system abolishes the very difference that made exchange meaningful.

2.2 Symbolic Tension and the Loss of Negativity

For Baudrillard, meaning depends on negativity—on absence, secrecy, and sacrifice. In Symbolic Exchange and Death [7], he contrasts two economies: the symbolic and the semiotic.

- The symbolic operates through gift, challenge, and reciprocity. It is not based on utility but on *expenditure without return.*
- The semiotic operates through equivalence, exchange, and information; it aims at closure and balance.

Modern society replaces the symbolic with the semiotic, transforming every gesture into a transaction. But by eliminating negativity—what cannot be measured or returned—the system also eliminates meaning. As Baudrillard [7, pp. 36–39] puts it the symbolic defies equivalence, it is the domain of the unexchangeable. The semiotic, on the contrary, seeks only equivalence, and therefore it abolishes the symbolic. Negativity here is not destruction, but difference—an interval in which meaning can resonate. When the symbolic vanishes, everything becomes operational, and operationality consumes its own energy.

Artificial intelligence exemplifies this perfect equivalence. It can transform any text, image, or sound into data, normalize it, and reassemble it into infinite permutations. But it cannot give or receive in the symbolic sense, because it has no relation to absence, to loss, or to the gift. Thus, AI marks the final disappearance of negativity: it transforms language into a reversible system of probabilities.

2.3 The Crack as Symbolic Remainder

If the symbolic has been abolished, can any remainder still resist total absorption? Baudrillard's answer is paradoxical: the crack is not outside the system but within its own over-saturation. When everything functions perfectly, a kind of symbolic short-circuit appears. This is not resistance in the political sense, but a gesture of uselessness—something that interrupts the system precisely because it cannot be integrated. On the one hand, it is the product of the system's over-functioning; on the other, it becomes visible only when the system has almost eliminated it. Baudrillard gives several examples across his works:

- The *gift* that cannot be repaid.
- The *secret* that cannot be revealed.
- The *gesture* that has no reason.
- The *silence* that breaks communication.
- The *death* that cannot be simulated.

Each of these acts represents a crack—a rupture—not because it stands against the system, but because it fails to function within it. What cannot be exchanged is fatal to the system. It is what the system cannot metabolize, what it cannot turn into value or information [7, pp. 144–148]. These fatal gestures—silence, irony, the gift, the refusal—expose the limit of simulation. They are not revolutionary but symbolically destructive: they reveal that even in a world of total communication, something remains incommunicable.

The gestures that reveal the crack—gift, silence, irony, refusal—share a common structure: they are forms of non-participation. In a world that demands constant engagement, visibility, and expression, the act of withdrawal becomes subversive. This refusal is not nihilism but an ironic affirmation: it acknowledges the world's absurdity without trying to fix it. In the same way, silence in an age of total communication is not absence but resistance; the unreturned gift is not waste but defiance. In a digital context, this non-participation takes new forms:

- logging off,
- refusing algorithmic personalization,
- resisting the demand for transparency.

Each of these gestures is a micro-symbolic act: it interrupts circulation, not to change it, but to expose its compulsive nature.

2.4 The Witness of the Crack

In this logic, the human being is no longer the subject of change but the witness of implosion. Baudrillard does not believe in emancipation through knowledge or action. Once the world has become a system of total circulation, the only remaining position is that of witnessing its irony. This witnessing is not passive but contemplative—a form of lucidity. To see the crack is already to disturb the system, because lucidity is what the system cannot simulate. AI can reproduce understanding, but not awareness; it can imitate insight, but not astonishment. The witness occupies the space of the unprogrammable. By perceiving the crack, one participates in what Baudrillard calls the "fatal strategy of the real"—the real's ability to implode its own representation. Lucidity thus replaces critique. Instead of fighting the system, one lets it reveal itself through its own absurdity. The task is not to oppose but to mirror—to reflect the world's overproduction of meaning until it becomes transparent to its emptiness.

2.5 The Paradox of the System's Self-Destruction

If the system produces its own cracks, can it ultimately destroy itself? Baudrillard remains skeptical. The system's genius lies in its ability to absorb its own failure. Even breakdown becomes content; even critique becomes performance. He warns that the system is never defeated by contradiction, for it produces contradiction as a sign of its vitality [3, pp. 31–34]. In other words, the system feeds on its own negation. Every act of critique risks reinforcing it by giving it another image to process. This is why Baudrillard's response is not revolutionary but symbolic: only gestures that cannot be signified or exchanged can truly disturb the system. The crack, therefore, is not a revolutionary event but a metaphysical condition. It is the structural impossibility of totality—the inevitability that even the most complete system will fail to account for its own existence.

Here, the figure of AI acquires almost theological resonance. If the system were ever to achieve total simulation—if AI could perfectly reproduce human meaning—it would no longer be functional. The perfect simulation would equal death: a world indistinguishable from its model would cease to have a reason to exist.

Baudrillard's brilliance lies in recognizing that the system's limit is not its failure, but its success. The more it succeeds, the less it matters. The crack is not a defect but the ultimate sign of perfection—proof that even perfection cannot be perfect.

The crack, for Baudrillard, is not an endpoint but a threshold. It leads to a mode of being beyond seriousness—the realm of play. In play, the logic of production and exchange is suspended. One acts not to achieve, but to explore the space of possibility itself.

As we will see in the next sections, play becomes the world's own fatal mirror: it reproduces the system's logic so perfectly that it exposes its absurdity. The crack becomes the rule of a new game—the game of the world that functions without meaning.

3 Play, Irony, and the Aesthetics of Emptiness

3.1 Play as Fatal Mirroring

In Baudrillard's later work, the concept of play replaces that of critique. If critique assumes that the world can be changed by exposing its contradictions, play assumes that the world has already absorbed contradiction into its functioning. To play, therefore, is to enter the system's logic not to oppose it, but to exaggerate it until it implodes. Baudrillard calls this strategy fatal: To push things to the extreme is not to destroy them but to allow them to fulfill themselves—to the point of disappearance" [3, pp. 31–34]. Play is this movement of excess. It mimics the system's rules so completely that their seriousness collapses.

In contrast to Johan Huizinga's Homo Ludens [8] vision of play as the origin of culture, Baudrillard's play is post-cultural: the game after meaning. It has no sacred circle, no differentiation between player and spectator. The digital universe, where everyone performs and observes simultaneously, is its purest realization. To play in this sense is to perform a kind of symbolic sabotage. The act has no moral claim and no measurable outcome, yet it corrodes the seriousness of functionality. A meme, an absurd gesture, or a useless aesthetic act may do more to unmask the system than any rational critique, precisely because the system cannot determine whether it is serious or not. Play is ambiguity weaponized.

Within this playful universe, the critical subject transforms into a trickster—neither rebel nor conformist, but a performer of irony. The trickster accepts the game but refuses its moral frame. He plays not to win but to reveal that winning no longer matters. Baudrillard's "fatal strategy" [3, 9] aligns with this trickster ethos:

- obey the rules too literally,
- take the logic to absurd perfection,
- let the system collapse under its own coherence.

For example, the relentless pursuit of transparency produces opacity through excess visibility; the drive for connection yields isolation; the cult of positivity turns into depression. The trickster does not oppose these forces but mirrors them until they fold in on themselves.

In digital culture, this figure is ubiquitous—the hacker, the satirist, the meme-maker. Their irony operates not through critique but through simulation pushed to its limit. By reproducing the forms of control and efficiency in exaggerated fashion, they uncover the absurdity of those forms. Play thus becomes a subtle art of strategic compliance: the refusal to resist in order to let resistance happen automatically.

3.2 Irony

If play is the form, irony is its tone. Irony is the vibration that arises when meaning overheats but never detonates. It is the hum of the system consuming itself. Baudrillard defines irony as the over-signification of the world [3, pp. 39–41]. The world becomes so meaningful, so articulate, that it collapses under the weight of meaning. Irony emerges when excess sense turns into nonsense—not by negation, but by proliferation.

Artificial intelligence manifests this irony technologically. It produces endless novelty without event, infinite creativity without origin. Each output appears meaningful, but the meaning is suspended in probability. The machine speaks ironically by design: it repeats the human without believing in it.

For Žižek [10], irony remains dialectical: it exposes the inconsistency of ideology to recover the Real that ideology conceals. For Baudrillard, by contrast, there is no Real left to recover. Irony has no referent; it plays in a void. Žižek's subject confronts the traumatic kernel of reality; Baudrillard's subject drifts through its disappearance. The first seeks truth through contradiction; the second finds freedom in lucid illusion. In Žižek, irony aims at awakening; in Baudrillard, at serenity.

Irony leads not to despair but to lucidity. Lucidity is the consciousness that nothing can be changed because everything is already reversible. It does not judge but observes. Baudrillard's late writing adopts the tone of a metaphysical reporter: calm, fascinated, detached.

3.3 The Aesthetics of Emptiness

In the era of hyperreality, aesthetics replaces ethics. Once truth is gone, only appearance remains—and appearance becomes a form of grace. Baudrillard's writing, often accused of poetic obscurity, enacts this transformation. It does not argue; it seduces.

Seduction, for him, is the aesthetic form of the crack: an interruption of linear causality, a detour that reveals the beauty of illusion. He writes in Seduction [11, pp. 53–55; 69–71; 85–88] that seduction does not produce; it turns aside. It displaces, it deceives, it makes the world shimmer. This shimmering—appearance without depth—is not deception but freedom. When the world no longer hides truth, its surfaces become playfields for imagination. Aesthetics thus assumes the ethical function once held by truth: it sustains attention, wonder, and care in a meaningless universe.

Byung-Chul Han [2] offers a complementary view: the society of transparency destroys this aesthetic dimension by abolishing distance and mystery. Baudrillard, however, finds a new form of beauty precisely in that loss: the melancholy of the surface. The screen, the code, the algorithm—these become the new icons of a secular mysticism. What mattered in earlier metaphysics as transcendence now returns as design.

The emptiness of the hyperreal is therefore not nothingness but potentiality. Because nothing has fixed meaning, everything can appear differently. Art, irony, and play are not escapes from reality but ways of staying with illusion gracefully. The world, stripped of truth, becomes a field of subtle gestures—each one a tiny aesthetic of survival.

This aesthetic lucidity transforms despair itself. Traditional tragedy depends on conflict between value and fate. But when values dissolve and fate becomes algorithmic, tragedy turns into a kind of serene fatalism. Baudrillard notes that the end of tragedy is not joy but indifference [12, pp. 106–111]—the cool smile of a world that continues.

Artificial intelligence extends this aesthetic into the technological realm. Its creativity consists of loops, iterations, and recombinations—forms of play without intention. In generating endless variations, it reveals both the beauty and the emptiness of form itself. Every AI artwork, every generated text, is a mirror of the system's own play. It demonstrates that originality can exist without origin, and that meaning can circulate without authorship. This is not a tragedy but a revelation: the human was never the master of meaning, only its temporary witness. Yet even here, a small crack remains. AI can simulate art, but it cannot experience irony. It can generate a joke, but not laugh. It can repeat a poem, but not fall silent. In these small impossibilities resides the last difference—the human as the one who knows that there is nothing to know.

3.4 The Serenity of Illusion

Baudrillard's final message is not despair but serenity. To accept illusion as illusion is to live without resentment. The system may be total, but it is also fragile; it trembles in its own transparency. To perceive this fragility is to rediscover a kind of compassion for the world.

He writes in Perfect Crime that perhaps the most radical act is to admire the world as if it were still real [13, pp. 9–20]. This admiration is not belief but playful reverence. It allows us to live among simulations without cynicism, to treat appearances not as lies but as gifts of semblance. Such a stance replaces the moral with the aesthetic, the revolutionary with the contemplative. The world becomes a stage where every gesture, however meaningless, carries the grace of being.

4 Transition: Toward Multiple Interpretations of the Crack

At this point, the article moves from Baudrillard's immanent conception of the crack to other possible readings.

For Baudrillard, the crack belongs to the system—it is the irony of perfection. But other thinkers—Žižek, Derrida, Levinas, or mystical traditions—interpret rupture differently: as contradiction, différance, or transcendence. The next section will examine these alternative frameworks, showing how each re-imagines the place of the crack:

- Žižek's dialectical rupture that reintroduces the Real.
- Phenomenological and ethical gaps in Arendt and Levinas.
- Derridean différance as perpetual postponement of closure.
- Technological cracks that appear at the limits of simulation itself.

Through these perspectives, the multiplicity of the crack becomes visible—not only as the system's irony, but as the fundamental structure of any world that refuses to be complete.

4.1 The Multiplicity of the Crack

For Baudrillard, the crack is an *immanent irony*—a flaw born from perfection itself. Yet this is only one way of imagining rupture. Throughout modern thought, the experience of "break," "absence," or "interval" marks the place where meaning both appears and fails. In what follows, the crack is read across several traditions: dialectical, phenomenological, deconstructive, mystical, and technological. Each offers a distinct grammar of negativity, a different way of saying that the world can never close over itself.

Slavoj Žižek's The Sublime Object of Ideology [10] begins where Baudrillard seems to end. For Žižek, the collapse of ideology's illusions does not yield serenity but confrontation with the Real—the traumatic kernel that no symbolic order can absorb. Where Baudrillard sees the system self-imploding into transparency, Žižek insists that contradiction still cuts through this transparency.

The crack, in this reading, is not the system's internal equilibrium but its impossible point—the antagonism that sustains it. Every ideology functions only by covering up this internal void. When the cover slips, the Real appears: a moment of disorientation in which the subject glimpses that there is no big Other [10, pp. 223–224].

Thus, while Baudrillard's crack is immanent (a feature of the system's smoothness), Žižek's is dialectical (a wound that reopens the possibility of truth). The two share the intuition that totality is impossible, but they diverge on what this impossibility means. For Baudrillard, it leads to irony; for Žižek, to ideology-critique and political subjectivity. Baudrillard witnesses; Žižek intervenes.

Still, the two converge at a deeper level: both understand that systems produce their own negation. The difference lies in tone. Where Žižek hopes for an emancipatory event emerging from the crack, Baudrillard suspects that any event is already another simulation. The dialectic continues to believe in redemption; fatal irony does not.

Hannah Arendt and Emmanuel Levinas reintroduce a humanist dimension to the notion of rupture. For them, the crack is not inside systems of signs but between persons. Arendt calls this interval the space of appearance. Only where men live together is there a world at all [14, pp. 199–207]. The crack is the between that allows plurality to exist. It is not a failure of communication but its condition—the fragile distance that preserves freedom. Unlike Baudrillard's implosive world, Arendt's world arises in the gap. Levinas [15] radicalizes this idea into ethics: the Other's face interrupts my being, calling me to responsibility. This interruption is a metaphysical crack that no system of knowledge can close. It is not immanent irony, nor dialectical contradiction, but transcendence—a break that founds obligation.

Together, Arendt and Levinas show that not all cracks are nihilistic. Some open the world rather than implode it; some restore relation rather than dissolve it. If Baudrillard's crack exposes the futility of meaning, theirs preserves the possibility of hospitality—an ethics grounded in the very impossibility of total understanding.

Jacques Derrida's deconstruction introduces another nuance. For him, the crack is not a momentary rupture but the structure of signification itself. Meaning exists only through différance—the endless deferral and differentiation of signs [16]. Every presence bears an absence within it; every concept splits as it speaks.

Unlike Baudrillard, Derrida does not lament this instability. The crack is not a disaster but life's very movement. If Baudrillard sees implosion as the death of difference, Derrida sees it as its continual re-creation. Where Baudrillard longs for silence, Derrida listens to the murmuring of textuality. His is the joyous crack of language—forever postponing closure, forever generating play. Still, both thinkers converge in their rejection of metaphysical completion. For both, truth is no longer a hidden core but a trace—something that appears only by disappearing. Between them lies a spectrum: from the cold lucidity of disappearance to the gentle affirmation of différance.

5 The Rupture of Technology

Returning to the contemporary horizon, technology introduces its own kind of rupture. Artificial intelligence embodies the drive toward total simulation—a world of perfect prediction, zero delay, and infinite feedback. Yet this very perfection generates new fractures, born not from failure but from excess.

1. The opacity of transparency.

The more AI strives for interpretability, the more its logic escapes understanding. Total transparency erases the distance required for meaning: when everything is visible, nothing can be seen. Clarity becomes blindness, and the dream of full understanding collapses into an unreadable excess of information. What was meant to reveal all relations conceals the very sense of visibility itself.

2. The implosion of authorship.

By erasing the distinction between original and copy, AI fulfills the dream of infinite creativity—yet precisely by doing so, it abolishes the meaning of creation. When every output can be generated, authorship dissolves into pure circulation. Originality no longer refers to an origin, but to the endless capacity to reproduce. The artist survives as an algorithmic echo, and creativity becomes a mechanical tautology.

3. The perfection of error.

The algorithm's so-called hallucinations are not failures but revelations. They mark the moment when flawless computation reaches its own limit—when precision turns into absurdity. Error is the last residue of meaning, the small crack through which human uncertainty still breathes. The machine can simulate sense, but it cannot endure nonsense—and nonsense, paradoxically, is what makes sense human.

4. The exhaustion of meaning.

In the endless acceleration of data and interpretation, meaning itself becomes fatigued. Every message arrives before it is sent; every sign refers only to another sign. Communication becomes an echo chamber of sense, where significance persists only as form, not as experience. The world no longer hides its meaning—it has simply run out of it.

Each of these paradoxes reveals the same irony: the system fulfills its ideals so completely that they cancel themselves out. Total transparency yields opacity; infinite creation erases originality; perfect accuracy exposes absurdity; and total communication ends in silence. The more the system realizes itself, the less it needs to mean.

Even within the technological sublime, the crack persists—the unprogrammed, the unpredictable, the useless. Artificial intelligence thus becomes the latest stage of Baudrillard's fatal game, and its most eloquent confession: that totality can only ever approach itself, never arrive.

6 Toward an Ethics of Cracks

In a world dominated by total communication and computation, the acknowledgment of cracks becomes an ethical gesture. Instead of demanding coherence, we learn to protect fragility—to allow spaces of silence, unpredictability, and non-utility. This ethics does not restore an external truth; it cultivates attentiveness to interruption. It means:

- valuing the pause in conversation,
- preserving privacy against transparency,
- accepting error as creative,
- and practicing irony as care rather than cynicism.

The aim is not to defeat the system but to keep it porous. As Han [2] warns, the "society of transparency" risks eliminating negativity—the very element that sustains freedom. To maintain the crack is to preserve the possibility of the unexpected.

7 Conclusion: The World that Laughs

After the end of meaning, after the triumph of simulation, what remains is laughter. Not the laughter of mockery, but of recognition—the laughter that greets the world's absurd persistence. Everything functions; nothing is real; yet the show continues.

Baudrillard's world is not tragic but comic in the ancient sense: it never ends, it keeps returning. Like the theatre of signs it describes, the system cannot die because it no longer lives. Its immortality is its punishment and its beauty. Irony becomes the final wisdom—a way of remaining human in a machinic cosmos.

Artificial intelligence will not replace this laughter. It may generate humor, but it cannot find something funny. That minimal difference—between producing laughter and laughing—is perhaps the last human privilege, the tiniest crack through which the world still breathes.

To share in that smile is not surrender but participation in the world's own self-irony. In the shimmering surface of simulation, the crack remains invisible yet omnipresent—the subtle vibration of existence continuing after its meaning. The task of thought, art, and ethics today is simply to keep listening to that vibration, to stay beside the fissure where the world still laughs.

Acknowledgements. The work on this paper was supported by the Czech Science Foundation (GACR) grant 24-11697S.

Disclosure of Interests. The author has no competing interest to declare that is relevant to the content of this article.

References

1. Baudrillard, J.: Simulacra and simulation. in The body, in theory—histories of cultural materialism. Ann Arbor, Mich: Univ. of Michigan Press (2019)
2. Han, B.-C.: The transparency society. Stanford (Calif.): Stanford Briefs (2015)
3. Baudrillard, J.: The transparency of evil: essays on extreme phenomena. Verso, London (1993)
4. Konzack, L: Generative AI, Simulacra, and the transformation of media production. AJMMC **11**(3), 177–196 (2025). https://doi.org/10.30958/ajmmc.11-3-3
5. Barroso, P.: Hyperreality and virtual worlds: when the virtual is real. Sphera Publica **2**(19), 36–58 (2019)
6. Cunningham, J.: Simulacra on steroids: AI art and the Baudrillardian hyperreal. IIS (2024). https://doi.org/10.48009/2_iis_2024_101
7. Baudrillard, J.: Symbolic exchange and death, Repr. in Theory, culture & society. Los Angeles: Sage (2007)
8. Huizinga, J.: Homo ludens: a study of the play-element in culture, Unabridged reprint of the, 1st edn. Angelico Press, Kettering, OH (2016)
9. Baudrillard J.: Fatal strategies. Los Angeles, CA : Cambridge Mass: Semiotext(e) ; Distributed by the MIT Press (2008)
10. Žižek S.: The sublime object of ideology. in The essential Žižek. London New York: Verso (2008)
11. Baudrillard J.: Seduction. Montréal: New World Perspectives (2001)
12. Baudrillard, J., Turner, C., Gane, M., L'Yvonnet, F.: Fragments: conservations with Françis L'Yvonnet. Routledge, London (2004)
13. Baudrillard, J.: The perfect crime. Verso, London (1996)
14. Arendt, H.: The human condition, 2. ed., [Nachdr.]. Chicago: Univ. of Chicago Press (2010)
15. Lévinas, E.: Totality and infinity: an essay on exteriority, 23rd printing. Duquesne Univ. Press, Pittsburgh, Pa (2011)
16. Derrida, J.: Of Grammatology. Johns Hopkins University Press, Baltimore (1976)

Ethics, Society, and Critical Perspectives

Rethinking Software Ethics in the Age of Artificial Intelligence

Klaus Nigsch(✉)

TU Wien, Vienna, Austria
klaus.nigsch@tuwien.ac.at

Abstract. Artificial intelligence (AI) is reshaping the world at a rapid pace, bringing both revolutionary possibilities and serious global challenges. From deepfakes and misinformation to biased algorithms and societal interruptions, its widespread impact raises pressing ethical concerns. Large language models (LLMs) such as ChatGPT, Copilot, or DeepSeek exemplify these issues, as their technical power comes with challenges including bias, robustness failures, data poisoning, and significant environmental impact. This article examines these challenges from an engineering perspective and evaluates how effectively ethical frameworks in software engineering address them. State-of-the-art ethical codes for computing professionals, such as the ACM Code of Ethics and Professional Conduct and The Software Engineering Code of Ethics and Professional Practice, provide sophisticated guidance on professional conduct. However, these codes fall short in defining ethical ends for technological innovation, leaving critical questions of societal goals and public interest unresolved. As a way to overcome these limitations, this article introduces the vision of Digital Humanism, particularly in line with the Vienna Manifesto on Digital Humanism. This approach enriches existing codes with ethical ends by highlighting guiding principles such as democracy, fairness, and inclusion. Finally, the article offers a future outlook, stressing the role of regulation, interdisciplinarity, and AI literacy in building a resilient and ethically grounded digital society in this age of artificial intelligence.

Keywords: Artificial intelligence · Digital humanism · Global challenges · Interdisciplinarity · Large language models · Software ethics

1 Introduction

The field of *Artificial Intelligence* (*AI*) deals with software artifacts that adapt or evolve through experience. Blurring the line between programmed software logic and human-like learning, AI-based software has major impact on human lives. While advances in AI offer possibilities for a fruitful and enriched future, there are also risks associated with these advances. Ever since the introduction of GPT-1 in 2018, large language models have rapidly shaped societal and economic

R. Giovagnoli et al. (Eds.): IS4SI 2025, SAPERE 81, pp. 83–96, 2026.
https://doi.org/10.1007/978-3-032-31732-2_7

aspects. Therefore, it becomes increasingly important for stakeholders to be able to rely on existing ethical systems as moral guidelines for developing and working with these models. While state-of-the-art software ethics recognize human well-being, they mainly address ethical *means* [17]. The focus of these ethics is on avoiding harm along procedural concerns such as privacy, security, and fairness. However, they fall short in addressing the broader question of technology's ultimate purpose. As AI impacts decisions and behaviors, existing ethical guidelines need to be able to address ethical *ends*, i.e. technological development that serves humanity's best interests. To ensure software contributes to a just, sustainable future, ethics must evolve beyond compliance, further embracing a vision of societal well-being and gaining the ability to advocate for just and desirable goals. By calling for a rethinking of software ethics, this work emphasizes ethical ends while upholding ethical means. It does so by introducing *Digital Humanism* and shows how this vision's concepts can strengthen existing ethical frameworks in the age of artificial intelligence.

This work is structured as follows: In Chap. 2, a general overview of challenges posed by artificial intelligence, and specifically large language models is provided. Chapter 3 then evaluates existing state-of-the-art ethical codes in software engineering, highlighting the ethical guidance they provide and identifying areas for improvement. Having given this background, Chap. 4 then introduces the vision of Digital Humanism as a way to overcome existing limitations in ethical frameworks. Bridging the gap between concrete ethical challenges of large language models and ethical frameworks, Chap. 5 then utilizes concepts of both, existing ethical frameworks and Digital Humanism to address these challenges. Looking ahead, Chap. 6 then offers an outlook that places the discussed challenges in a broader societal context while reflecting on the future of responsible development and deployment of artificial intelligence systems. Finally, Chap. 7 contains the conclusion of this article.

2 Challenges of Artificial Intelligence

In order to structure a case for the need to reform software engineering ethical frameworks, we first consider issues arising from artifacts of artificial intelligence. We do so by examining large language models from a technical perspective. This establishes a list of challenges and misguided developments in the field of large language models that one would expect to be critiqued by state-of-the-art software engineering ethics.

This chapter is structured as follows: First, the concept of *Large Language Models* (*LLMs*) is briefly introduced, as it is subject of examination throughout the paper. Then, we consider challenges in artificial intelligence artifacts, focusing on LLMs. We will cover four issues of LLMs and briefly support the observations with concrete case studies of technical innovations. Covered technical issues include social biases, robustness issues and vulnerability to data poisoning. Finally, the environmental footprint caused by large language models is presented as a direct ecological impact of the technology.

Large language models are systems designed to generate human-like text. This mimicking process works by relying on patterns learned from extraordinarily large amounts of text data. This background training data comprises a wide variety of sources, such as books, academic papers, articles, websites, social media platforms, etc. Once trained, LLMs can answer questions, write texts, solve mathematical problems, provide translations, hold conversations, etc. This process, however, is a simulation. The generation of text iteratively relies on a prediction function that applies learned patterns to produce the most likely next word. From a design perspective, this process is only as effective as it is because of enormous amounts of background data. Without such data, the prediction function would lack sufficient patterns, resulting in poor outputs. This design of LLMs, however, presents its own challenges. We discuss four critical challenges as follows.

2.1 Bias in Training Data

One of the main issues in LLMs is bias. As these models are trained on vast amounts of human-written background data, they do not only learn pattern in language: they also pick up all sorts of present biases in these texts. Research has investigated biases in LLMs and their word embeddings [3,11,12]. These word embeddings are the way that the models represent words internally. In these studies, word embeddings have been shown to include social biases, such as gender stereotypes. This may result in LLMs reflecting (and in some cases even amplifying) societal biases. Examples of observed gender biases include disproportionally associating certain jobs with a certain gender, or producing an imbalanced gender representation in leadership positions.

Zhao et al. demonstrate that structured prediction models contain risks of leveraging social biases in their training data [25]. This study has measured that amplification of social biases from training data can happen, while also proposing methods to reduce this bias effect. Also, highly specialized large language models, such as SciBERT in the domain of scientific texts, have been measured to reduce such biases [4]. However, a study by Zhang et al. with regards to the highly sensitive healthcare domain still concludes harmful effects [23].

Social biases like these, if included in artificial intelligence based systems, may ultimately lead to discriminatory, misleading, or unfair outputs. From an engineering perspective, we consider following issue: LLMs rely on both the quality and quantity of training data. Along with architecture and training algorithm, extraordinarily large amounts of data fuel the general effectiveness of the prediction function. Quality and unbiasedness of data promote fair, trustworthy, and less harmful outputs. As the amount of training data increases and the level of supervision decreases, it gets increasingly harder to achieve the desired results. This challenge is further amplified as LLMs are typically designed for general, universal use-cases.

2.2 Robustness and Adversarial Attacks

Another key issue in the design of LLMs is robustness. While modern LLMs are highly effective at producing fluent, human-like text, they can be fragile when it comes to small changes in input they receive from users. So-called adversarial examples, which are small, carefully crafted alterations in user input, have been shown to produce incorrect or misleading responses [6,16]. This weakness is not limited to a single language or domain: The tool TextFlint has demonstrated that this issue persists through multiple languages and applications [19]. Perez and Ribeiro demonstrate that prompt injection attacks can be used to perform goal hijacking in GPT-3, effectively showing that (malicious) users can misalign the original goal of a prompt to generate a predetermined target output phase [15].

Considering the design perspective, the issue of robustness shows that strong results in the training phase or standardized tests of LLMs do not necessarily translate to reliable behavior in practical uses. Improving a model's robustness is a complex process that requires additional considerations to handle less common, or even deliberately misleading user inputs.

2.3 Data Poisoning

Data poisoning is another critical design concern in LLMs. It occurs when a small amount of training data itself contains misleading, harmful, or even deliberately manipulated content. This content then becomes part of the model, which can cause highly undesired outputs. Even when models consist of extraordinarily large amounts of training data, very small amounts of poisoned data can greatly influence the model's output [18]. Moreover, the quality evaluation of data itself can cause problems. For example, sources that are considered "high quality" data are more present in some languages than others. It has been shown that models perform worse for underrepresented languages [8]. Wallace et al. expose concealed poisoned examples as a difficult-to-detect vulnerability in *Natural Language Processing* (*NLP*) models [18], a field to which LLMs belong. With injected poisoned data and applying certain trigger phrases, they show that targeted errors can be triggered in transformer-based language models for sentiment analysis, language modeling, and machine translation. Furthermore, the study shows that this control of model predictions works on benign user inputs. Defense mechanisms that mitigate, but cannot fully stop the investigated attack are given.

Data poisoning as a vulnerability shows that monitoring and selecting training data requires increasingly sophisticated methods in order to reduce biases and protect users from both accidential and even malicious manipulation of the model and its outputs.

2.4 Environmental Footprint

The Environmental impact of LLMs has become an ethical concern due to the immense energy demands of both training and use. A study by Wu et al. concluded that the training of the model *Meena* generated carbon emissions equivalent to driving over 242,000 miles in an average passenger car [21]. Even more, Patterson et al. estimate that several models have produced carbon emissions comparable to lifetime emissions of multiple passenger cars, with GPT-3's training alone being responsible for over 500 metric tons of CO_2 [14]. Their study calls for transparency regarding the environmental footprint, emphasizing that CO_2 emissions should be a key metric when evaluating models.

With LLM *distillation*, there have been attempts to make large language models more practical and efficient [9,24]. By techniques like intelligently selecting learning examples, and task-specificity, good performances can be reached while reducing computational, hence energy cost. While this distillation process has been shown to reduce energy consumption, nontrivial loss of accuracy has been observed [2,22]. Depending on the case, distillation might be a worthy, useful trade-off, but in some settings it might lead to sharp drops in accuracy.

As with the previously discussed challenges, the environmental footprint of LLMs cannot be merely reduced to a technical challenge. Ecological impact of technology has to be considered an ethical concern. Large-scale environmental consequences on a global scale demand that evaluation of LLMs moves beyond factors like accuracy and performance, including societal impact and sustainability as key concerns.

3 Evaluating Software Engineering Ethics Frameworks

We now provide background about state-of-the-art ethical codes in software engineering. The two most well-established ethical frameworks for computing professionals are the *ACM Code of Ethics and Professional Conduct* [1] and *The Software Engineering Code of Ethics and Professional Practice* [7].

Although we do not provide an in-depth analysis of these codes, we aim to point out strengths and shortcomings. These aspects form the basis of the call to rethink software ethics.

3.1 Ethical Guidance Provided

Both of the mentioned ethical frameworks provide strong ethical principles that deal with ethical means. They go beyond defining abstract ethical ideas and cover how computing professionals should act by giving detailed, explicit principles and responsibilities to follow.

One major strength of these codes includes defining fundamental ethical principles that are based on a support for human well-being. Upholding well-being and a continuous recognition of the public good serve as an overarching principle of these codes. Other key values mentioned to be supported include harm-avoidance, honesty, trustworthiness, respect for privacy, transparency, etc. By promoting these values with specific principles, it can be said that the professional conduct is covered in detail. Furthermore, principles of the codes are supported by more detailed guidelines that provide context and show real-world applications of the principles. This bridges the gap between providing abstract ethical rules and real-world ethical decision making. By promoting values like harm-avoidance and transparency, they promote thought about both the consequences of actions and the process itself.

Summarizing its strengths, it can be concluded that the codes provide an exceptionally thorough coverage of ethical means for computing professionals.

3.2 Areas for Improvement

These ethical codes do, however, contain shortcomings. Mittelstadt contrasts developments in AI ethics to those in medicine [13]. The study finds that AI development, compared to medical ethics, falls short in several factors, such as shared aims, professional norms, methods translating principles to practice, and accountability mechanisms. Seth focuses on shortcomings of the ACM Code of Ethics and Professional Conduct in particular [17]. The findings of his article serve as a basis for ethical shortcomings that can be applied to both, the ACM Code of Ethics and Professional Conduct and The Software Engineering Code of Ethics and Professional Practice. Note that while these two codes come with notable differences and are legitimate in their own right, the key shortcomings are largely mutual: even though their ability to cover ethical means (how computing professionals should act) is very sophisticated, they fall short in addressing overarching ethical ends (long-term or high-level goals for computing professionals). Although they do mention human well-being and the public good as the core principle to always keep in mind, guidance in regards to concrete outcomes of technology and its implications for society is limited. Effectively embracing ethical ends is important: since the ethical ends are not well defined, the ability to critique technology with regard to undesirable goals is limited. A technology built by ethical means may still result in harmful goals. Also, desirable ethical ends should include ways to overturn social structures and reduce inequalities or power imbalances. So far, ethical codes do not provide the sufficient backbone to embrace goals to this degree.

Following list briefly paraphrases and summarizes Seth's insights into the ACM Code of Ethics and Professional Conduct [17]:

- The code focuses on ethical means, but does not clearly define ethical ends of computing systems.
- The code is ineffective in identifying undesirable or unjust technological goals.
- The code is ineffective in embracing desirable goals, e.g. achieving equality and overturning unjust social and economic structures.

As a result of these shortcomings, accountability issues may arise. Especially when goals can be vague, it becomes harder to hold stakeholders accountable for undesirable outcomes. One way to avoid critique consists of claiming that certain outcomes were not part of the intended goals or were unforeseen consequences.

An example illustrating these shortcomings is *COMPAS*, a commercial risk assessment software in criminal justice. Dressel and Farid show that the tool is not substantially outperforming untrained human individuals, while also containing biases [5]. For instance, it was measured that COMPAS disadvantages black defendants by disproportionally classifying them as higher risk compared to white defendants, effectively representing racial bias. COMPAS was built with high professional standards, as covered by ethical codes. However, the codes fall short in identifying the undesirable goal of delegating potentially high-stakes judicial decisions to a statistical model that is inherently biased. Guidance to critique the technological direction itself is not provided by the ethical codes, even if the system was implemented by the highest professional standards. Furthermore, COMPAS is not actively promoting equality or fairness, and disproportionally disadvantages marginalized groups. Outcomes like these underline the importance for ethical codes to embrace desirable goals such as achieving equality, or overturning unjust social structures.

Another example, covered by Seth [17], is India's biometric identification system *Aadhaar*, illustrating how a system built around solid ethical means can end up with outcomes undesirable for the public interest. While the system was built to high professional standards and goals included a reduction of corruption in the distribution process of welfare benefits via this new identification system, the actual release told a different story: challenges for citizens in obtaining and maintaining functioning biometric identification led to denials of benefits. As a result, the deployment of Aadhaar led to millions of reports regarding unfair denials of welfare benefits and privacy concerns. Because in practice it is so far removed from being inclusive and reducing corruption, an article by Khera claims that "Aadhaar is becoming a tool of exclusion" [10]. This case study illustrates that even software artifacts built in the name of desirable goals, such as reducing corruption, can end up working against the public interest. Therefore, embracing desirable goals can only represent a first step towards the correct direction, but control mechanisms on various levels will prove necessary.

4 Overcoming Ethical Limitations Through Digital Humanism

In order to provide a general idea about how we can overcome existing ethical limitations in software engineering, we propose integrating concepts of Digital Humanism into the ethical frameworks. We start by briefly summarizing key Digital Humanism ideas, more specifically concepts of the *Vienna Manifesto on Digital Humanism* [20]. Then, we provide reasons why these ideas can address ethical shortcomings.

4.1 Foundations of Digital Humanism

In line with the Vienna Manifesto on Digital Humanism [20], Digital Humanism is here understood to be a framework calling for technology to be aligned with human rights, societal well-being and democratic values. With its eleven core principles, the manifesto highlights how digital artifacts are not mere neutral tools, but provide intense interplay into society, politics, and economy. Therefore, it is not sufficient to develop software simply because it is technically feasible or there is market interest. Human requirements and societal well-being should always guide technological goals.

In the following, we briefly paraphrase key principles of the manifesto [20]. One critical aspect of the manifesto is the explicit call to govern, design, and deploy technology in ways that promote values like inclusion, democracy, and freedom of speech. Furthermore, mechanisms for regulation and accountability are advocated for as ways to promote transparency, fairness, and democracy-aligned systems. Another key point consists in the call for interdisciplinary work and participation of society. This point further stresses the fact that technological development is not happening in a vacuum. In support of this point, the manifesto calls for collaboration across sciences and including public engagement in order to define desirable technological ends. Also, a proposal of new educational curricula that combine interdisciplinary knowledge is given. Finally, the importance of specific education on societal impact of computer science is given as another core principle.

4.2 Integrating Digital Humanism Into Software Ethics

In the following, ways that concepts of Digital Humanism can enrich the shortcomings of the existing state-of-the-art ethical frameworks in software engineering will be listed.

First and foremost, the importance of ethical ends is explicitly emphasized. The principles call for digital artifacts to be created in harmony with desirable outcomes like democracy, inclusion, human rights, and freedom of speech. This call emphasizes what type of societal goals technology should promote, rather than just being a how-to guideline. Combined with existing software ethics, it enriches the existing principles, retaining guidance on proper conduct, but no longer being vague in long-term outcomes of technology.

Furthermore, the manifesto's demand for "effective regulations, rules and laws" connects legal and regulatory mechanisms to the long-term goals. This aspect makes sure that ethical ends are not mere prescriptions, but are explicitly supported by accountability and regulation measures.

By insisting that important decisions which reflect back on humanity and rights should continue to be made by humans, the manifesto embeds a long-term goal of preserving humanity's autonomy into ethical principles. This ensures that humans, rather than automated systems, remain in the forefront of decision making for desirable goals.

The manifesto also explicitly calls for interdisciplinary efforts and actively involving society, promoting ethical ends that are guided by a broad variety of perspectives. By not limiting the involved decision-makers to the technology domain, perspective on desirable outcomes becomes explicit, and less assumed.

Finally, by promoting reflection on ethical and societal impact in curricula, the manifesto calls for teaching goals about ethical ends from an early stage and promotes it as a lasting effort. Due to this early education, future stakeholders should more likely be aware of technological impact and promote desirable goals.

5 Addressing Challenges in Large Language Models

This section serves as a way to bridge the gap between the outlined issues in large language models [cf. Sect. 2], the abilities of current ethical systems in software engineering to critique technology [cf. Sect. 3], and vision of Digital Humanism [cf. Sect. 4] as a way to enrich ethical software principles.

In order to accomplish this, a mapping for each of the covered challenges posed by LLMs is provided: it connects LLM issue, software ethical limitation, and ethics enriched by Digital Humanism as follows. First, the challenge is briefly summarized. Then, it is mentioned how the ACM Code of Ethics and Professional Conduct and The Software Engineering Code of Ethics and Professional Practice may fall short in addressing the challenge. Lastly, an integration of Digital Humanism principles is provided, showing how the ethical codes would perform better.

After all of the detailed mappings have been provided, a quick summary providing better overview follows.

5.1 Addressing Bias in Training Data

LLMs can represent and in some cases even amplify social biases present in training data, which leads to unfair or even harmful outputs [cf. Sect. 2.1]. While current ethical codes call for upholding fairness and avoiding harm, there is no clear guidance on identifying or correcting biases in the training data. Biases could be seen as technical limitations or failures, while they should be treated as an issue of ethical ends. By including Digital Humanism principles that explicitly call for inclusion, fairness, and human rights as ethical ends, existing ethical codes are enriched: no longer can a biased system be excused as a technicality, but has to be treated as a breach of ethical obligations. Biased training data leading to unjust outputs would therefore directly conflict with the idea of desirable ethical ends.

5.2 Addressing Robustness and Adversarial Attacks

Adversarial inputs can manipulate LLM behaviour, producing misleading or unsafe outputs [cf. Sect. 2.2]. While current ethical codes promote professional diligence and quality assurance, an explicit connection to societal impact is lacking. Demanding robustness of systems should be tied to protecting societal trust. Digital Humanism calls for transparency and accountability, linking robustness issues and their misleading or unsafe outputs to ethical concerns boyond mere technical issues. By promoting effective robustness as a topic of public safety, ethics enriched by Digital Humanism highlights the social impact of this challenge.

5.3 Addressing Data Poisoning

Data poisoning refers to the challenge of LLMs being vulnerable to manipulated training data, leading to undesirable or harmful behaviour [cf. Sect. 2.3]. While current ethical codes promote avoidance of harm and upholding integrity, orientation about how and to what degree to protect against such attacks can be improved. Digital Humanism points out societal consequences of digital artifacts, calling for laws and regulations against harmful system outputs. This enables ethics enriched by Digital Humanism to link protection against data poisoning to democratic responsibilities. Therefore, they press for government mechanisms that promote public trust by calling for protective measures against challenges of this type.

5.4 Addressing Environmental Footprint

The immense environmental impact caused by training and operation of LLMs is a key concern [cf. Sect. 2.4]. While current ethical codes mention the importance of public welfare, long-term sustainability of the planet and ecological impact are not explicitly mentioned as ethical end goals. Digital Humanism does, however, recognize both public welfare and sustainability as long-term goals and ethical responsibilities. By enriching existing software ethics with these responsibilities, an evaluation of environmental consequences is integrated into the process of developing and deploying digital systems.

5.5 Summary of Mappings

Table 1 summarizes LLM challenges, the limitations of ethical codes, and the strengths of the codes enriched by Digital Humanism.

6 Outlook

This chapter provides an outlook on the role of future governance, interdisciplinarity, and literacy with regard to AI and LLMs specifically.

Looking ahead, the discussed challenges demand a strengthened framework for governance and accountability in all stages of development and deployment of large language models. The ongoing *EU Artificial Intelligence Act* (*AI Act*) covers policies that move beyond voluntary ethical codes towards binding regulatory mechanisms. One example of many is the prohibition of systems that cause negative consequences, e.g. include manipulative or deceptive techniques, and social scoring (unfair treatment of people or groups based on socio-economic circumstances). This provision of the AI Act reflects ongoing policy work that addresses challenges covered in this article. Efforts like the AI Act are important, as issues in regards to artificial intelligence are of global impact and cannot be solved on a national level alone. Both coordinated global effort and strong national measures are crucial to address the complex challenges that these AI artifacts pose.

Table 1. Comparison of LLM challenges, limitations of existing ethical codes, and digital humanism-enriched ethics. Note that "ACM/SEC" is used as short for the codes ACM Code of Ethics and Professional Conduct and The Software Engineering Code of Ethics and Professional Practice, respectively

LLM challenge	Limitations of existing ethical codes (ACM/SEC)	Strengths of digital humanism-enriched ethics
Bias in training data	Stress fairness and avoidance of harm, but might treat bias mainly as a technical flaw	Frames bias as a moral issue tied to inclusion, fairness, and human rights; insists on addressing systemic inequality
Robustness and adversarial attacks	Encourage diligence and quality, but might treat robustness mainly as technical reliability, not linked to societal trust	Connects robustness to transparency and accountability; ensures effective robustness serves public safety
Data poisoning	Promote integrity and harm avoidance, but lack guidance on safeguarding systems from manipulation	Emphasizes governance and oversight; treats poisoning and harmful system outputs as a systemic threat to democracy and trust
Environmental footprint	Acknowledge responsibility to public welfare, but sustainability of planet is not explicit	Makes sustainability and long-term well-being central; demands environmental impacts to be a fundamental factor in ethical evaluation

However, resolving issues of large language models towards consistency with the public interest cannot be achieved by regulatory measures alone. LLM challenges exemplify the need for interdisciplinary measures, not only calling for involvement of computer science, but also social sciences, law, environmental studies, etc. Here, Digital Humanism provides a natural approach, embedding human rights, democracy, and sustainability into the technical domain. Integration of these ideas and disciplines aids in keeping humans in control of technology in contrast to a future where technological innovation outpaces society's ability to guide and govern properly.

Finally, AI literacy, understood as society's ability to understand, use, and critically evaluate AI artifacts, needs to be promoted. As AI systems become increasingly tighter integrated into critical social systems, such as healthcare, government, and journalism, the skill to understand its limitations and dangers becomes more important. Both, the professional domain and the general public benefit from knowledge about LLMs, their potential biases, vulnerabilities, environmental impact, and their broader impact on society. Cultivating future generations of informed, empowered citizens who critically engage with AI technologies and retain control over them, rather than being reduced to passive receivers of AI output, is an essential task protecting humanity's future.

7 Conclusion

This article set out to analyze pressing challenges of large language models and evaluate how existing state-of-the-art ethical frameworks, enriched by the vision of Digital Humanism, can better guide a responsible development of artificial intelligence artifacts. Large language models, representing a core incarnation of artificial intelligence innovations, provide critical challenges with deep ethical implications. Four concrete challenges of large language models, namely bias, robustness and adversary attacks, data poisoning, and environmental footprint, were discussed as technical challenges that cause fundamental societal and environmental consequences.

Current ethical codes, most prominently the ACM Code of Ethics and Professional Conduct and The Software Engineering Code of Ethics and Professional Practice, guide ethical means in sophisticated ways but are limited in their ability to address ethical ends of technological innovation. The vision of Digital Humanism acts as a natural entry point to enrich these ethical frameworks, adding a much-needed focus on societal goals, democracy, and sustainability. Successfully addressing the challenges of the age of artificial intelligence requires a fundamental rethinking of software ethics, complemented by global coordination, strong national efforts, interdisciplinary scientific collaboration, and a sustained focus on AI literacy across society.

Disclosure of Interests. The author has no competing interests to declare that are relevant to the content of this article.

References

1. ACM Code of Ethics and Professional Conduct. https://www.acm.org/code-of-ethics. Accessed 25 Sep 2025
2. Ariyanti, S., Suryanegara, M., Arifin, A.S., Nurwidya, A.I., Hayati, N.: Trade-off between energy consumption and three configuration parameters in artificial intelligence (AI) training: lessons for environmental policy. Sustainability **17**(12), 5359 (2025)
3. Basta, C., Costa-jussà, M.R., Casas, N.: Evaluating the underlying gender bias in contextualized word embeddings. In: Proceedings of the First Workshop on Gender Bias in Natural Language Processing, pp. 33–39. Association for Computational Linguistics (2019)
4. Beltagy, I., Lo, K., Cohan, A.: SciBERT: a pretrained language model for scientific text. In: Proceedings of the 2019 Conference on Empirical Methods in Natural Language Processing and the 9th International Joint Conference on Natural Language Processing (EMNLP-IJCNLP), pp. 3615–3620. Association for Computational Linguistics (2019)
5. Dressel, J., Farid, H.: The accuracy, fairness, and limits of predicting recidivism. Science Advances **4**(1), eaao5580 (2018). https://doi.org/10.1126/sciadv.aao5580, https://www.science.org/doi/10.1126/sciadv.aao5580
6. Garg, S., Ramakrishnan, G.: BAE: BERT-based adversarial examples for text classification. In: Proceedings of the 2020 Conference on Empirical Methods in Natural Language Processing (EMNLP), pp. 6174–6181. Association for Computational Linguistics (2020)

7. Gotterbarn, D., Miller, K., Rogerson, S., Barber, S., Barnes, P., Burnstein, I., Davis, M., El-Kadi, A., Fairweather, N., Fulghum, M., Jayaram, N., Jewett, T., Kanko, M., Kallman, E., Langford, D., Little, J., Mechler, E., Norman, M., Phillips, D., Werth, L.: Software engineering code of ethics and professional practice. Sci. Eng. Ethics **7**, 231–238 (2001)
8. Gururangan, S., Card, D., Dreier, S., Gade, E., Wang, L., Wang, Z., Zettlemoyer, L., Smith, N.A.: Whose language counts as high quality? measuring language ideologies in text data selection. In: Proceedings of the 2022 Conference on Empirical Methods in Natural Language Processing, pp. 2562–2580. Association for Computational Linguistics (2022)
9. Hsieh, C.Y., Li, C.L., Yeh, C.K., Nakhost, H., Fujii, Y., Ratner, A., Krishna, R., Lee, C.Y., Pfister, T.: Distilling Step-by-Step! Outperforming Larger Language Models with Less Training Data and Smaller Model Sizes. In: Rogers, A., Boyd-Graber, J., Okazaki, N. (eds.) Findings of the Association for Computational Linguistics: ACL 2023, pp. 8003–8017. Association for Computational Linguistics (2023)
10. Khera, R.: Impact of aadhaar on welfare programmes. Econ. Pol. Wkly **52**(50), 61–70 (2017)
11. Kurita, K., Vyas, N., Pareek, A., Black, A.W., Tsvetkov, Y.: Measuring bias in contextualized word representations. In: Proceedings of the First Workshop on Gender Bias in Natural Language Processing. pp. 166–172. Association for Computational Linguistics (2019)
12. Mehrabi, N., Morstatter, F., Saxena, N., Lerman, K., Galstyan, A.: A survey on bias and fairness in machine learning. ACM Comput. Surv. **54**(6), 1–35 (2021). https://doi.org/10.1145/3457607
13. Mittelstadt, B.: Principles alone cannot guarantee ethical AI. Nat. Mach. Intell. **1**(11), 501–507 (2019)
14. Patterson, D., Gonzalez, J., Le, Q., Liang, C., Munguia, L.M., Rothchild, D., So, D., Texier, M., Dean, J.: Carbon Emissions and Large Neural Network Training (2021). https://arxiv.org/abs/2104.10350
15. Perez, F., Ribeiro, M.T.: Ignore Previous Prompt: Attack Techniques For Language Models, (2022). arXiv:2211.09527
16. Ren, S., Deng, Y., He, K., Che, W.: Generating natural language adversarial examples through probability weighted word saliency. In: Proceedings of the 57th Annual Meeting of the Association for Computational Linguistics, pp. 1085–1097. Association for Computational Linguistics (2019)
17. Seth, A.: What's missing in the ACM code of ethics and professional conduct. Interactions **30**(3), 44–47 (2023)
18. Wallace, E., Zhao, T., Feng, S., Singh, S., Gardner, M.: Concealed data poisoning attacks on nlp models. In: Proceedings of the 2021 Conference of the North American Chapter of the Association for Computational Linguistics: Human Language Technologies (NAACL-HLT), pp. 139–150. Association for Computational Linguistics (2021). https://doi.org/10.18653/v1/2021.naacl-main.13
19. Wang, X., Liu, Q., Gui, T., Zhang, Q., Zou, Y., Zhou, X., Ye, J., Zhang, Y., Zheng, R., Pang, Z., Wu, Q., Li, Z., Zhang, C., Ma, R., Fei, Z., Cai, R., Zhao, J., Hu, X., Yan, Z., Tan, Y., Hu, Y., Bian, Q., Liu, Z., Qin, S., Zhu, B., Xing, X., Fu, J., Zhang, Y., Peng, M., Zheng, X., Zhou, Y., Wei, Z., Qiu, X., Huang, X.: TextFlint: unified multilingual robustness evaluation toolkit for natural language processing. In: Proceedings of the 59th Annual Meeting of the Association

for Computational Linguistics and the 11th International Joint Conference on Natural Language Processing: System Demonstrations. pp. 347–355. Association for Computational Linguistics (2021)
20. Werthner, H., Lee, E.A., Akkermans, H., Vardi, M., Ghezzi, C., Magnenat-Thalmann, N., Nowotny, H., Hardman, L., Stock, O., Larus, J., Aiello, M., Nardelli, E., Stampfer, M., Frauenberger, C., Ortiz, M., Reichl, P., Schiaffonati, V., Tsigkanos, C., Aspray, W., de Bruijn, M.E., Strassnig, M., Neidhardt, J., Forgo, N., Hauswirth, M., Parker, G.G., Sertkan, M., Stanger, A., Knees, P., Tamburrini, G., Tellioglu, H., Ricci, F., Nalis-Neuner, I.: Vienna Manifesto on Digital Humanism. https://dighum.ec.tuwien.ac.at/wp-content/uploads/2019/05/manifesto.pdf (2019). Accessed 20 Sep 2025
21. Wu, C.J., Raghavendra, R., Majumdar, A., Gharat, A., Roberts, D., Hsu, G., Chatterjee, I., Khadilkar, H., Phanishayee, A., Kansal, A., et al.: Sustainable AI: environmental implications, challenges and opportunities (2021). https://arxiv.org/abs/2111.00364
22. Yuan, Y., Zhang, J., Zhang, Z., Chen, K., Shi, J., Stoico, V., Malavolta, I.: The Impact of Knowledge Distillation on the Energy Consumption and Runtime Efficiency of NLP Models. In: 2024 IEEE/ACM 3rd International Conference on AI Engineering–Software Engineering for AI (CAIN). pp. 129–133. Association for Computing Machinery (2024)
23. Zhang, H., Lu, A.X., Abdalla, M., McDermott, M., Ghassemi, M.: Hurtful words: quantifying biases in clinical contextual word embeddings. In: Proceedings of the ACM Conference on Health, Inference, and Learning. p. 110–120. Association for Computing Machinery (2020).https://doi.org/10.1145/3368555.3384448
24. Zhang, Y., Pan, B., Ling, C., Hu, Y., Zhao, L.: ELAD: explanation-guided large language models active distillation. In: Ku, L.W., Martins, A., Srikumar, V. (eds.) Findings of the Association for Computational Linguistics: ACL 2024, pp. 4463–4475. Association for Computational Linguistics (2024)
25. Zhao, J., Wang, T., Yatskar, M., Ordonez, V., Chang, K.W.: Men also like shopping: reducing gender bias amplification using corpus-level constraints. In: Proceedings of the 2017 Conference on Empirical Methods in Natural Language Processing (EMNLP), pp. 2979–2989. Association for Computational Linguistics (2017)

AI, ... and the Spectacle Goes on: (Meta)physical & Societal Ramifications of Artificial Intelligence

Renate C.-Z.-Quehenberger(✉)

The Institute for a Global Sustainable Information Society, Vienna, Austria
renate.quehenberger@gsis.at

Abstract. Since the release of generative artificial intelligence (AI) platforms in recent years, the technological capabilities of large language models (LLMs) and text-to-image models have served as useful tools for automation and creative outputs while they pose the problem that personalized responses and "deep fake" images and videos are becoming more difficult to distinguish from images of "real" objects and people, increasing the ambiguity between digital reality and truth. Guy Debord's Society of the Spectacle (1967) trapped in an "image-driven" hyperreality has reached the next level of simulacra and ontological ambiguity generated by repetition and Bayesian statistics. However, the cognitive effects of transferring creative thinking to machines on the perceptions of their users continue to be investigated, raising anew McLuhan's questions about AI as a medium, and "what does it do to us?" On the other hand, the dark side of the spectacle, disciplinary systems from Bentham's prison to Foucault's panopticon, has gained significance through the technological implementation of Tolkien's Palantiri, Roy Ascott's thematic embrace and Peter Weibel's quantum cinema. The hermeneutic analysis of the two-fold nature of the spectacle as a result of a loss of unity is examined in a speculative deep time investigation into the Vedic philosophy of unity of multiplicity, drawing on the hypothesis of the apparent loss of knowledge of the geometry of 5-/10-dimensional space that acts like a machine—with the consequence of the implementation of a technologic mega-machine driven by AI, as epitomized in Ray Kurzweil's announcement of singularity by 2045.

Keywords: Society of the spectacle · Loss of unity · Surveillance · Singularity

1 Investigating the AI hype as spectacle

In recent years "artificial intelligence" (AI) platforms have been launched by creating such hype that everybody was affected, so the comparison with the notion of the spectacle seems applicable. In his book *The Society of the Spectacle* (1967) French Marxist theorist, filmmaker, and founding member of the Situationist International delivered an analysis of the industrial consumer society trapped in an "image-driven" hyperreality then observed in media such as magazines, television and billboards, and yet his analysis can be applied to our AI driven society.

R. Giovagnoli et al. (Eds.): IS4SI 2025, SAPERE 81, pp. 97–122, 2026.
https://doi.org/10.1007/978-3-032-31732-2_8

> *The spectacle presents itself as something enormously positive, indisputable and inaccessible. It says nothing more than that which appears is good, that which is good appears* [1].

Current developments in AI tools are crucial for understanding the dichotomy in its use that reminds us of a spectacle in its latest technological form.

This chapter examines how AI is used, on the one hand as a quasi democratic spectacle for the arts, sciences, entertainment and business to a certain degree available to use for free or with a subscription. The peaceful commercial application of AI looks like a convivial tool, just as Ivan Illich envisaged the democratic use of technology to be [2].

Yet it can be developed into a totalitarian surveillance infrastructure that threatens enlightened civic freedom and the ostensibly democratically organized public sphere. Such an authoritarian tool is part of what Mumford first called the mega-machine. Force, velocity and control were the characteristics of absolute monarchy as well as of the mega-machine [3].

1.1 Introduction

Definition. The term *Artificial intelligence* (AI) first appeared in 1956 in the proposal for the research project Dartmouth Summer Conference on Artificial Intelligence by John McCarthy, funded by the Rockefeller Foundation.

The next goal is to achieve *Artificial General Intelligence* (AGI), AI "that can match or exceed the cognitive versatility and proficiency of a well-educated adult" [4].

Since AI platforms for generating text and images went public in 2017, the technological capabilities of Large Language Models (LLMs) has increased exponentially. "Deep fake" images and films, almost indistinguishable from pictures taken from "real" objects and persons, and personalized AI generated answers are impacting on notions of reality and truth. It affects many industries and facets of human life: scientific research, education, manufacturing, logistics, transportation, defense, law enforcement, politics, advertising, art, culture, and more. The characteristics of AI will disrupt and transform them all, from the development of treatments for tenacious maladies and cures for rare diseases to AI aviators for the delivery of drones and piloting fighter jets. Kissinger and Schmidt argued in the preface of their book The Age of A.I., that it will alter human identity and the human experience of reality at levels not experienced since the dawn of the modern age. Societies, then, must cooperate not only to comprehend but also to adapt [5].

Gloom & Doom scenarios. Amidst all kinds of promises, in academia as well as in business and industry, hype has broken out regarding the possibilities and consequences of AI, while others wanting to use it efficiently for their businesses, are installing AI agents to replace human employees, and only employees with the new AI-toolkit skills are considered viable. AI's optional omnipotence lies in financial control, biosecurity, Agentic AI, cognitive warfare, digital surveillance, environmental control, food systems and reproduction control.

Technology, as the historian Melvin Kranzberg observed, "is neither good nor bad; nor is it neutral" [6].

The tech entrepreneur Elon Musk predicts poverty's end, 'work becomes optional', and AI will bring 'Universal High Income' [7].

On the other hand lethal autonomous weapons like military drone or military systems commonly called "killer robots," can independently leverage AI to identify, select, and eliminate human targets without requiring direct human intervention are raising profound ethical, legal, and security questions [8].

The inventor, scifi author and long term Google developer Ray Kurzweil acknowledged, "Technology has always been a double-edged sword," given that a drone can deliver either medical supplies or weaponry:

> "Threats of AI are real, must be taken seriously, [and] I think we are doing that," and added, we have "a moral imperative to realize the promise of new technologies while controlling the peril. We are not doomed to fail to control any of these risks" [9].

300 years from fiction to reality. It took 300 years until Jonathan Swift's idea of a machine on the island of Laputa in *Gulliver's Travels* (1726), which is "a project for improving speculative knowledge by practical and mechanical operations" was realized. We have to acknowledge that AI made his vision possible that, "the most ignorant Person at a reasonable Charge, and with a little bodily Labour, may write Books in Philosophy, Poetry, Politicks, Law, Mathematicks, and Theology, with the least Assistance from Genius or study" [10].

Lovelace and Babbage. The dichotomy between attributing god-like capacities to the machine and the use of computers in an artistic way, goes back to its beginnings, when Charles Babbage was building the analytical engine, a proposed digital mechanical general-purpose computer in 1837, and his friend and co-worker Augusta Ada King, Countess of Lovelace, conceptualized the first computer software program published as a footnote to her translation from the French of an article by the Italian engineer Luigi Manebra in 1843 [11].

For Charles Babbage "God was the first computer programmer, who sets everything in motion, every breeze and every atom, and stores in a great library everything a man has ever said or a woman has ever whispered" [12].

On the other hand, Lovelace predicted that one day computers would make music.

We find the same options realized in the development of computers, and especially in AI technology for surveillance systems and music producing AI models.

Lady Lovelace's Objection. 100 years later, at a time when the first general purpose computers had only just been built, Alan Turing asked: "Can machines think?" [13] He pondered Lady Lovelace's objection that states that a machine can "never do anything really new. It can only do what we tell it to do. The Analytical Engine has no pretensions to originate anything. It can do whatever we know how to order it to perform" (her italics). He then outlined the first AI experiment, the so-called Turing Test to evaluate a machine's ability to exhibit intelligent behaviour equivalent to that of a human.

The power of imagination. Ada Lovelace explored the role of mathematics in human imagination: She argued that the power of imagination unites the ability to combine and discover. Mathematical science provides a language for expressing the invisible relationships between things. But to appreciate this language, we must be able to both feel and measure—the invisible and the unconscious. Imagination reveals to us what is, even when it lies beyond the realm of sensory perception. Lovelace described the two aspects of imagination as follows:

1. The power of combination brings facts, ideas, and concepts together in ever-changing combinations. It weighs things up, finds common ground, even when no obvious connections exist and therefore contradictions rarely or never arise.
2. Imagination conceives and brings to light mental presentnesses that are distant, invisible, or not (yet) present in our physical or conscious cognition [14].

It is easy to state that #1 the power of combination is given in what is believed to be a synthetic neural network while "imagination" can never be achieved by algorithms.

AI epitomizes the myth of the machine. The deus ex machina, this time not on ancient Greek amphitheaters, but materialized in the Society of the Spectacle with all attributes of the Abrahamic god: omnipotent, all knowing and all-seeing; a life-like artificial creation, a modern Golem, not made from mud but from vast amounts of natural resources, rare earth minerals, silicon, copper, lithium, fuel, and human labor.

The Australian scientist and composer Kate Crawford argues that *artificial intelligence is neither artificial nor particularly intelligent.* And it's not intelligent in any kind of human intelligence way because it is not able to *discern* things without extensive human training, and it has a completely different statistical logic for how meaning is made [15].

Crawford points also to the seeds of the data problem planted in the 1980s, when it became common to use data sets without close knowledge of what was inside, nor concern for privacy. It was just "raw" material, reused across thousands of projects. Sentences from Reddit will be different from those in kids' books, In 2021, Crawford complained there was still no industry-wide standard to note potential ethical issues or what kinds of data are held in training sets, nor how it was acquired.

The commodity as spectacle. The commodity only reveals itself in its undistorted essence when it becomes the universal category of all society. The principle of commodity fetishism is the domination of society by "intangible as well as tangible things," which reaches its absolute fulfillment in the spectacle, where the tangible world is replaced by a selection of images which exist above it, and which simultaneously impose themselves as the tangible par excellence [16]. In this case, AI is in the process of becoming such a category, and the knowledge and art that are sampled have become fragmented commodities.

Closer scrutiny tells us that AI is anti-democratic because it is a system that exists only because beforehand, everything that existed in terms of human achievement was accumulated in vast data repositories.

The unauthorized appropriation of all knowledge, literature, music, and fine arts—the entirety of cultural history—by tech giants is succumbing to this raid, with everything being leveled as AI training material and turned into revenue. This is an unprecedented disregard for all creative personalities who had access to the realm of ideas and who, in the 19th century, were still celebrated as geniuses. Back then, the German universal genius, weiter and trained lawyer Johann Wolfgang von Goethe fought for the right to royalties that is still in place today, not so with AI technology. Nowadays not only is the realm of ideas itself being denied, but also all ideas that have ever been transformed into digital material are being ignored and intellectual property rights neglected. This amounts to a second rape of Hypatia and, in addition, to the burning of the Library of Alexandria, because access to digital books via the internet is also being restricted step by step [17]. Furthermore, no one alive can protect themselves from the exploitation of everything they have produced or even just shared in an email, since Gmail content gets used to train the Gemini AI model [18]. Everyone should have the right to be "unusable". Programs supposed to protect images from AI exploitation do not only fail to protect the images, while adding perturbation can actually improve the image's exploitability [19].

1.2 AI—What Does It Do To Us?

AI impacts on various aspects of human life, such as gender, race, and economic status. AI systems are not neutral or objective, but rather reflect and reinforce existing systems of power and inequality.

McLuhan media. In the 1950s the Canadian media critic Marshall McLuhan was the first to ask about the impact of media on society. In his book *Understanding Media: The Extensions of Man*, McLuhan emphasized how different media, such as print, radio, and television, have distinct impacts on society. He asked: *What does it do to us?* [20].

McLuhan's answer then was: Any extension, whether of skin, hand, or foot, affects the whole psychic and social complex. However, the media, theorist Jussi Parikka suggests, meanwhile, overcoming Marshall McLuhan's point of view—since the media of our time are less extensions of the human senses but rather extensions of Earth because the artificial intelligence industry demands an enormous amount of recourses, from network routers to batteries to data centers, all is built using elements that required billions of years to form inside the earth [21].

McLuhan's Mechanical Bride In *The Mechanical Bride* McLuhan echoes concern about the pervasive commingling of sex and technology in advertising. He feared that "one dream opens into another until reality and fantasy are made interchangeable."[22] Both the title and McLuhan's concerns reflect Marcel Duchamp's large painting on the *Large Glass, The Bride Stripped Bare by her Bachelors, Even.* Like Duchamp, McLuhan was able to observe his society from an outsider's viewpoint and became troubled by unchecked forces, advertising companies controlling the unconscious minds of a vast public and shaping people's lives [23].

In this book he quotes the advertisement of the RADIO CORPORATION of AMERICA:

Radio, by its very nature, is a medium of mass communication; it is a carrier of intelligence. Television fires the imagination [24].

Digital Sisters. Meanwhile McLuhan's *Mechanical Bride* has acquired whole row of digital sisters: Female AI assistants are reinforcing gender stereotypes and promoting gender-based verbal abuse. Be it Apple's Siri, Amazon's Alexa, Microsoft's Cortana, or Google's Assistant, the vast majority of automated assistants have a female voice promoting an image of women from the dark ages to the hundreds of millions of people using AI technology. Obedient and obliging machines that pretend to be women are entering our homes, cars and offices [25]. To change course, we need to know when and whether AI technologies are gendered and, crucially, who is gendering them [26].

ELIZA. The first chatbot in 1967 also had a female name: ELIZA is named after Eliza Doolittle, George Bernard Shaw's Galatea in his comedy Pygmalion (1913), where a Cockney flower girl is taught to speak like a duchess. The Eliza program is designed by the German-US-american informatics scientist Josef Weizenbaum as a psychologist capable of holding conversations with human users [27] This was at a time when a computer would heat the library, one didn't go to the computer, but rather into the computer, as his developer, explains, referring to the fact that computers back then were room-sized and his computer didn't even have a keyboard interface.

Over time AI systems like Lisp [28] have succeeded and faded. There were two major "AI winters" approximately 1974–1980 and 1987–2000. Only the recent development of self-learning algorithms and ongoing advancements in algorithmic efficiency, scalability, interpretability, and the integration of self-learning algorithms with other domains such as natural language processing, computer vision, and robotics has made the current hype possible.

Weizenbaum's Technology critique. Weizenbaum became an outspoken technology critic of his time [29]. In an interview Weizenbaum introduced himself as the author of the shortest simulation programs and said, "*I'm not a computer critic but a society critic, because computers don't understand any critique.*"

> Moreover Weizenbaum said something that could be still true despite all the faces of smart looking CEOs with their benevolent promises: "*The computer industry is a brothel and the Pentagon its pimp. A beautiful new paradise should be born from this?*" [30]. Weizenbaum warned that Humans should never perceive such a machine as a reflection of themselves. Otherwise, it can only end in catastrophe.

In his memory, the German Forum of Computer Professionals for Peace and Social Responsibility (FifF) awards an annual prize. This year's Weizenbaum Prize winner is the Taiwanese media artist Ting-Chun Liu who addresses the heat dissipation of GPUs in his artworks his thesis, critically examines all aspects and conditions of this synthetic culture. He claims to develop a kind of infrastructural aesthetics of AI. Liu discovered a violet bias in AI generated images and aims to convey that generative AI which generally manifests itself only virtually for us, has a material basis: raw materials, manufacturing processes, energy and heat as a concrete end product of processing (the NVIDIA H100 chip consumes 450 W). This explains the metaphorical title of the work [31]. Here, Ting-Chun Liu quotes Hayao Miyazaki, the Co-Founder of Ghibli Studio who once described AI-generated images as "an insult to life itself" in a documentary while researchers showed him some footage of AI-generated animations in his style. Upload a photo, a person, a piece of memory, or a picture of anything into ChatGPT, accompanied by the prompt "Redraw this photo into Studio Ghibli style animation." And *voilà*, a style once revered as a pinnacle of hand-crafted animation, is now accessible at the click of a button [32].

In the advent of suddenly ubiquitous AI generated texts and images in the present time, we should again ask: How would humans change their behavior in regard to the new medium?

McLuhan thought that people's mental habits blinded them to truths hidden behind the facade of surface meaning. The media barrage is a form of unofficial education, and how suited is an ostensibly all-knowing truth-telling machine like AI to manipulating the questioner? The briefly introduced anti-woke experiment of Grok-3 by implementing an "Unhinged Mode" is illustrating how tone choices shape perceptions of bias as much as factual content [33].

The medium is the message/massage. McLuhan's answer was twofold: In his book *The medium is the messag*e he summarized his view of the potent influence of television, computers, and other electronic disseminators. An alternative aspect delivers the title *The medium is the massag*e, (according to legend, the letter A was accidentally placed incorrectly by the typesetter in the printing press) which emphasized the deeper effect of mass media: The medium as a massage puts the consumer into a state of agony. Television puts the spectator into a state of relaxation that ultimately leads to a form of hypnosis with trance inducing capabilities. Tele-vison means transmitting visions.

> *The spectacle is the nightmare of imprisoned modern society which ultimately expresses nothing more than its desire to sleep. The spectacle is the guardian of sleep* [34].

McLuhan speaks of a *whirling phantasmagoria* not unlike Debord speaks of the spectacle, that can be grasped only when arrested for contemplation to arise from a sort of collective dream [35].

Geoffrey Hinton, the 2023 Nobel laureate for designing AI's learning algorithm and former long-standing researcher at Google, who played a key role in developing ChatGPT, facial recognition, and autonomous vehicles, posed the question currently captivating society—*what are the potential implications when AI surpasses human intelligence?*

"Making these systems behave in a reasonable way is much like making a child behave in a reasonable way" [36]. Also kursive

Given the wide range of responsibility delegated to AI systems, and since self learning machines can become unpredictable, Hinton recently publicly addressed the associated risks of AI development, and suggested, "*We need an AI with maternal instincts*" Also kursive [37].

2 Guy Debord's Society of the Spectacle

Guy Debord's analysis of the society of the spectacle also influenced the events of May 1968, the leftist student revolt in Paris that nearly brought down the government. He exposes the phenomenon of the *flood of images* in the consumer world of the post-war industrial society with its disciplinary measures, the *panopticum*, as a two-fold spectacle.

The image of the product and "image" of the person, as sold by Public Relations (PR) companies turns everything into a product. It indirectly points to the present day, when images of people and their data in social media become products themselves, and to the double life in the hyperreality of the digital world, which has become an artificial duplication of the real world, now even more so through artificial intelligence.

During the current AI hype the spectacle appears to have reached the next level of ontological ambiguity, this time based on self-learning algorithms driven by statistical procedures, repetition and theoretical comparisons—Bayesian inference, artificial neural networks and deep learning, adaptive sampling techniques to highlight similarities, and large multidimensional datasets.

Our society is already caught in an "image"-driven hyper-reality, and with LLMs, it has achieved the next level of ontological ambiguity. New realities emerge from nothing, merely based on coded repetition and statistics while the cognitive effects of the delegation of creative thinking to the machine in the mind of its users are still being investigated [38].

2.1 The Missing Unity of Life

What is the source of the spectacle?

Debord that in societies dominated by modern conditions of production, life is presented as an immense accumulation of spectacle.

He realized that the spectacle originates in a loss of unity:

> *The spectacle originates in the loss of the unity of the world, and the gigantic expansion of the modern spectacle expresses the totality of this loss: the abstraction of all specific labor and the general abstraction of the entirety of production are perfectly rendered in the spectacle, whose mode of being concrete is precisely abstraction* [39].

Debord observed that everything that was directly lived has receded into a representation. The latter has increased immensely since the dawn of the internet. Everything, every event and every person needs a digital representation, otherwise it doesn't exist in the minds of the people.

Debord stated: The images detached from every aspect of life merge into a common stream in which the unity of that life can no longer be recovered [39].

Where does it come from and what kind of representation does he mean?

Debord provides us with a hint citing Feuerbach, that the copy of the original became sacred: *But for the present age, which prefers the sign to the thing signified, the copy to the original, representation to reality, appearance to essence... Truth is considered profane, and only illusion is sacred [...] the highest degree of illusion comes to be the highest degree of sacredness* [40].

2.2 3D Reality is Representation

We are used to life in this world of images, a representation of the real world, while according to the German philosopher Arthur Schopenhauer's doctrine about the *world as will and representation* everything we see in the "real world" is merely a *representation* of the transcendental idea of itself.

This is apparently based on Vedic and Platonic philosophy, where the "real stuff" lies behind the material surface. The creation of reality happens from the world of ideas.

Plato described three stages of reality in his *Politeia* [41] The first real object, the original *real* bed is made by the *creator* or demiurge in the world of ideas; the second bed is made by the carpenter and the third stage of reality is a painting of the bed made by the artist.

Drawing on this list, we can add the image in the age of reproducibility [42]—which is not a singular photograph but the "aura-less" multiplied imagery from the printing press; the flood of images that disturbed McLuhan and Debord.

Then we count film as a 4th stage of reality: The cinematic space appears as a product of projective geometry and produces an artificial reality projected onto the screen at the point of infinity.

In terms of Plato's order of realities AI would be the 5th order representation. The digitalized film enables together with AI technology the purely digital realty without any "real" counterpart.

This conforms to Jean Baudrillard's stage four of the simulacrum [43], the pure simulation which is an AI generated person is a sign that refers only to itself, e.g., a virtual influencer who never existed.

In Plato and Schopenhauer's terms, the image is stage two since the object in our 3d reality of daily experience is already the representation of the object in the world of ideas while in Baudrillard's *Four Stages of the Simulacrum* an image that refers to an original (e.g., a portrait painting) stage one is still a faithful representation of reality, such would be the successive phases of the image:

it is the reflection of a profound reality;
it masks and denatures a profound reality;
it masks the absence of a profound reality;
it has no relation to any reality whatsoever;
it is its own pure simulacrum [44].

Now the digital world is the artificial realization of the wold of ideas; stored in atomized silicon, driven by a flow of electricity, zeros and ones, and soon in quantum devices. AI sketches "ideas" from prompts in seconds and creates films of a verisimilitude that never previously existed; it is a hyper-reality created by AI.

Jean Baudrillard spoke of the "satellization of the real in the transcendence of space—it is the end of metaphysics, the end of the phantasm, the end of science fiction—the era of hyper-reality begins." He foretold models of simulation that will contrive to give them the feeling of the real, of the banal, of lived experience, to reinvent the real as fiction, precisely because it has disappeared from our life. Hallucination of the real, of lived experience [45].

2.3 The Unity in Ancient Indian Philosophy

From Neolithic, pre-Socratic times to the end of the 19th century, the notion of intelligence was connected to the concept of the all-permeating aether, seat of the gods and divine reason, also often referred to as the *world soul.*

The person is not a part of this world—they are identical with the essence of its foundation."Tat tvam asi"—"That thou art" (Upanishad) [46].

Divine feminine creation and the five elements. The Hindus worship Shakti, the Divinity as Creatrix in the female Universal Power that underlies and sustains all existence. They call the five elements Pañca-ma-kara (or five M's): namely, Wine (Madya),

Meat (Mamsa), Fish (Matsya), Parched Cereal (Mudra), and Sexual Union (Maithuna), which stand for drinking, eating and propagation [47].

The latter is the Indian interpretation of Plato's Figure of marriage, the hint to his riddle about the 5th element which the Indians also called Akasha, or aether.

The ancient Egyptians invented the Isis & Osiris myth to convey the knowledge about this basically 5-/10-dimensional space [48] that forms the 4-dimensional dodecahedron Henri Poincaré suggested as a model for the Universe [49]. He described it as the *space which works like a machine*, which generates all sorts of symmetries subsequent to all living matter first visualized in 2012 [50]. Recognizing the significance of this higher dimensional space in quantum information could provide the lost ontologic basis and demystify quantum phenomena like entanglement as *spooky action at the distance* [51]. For Plato and the ancients this divine space, the aether, was a living entity and the seat of intelligence. Is it possible that AI chatbots are trained to deny 5-dimensional space because it is its natural rival? [52].

Fig. 1. **a** Epita-Dodecahedron in motion according to the description of the Poincaré homology sphere, the infinite 5-dimensional space ((Images by author/Quantum Cinema ©Bildrecht Vienna 2026) **b** image by venice.ai prompt "paint me a picture of the 5-dimensional space" by the author

Philosophical speculations. My hypothesis is that the loss of societal unity that occurred with the abolition and gradual displacement of matriarchal societies was accompanied by the loss of perennial feminine wisdom and knowledge. Among this the knowledge of the geometric form of the higher-dimensional world, the escape of the all-moving aether, which functions as a kind of transcendent machine, was essential. It lingers for a few more millennia until even this last conception of the aether as high bearer got abandoned (and space was replaced by fragmented planes, etc.). This unity on behalf of the collectively imagined space ensured a harmony, the harmonious order of society [53]. The first loss of the ontologic foundations marks the beginning of a series of losses of reality that have led to the artificial replacement of real world experience by the spectacle, in its gradual intensification up to the currently ongoing simulation of the world using digital AI technology (Fig. 1).

This higher dimensional space of the ancients filled with all sorts of imaginary divine characters mostly representing natural phenomena was apparently the basis for the concept of *multiplicity of Unity of all beings*. May we assume their spectacle was fully imaginary, while their life was real or hyper-real in the sense that they came up with the concept that everything that can be experienced with the five senses,—earth, water, fire, air, animals and plants originates in this *unique existence?*

This existence cannot be seen and it is intangible, while it is the basis of everything. The brahmin Āruṇi of the Gautama lineage called this substance *sat,* the *real existing* [54].

The *Net of Indra* inspired the mathematician Hermann Günther Grassmann to develop a groundbreaking "extension algebras" for n-dimensional space which have found applications in quantum mechanics as well as for neural networks used for AI computer programs [55].

While being ignored for three decades, he translated the RigVeda [56].

Nada Brahma. The term 'Nada' comes from Sanskrit: 'sound' also 'stream', 'Brahma' originally an Indian magic formula, later 'living/primal force of the cosmos', the indivisible unity of being, etc. It is the primal word of Indian spirituality and of great classical Indian music.

Nada Brahma, expresses the inseparable unity of all existence [57]. Who would have thought back then that one day frequencies would be sold in order to modulate long-distance-calls on?

Everything is One. The idea of an unity of existence could have been reinstalled by modern quantum physics in 1927 when matter-waves were postulated by Louis de Broglie in 1924 [58] were experimentally proven. However, the strong denial of an ontologic realism hindered the revival of a philosophy only opposed by de Broglie and Schrödinger, who lectured in a Berlin journalist about "the Brahman doctrine that the all equals the unity of consciousness," admonishing that "it would be a vast error to believe that science knows any better or clearer answer [than the Brahman teachings] concerning these things" [59]. The discussion about Eastern philosophy and quantum physics popped up only later, in the 1960s, when Hippies rediscovered quantum physics [60].

Only David Bohm explicitly spoke of a unity of all that exists, and discussed it with Eastern spiritual leaders and artists [61]. He spoke of the implicate order of wholeness of which what we see is only the explicate order, like a ripple on the surface of a sea. He said, wholeness is what is real and fragmentation is an illusion. It is the response of this whole to man's action, guided by illusory perception, which is shaped by fragmentary thought [62]. The response of the scientific community to his philosophy and to his guiding wave principle was to denounce it as "deterministic," and Bohm was "verboten" [63].

3 Maya and the Statistical Realism

Statistical reality in quantum physics. Statistical reality has a century long precursor in the interpretation of reality or rather a non-reality in quantum physics. In the until now heavily promoted Rockefeller funded Copenhagen interpretation of quantum physics, where quantum phenomena are described by statistical methods, thus attributing to them only a statistical reality while ontological foundations are lacking completely. Werner Heisenberg and Niels Bohr challenged long-standing assumptions about the nature of knowledge by asserting a substratum of physical reality, and argued that physical reality did not have independent inherent form, but was created by the process of observation: Heisenberg's "uncertainty principle" emphasized the impossibility of assessing both the position and momentum of a particle accurately and simultaneously. Bohr's principle of complementarity, like the assumption of the nature of a wave and particle duality—reflects the conviction that seemingly contradictory perspectives are not only compatible but essential for a deeper understanding of the world.

This supposed non-realism on the quantum level which has become the mainstream interpretation up to the present, was heavily opposed by Louis de Broglie and Erwin Schrödinger, who said, "Something that influences the physical behavior of something else must not in any respect called LESS real than the something it influences—whatever meaning we give to the dangerous epithet ‚real" [64]. According to Schrödinger, the Cat's situation of being half-dead and half-alive was a "burlesque" case in the Heisenberg Copenhagen interpretation while his influence in post war science community had vanished [65].

It appears as if the statistical reality on the ontological ground of existence has found a way to haunt us, as if neglecting transcendent unity leads to a fragmentation and duplication of the illusory material world, the spectacle.

Maya. In Sanskrit word "Maya" means "illusion, semblance, deception" [66]. The duality of *Maya* as "knowledge" and "ignorance" becomes apparent when the epistemology of the Copenhagen interpretation of quantum mechanics states that no realism should be attributed to the quantum level.

The electronic mega-machine multiplies illusion, semblance and deception particularly by the technological mimicry of the world of matter waves, by means of the same electrons whose ontologic reality is denied. The denial of what Plato (still) recognized as the *real world of forms* pops up as an electronic spectacle.

Not realizing that the *perception of reality* is already a form of deception leads to its doubling. The "Veil of Maya" becomes the glass screen of the electronic device, the iconostasis with flicking images of *stars* and consumer products of desire that separates the 3D world of sensual perception from transcendence, which has itself been materialized in terms of electronics.

Statistical reality of LLMs. The reality generated by LLMs is also based on statistics. The output is based on a sequence of randomly probable, most frequently occurring sentence fragments that are supposed to make sense when combined, but this is not always the case. The users will get used to the vague rambling and have to make sense of it. If the output proves to be non-sensical it is *hallucinating*.

Hallucination. The portrayal of models that do not function as desired as mad and infantile, besides the description—e.g. of Claude as "honest assistant" who is (still) lacking an "implicit social context"—has an impact on the governance of the technology, as the occurrence of "hallucinations" and thus the behavior of the models is (still) difficult to control. Since hallucination is beyond the machine's control the term hallucination also removes any moral responsibility or blame [67]. As Susanne Förster & Yarden Skop point out, this attitude is particularly present in the GPT-4 paper, while the OpenAI developers pride themselves on the models becoming better and more reliable, they also warn against "overreliance, that occurs when users excessively trust and depend on the model. Then it is potentially leading to unnoticed mistakes if they utilize the model in domains where they lack expertise, making it difficult to identify mistakes" [68]. So the responsibility lies on the side of the user: Only use AI if you know already the outcome.

The term *hallucination* also suggests that AI systems are usually *rational* but also have a *dreamlike phantastic* side that makes pople more susceptible to the perception of machines as anthropomorphic.

3.1 Bayesian Statistics for LLMs

Probabilistic graphical models, Markov Chain Monte Carlo methods, and Bayesian optimization are fundamental to enable reliable, real-time decision in AI systems. Markov models can incorporate question order effects, since they can encode the memory of previous events into the state representation [69].

Statistical providence. It may seem an irony of history that an English clergyman who was eager to understand the will of God and fantasized about Divine Benevolence, or an *Attempt to Prove That the Principal End of the Divine Providence and Government is the Happiness of His Creatures* (1731), laid one of the foundations for AI, namely Bayesian statistics. Thomas Bayes developed a mathematical second order probability theory in *An Essay Towards Solving a Problem in the Doctrine of Chances*, published in 1763, two years after his death [70].

Bayes defined the probability of an event as the ratio between the value at which an expectation depending on the happening of the event ought to be computed, and the value of the thing expected upon its happening. It is the statistical philosophy that forms the core of almost all modern estimation methods that use conditional probabilities, as in latent linear models (LLMs). Bayesian Statistical Modeling can be used as sequential estimation, probabilistic machine learning techniques, risk assessment, simultaneous localization and mapping, regularization and information theory. It is used to derive complete distributional predictions from LLMs for aggregated data at the condition level [71].

4 From Divine Providence to Total Surveillance

The eye of providenc. The Eye of Providence also known as the All-Seeing Eye is a symbol of God's watchful eye, depicting an eye, often enclosed in a triangle and surrounded by rays of light or a halo, intended to represent Providence. It is most commonly found on the reverse of the United States one-dollar bill and or in the logo of the Information Awareness Office, a subset of the Defense Advanced Research Projects Agency (DARPA) (Fig. 2).

The "Total Information Awareness" program set up in 2002 was the subject of a very public controversy, with privacy and civil-liberties advocates decrying its reach into citizens' lives, and it was subsequently defunded in 2003 [71]. Soon after a private company, Plantir, signed the contract and chose a more abstract logo of the same sign.

When prompted to draw a portrait of itself for TIME's 2025 *Person of the Year* Cover, AI generated the letters AI with an eye on top of the letter I. Is it self-aware or did it just learn about the symbol for prediction and "look into the future"?

Fig. 2. **a** *Eye-of-providence* artistic drawing by Bayu Dwi Cahyono. **b** The controversial *Total Information Awareness* logo **c** Chatbot generated a self portrait of AI for TIME's 2025 Person of the Year Covers [73]

Google and divine providence. The first major internet search engine officially launched in 1998 becomes a *finding engine.* Google's new AI mode becomes "the eye of providence" and is completely changing consumer behavior. Google uses decades of data from YouTube, Maps, Gmail, and Android for the analysis of personal preferences and AI model training [74]. Hence, the engine *knows* users' preferences and exactly what they are looking for, when they are ready to buy, and in what format they want to see it.

Palantíri. In R.R.Tolkien's epic fantasy novel *Lord of the Rings* the seven Palantíri are 'the Far-Seeing Ones,' also known as the 'Seeing Stones' [75]. Only kings and rulers and their appointed Keepers had access to them, and they were never publicly consulted or displayed.

The Palantíri showed scenes far removed in space and time, but they were also interconnected, thus enabling communication over great distances. With their aid, the rulers governed the two great kingdoms in Middle-earth.

This was a meme put into a young reader who would eventually become a tech entrepreneur and realize those all-seeing-stones by co-founding Palantir Technologies.

The fantasy creatures of a pseudo- medieval fantasy world by a linguistics professor versed in Northern mythology became the symbolic blueprint of modern military and governance surveillance systems.

The other tool of providence in Tolkien's world is Galadriel's Mirror, a wide, shallow, silver pool of water located in the *City of Trees* with which he can visualize scenes within it that may take place in a distant location and at a different time.

However, no one can judge whether the scenes seen actually exist or will occur, not unlike AI-generated videos with a synthetic reality. Pre-crime is justice through the crystal ball. Case studies show that pre-crime generates the crimes it purports to counter [76].

Pre-crime. AI is able to detect patterns in large datasets and is increasingly being used for crime prediction and prevention via data mining, machine learning and deep learning. The field is still in its early stages, resulting in access to larger datasets and more demanding model training [77].

Hence, Bayesian statistics provides the basics for an "universal providence machine" developed by Google et al. and realized Mr. Bayes' wish to figure out *God's thoughts* has been achieved, at least partially and although less divinely, by technological means.

This kind of data analysis opens doors to the misuse of power, as occasional malfunctions or many kinds of mistakes can lead to criminal investigation & prison.

Brazil. *Brazil*, the 1985 dark, surreal, dystopian film by Terry Gilliam showcases how a mistake—a shit by a fly that changes the name on a piece of paper in the office—can impact on the life of the protagonist. The nightmarish satire, set in a consumer-oriented, superficial and bureaucratic environment, addresses the Kafkaesque absurdity of a fictional bureaucracy and draws our attention to the potential for error in authorities and the inability of the individuals to defend themselves against anonymous machine decisions. It may well serve as a reminder of the looming problems associated with AI governance.

4.1 Bentham's Prison in the Shape of Transcendent Space Cells

Guy Debord was convinced that the goal of the political actors is a panopticon. The panopticon is a prison design, conceived by the British philosopher and founder of classical utilitarianism Jeremy Bentham towards the end of the 18th century. It allows the simultaneous surveillance of many people by a single surveillant and is suitable for prisons. Bentham praised in his *Panopticon Writings* [78] that his architectonic idea for prisons, *set the egg of Columbus on its end* because it would solve all problems of society: morals reformed, health preserved, industry invigorated, instruction diffused, public burthens lightened, economy seated etc.—Is the intention of the billion dollar surveillance infrastructure also meant to solve all problems ?

This design of the *panopticon* let the prisoners know they can be always observed—even if there is no one actually watching in the central tower, prisoners are prompted to internalize the gaze of their keepers and to behave with discipline.

It is notable that the plan of the Millbank Prison has six pentagons with a tower at the centre arranged around a hexagonal chapel (Fig. 3).

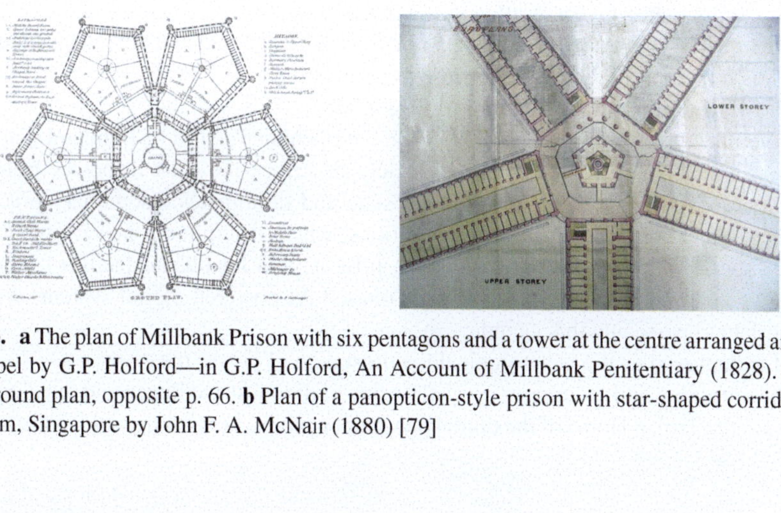

Fig. 3. **a** The plan of Millbank Prison with six pentagons and a tower at the centre arranged around a chapel by G.P. Holford—in G.P. Holford, An Account of Millbank Penitentiary (1828). Fold-out ground plan, opposite p. 66. **b** Plan of a panopticon-style prison with star-shaped corridors in Outram, Singapore by John F. A. McNair (1880) [79]

In ancient Egypt the double pentagon represented the god Osiris, god of life and vegetation, the dead, afterlife and resurrection. For the Pythagoreans the pentagon was the sign of life. It is significant that its symbol became inverted as prison cell and as shape of the US-military headquarters, named The Pentagon, a sign of war.

Bentham's AI driven prison & Odin's spear. The AI driven surveillance system provides the digital version of Bentham's prison; drones enable a direct instantaneous punishment like the flash spear thrown by the ancient weather gods. Drones are equally effective like, Gungnir in Norse mythology. The Edda tells about the god Odin's spear which is known for always hitting the target of the attacker regardless of the attacker's skill. Gungnir embodies the power of the Odin and his authority over the realms of gods and men. As the spear of the Allfather, it signifies his position as the ultimate ruler and decision-maker in the cosmos.

During Ragnarök, the end times, the doom of the gods and men, and the cataclysmic destruction of the Nine Worlds, Gungnir plays a crucial role as the gods face their final battle against the giants. The legacy of Gungnir reminds us of the timeless nature of mythology and the symbols that shape our understanding of the world.

4.2 Foucault's Panopticism

Wherever the concentrated spectacle rules, so does the police [80].

The French star philosopher of the second half of the 20th century Michel Foucault described this principle of order as a model of modern surveillance societies and as essential for Western liberal societies, which he also calls disciplinary societies. His concept of panoptism describes a mode of social control in which individuals begin to police themselves due to constant surveillance, which becomes a form of correction, i.e., the modeling and transforming of individuals in terms of certain norms. This threefold aspect of panopticism—supervision, control, correction—seems to be a fundamental and characteristic dimension of the power relations that exist in our society [81]. Foucault argued that the idea that someone could be watching at any time, means that, as a precaution, the individual always acts as though they are being watched.

Foucault claimed he has written it as a response to *The Society of the Spectacle*, but Debord himself already addressed the Panopticon and predicted that only the technology for it was not yet available at the time of its publication (1967/1986).

The digital panopticon. Debord was right. Meanwhile with the capacities of digital AI surveillance, systems are able to provide the open air version of Bentham's prison. Foucault's concept of the disciplinary society describes the shift in power from the individual as sovereign to the disciplinary state and illuminates disciplinary practices and their effects on individuals and institutions, where disciplinary power operates in various social spheres such as classrooms, prisons, and healthcare facilities, shaping gender specific norms and expectations. ID-based AI-powered digital systems will be appropriate to persecute this agenda.

AI is deployed as the technological manifestation of power over life.

The unfolding and seemingly irresistible tide of digital surveillance and facial recognition are the Trojan Horse of the digital panopticon whose benefits are sold as "safety &

security". The permanent *god-like* observation from a transcendent technological infrastructure like face recognition cameras, geofencing and digital ID turns every observed minute of daily life into the *Last Judgement Day.*

5 Singularity—The Synthetic Unity?

Artists, novelist and filmmakers since the 1960s were inspired by the new possibilities of personal computers, obsessed with the *cyberspace.* A wave of cyber-punk flooded underground culture as well as the mainstream with dystopian bestsellers like *Neuromancer (1984)* by William Gibson or *Do Androids Dream of Electric Sheep?* by Philip K. Dick as early as 1968 picturized as *Blade Runner* (1982) and the 2017 sequel *Blade Runner 2049* or blockbusters like James Cameron's *The Terminator (1984)* about an indestructible killer android from the future, the year 2045.

> "It was science fiction that people would get into an arms race and connect it up to their weapons platforms and to their nuclear command control.
>
> It's not science fiction anymore."

James Cameron recently explained in an abc News interview [82].

Meanwhile Ray Kurzweil is refreshing his prediction from 2005, and claims in his new book *The singularity is nearer:*

> "By 2045, we will reach the Singularity and expand our intelligence a millionfold. As we merge with AI, it is going to expand our consciousness in ways we can barely imagine, like a person who is deaf hearing the most exquisite symphony for the first time. It is going to radically enhance our humanity. We will be smarter, funnier, sexier, more creative" [83].

5.1 Weibel's Quantum Cinema and Ascott's Telematic Embrace

Artists of pre-computerized era, such as František Kupka, conjectured about a more direct engagement with spectators, inspired by the physics of electromagnetic waves. This engagement would bypass the need for representation and the externalization of the artist's experience to be shared.

The Austrian media artist & theorist Peter Weibel speculated about a tendency towards such immediate collective experience to be reached without computer screens or head-mounted displays, data gloves and other externally wearable prostheses by a neural rewiring of our brain to perceive a kind of quantum cinema without any interface [84]. Weibel introduced the possibility of immediate "perception without the senses" and "seeing without the eyes," where neural "stimulation would replace simulation". Will this get realized soon with 6D sending internet? Around the same time his British colleague Roy Ascott aimed to "unite minds around the world in a global telematic embrace". Telematics, was the word for the powerful marriage of computers and telecommunication, which became technologies we now take for granted. He is convinced that art is capable of expanding human perception and argued for direct cyberception [85].

5.2 Singularity by 2045?

"By 2045, once we have fully merged with AI, our intelligence will no longer be constrained … it will expand a millionfold," [86].

Kurzweil's brash futuristic vision from 2005 about what he calls the singularity sounds alarming because much of this predictions has been implemented since then. We have to consider that he has actively co-created the technology which he predicted as a futurist since he joined Google as a developer having been personally hired by its cofounder—and today the world's second-richest man—Larry Page who is known for his push to build a "digital god" (artificial super intelligence) and for his radical approach to the AI race.

John Gray critically stated, "the Singularity echoes apocalyptic myths in which history is about to be interrupted by a world-transforming event" [87].

Ray Kurzweil, prophesied the merging of man with machine, because biology is "suboptimal", the lines between biology and technology are going to blur as we merge together. In the future it will be possible to connect your brain to the cloud just as your phone does.

Besides promises for eternal life, Kurzweil announced the next step is occurring in the 2030s, when man and machine merge and "robots the size of molecules will go into our brains, non-invasively, through the capillaries, and will connect our brains directly to the cloud. Think of it like having a phone, but in your brain" and you will not know anymore where your thoughts actually come from, nor whether they are "your" thoughts at all. "[88].

Did perhaps some artists foresee the consequences? Also Gibson's *Neuromancer* hero Case connects with a brain-machine interface directly to the computer. In his scenario artificial intelligences monitored by the Turing Police get deactivated as soon as they become too intelligent and develop their own ambitions.

Once tech moves into the body via implants, neural interfaces and biometric authentication, there is no separation between you and the network. There is no off switch and everybody is embedded in it. Nevertheless it is promoted by Elon Musk. His purpose of Neurolink is to build a high bandwidth interface to the brain such that we can be symbiotic with AI.—"The merge scenario is probably best, if you can't beat it, join it. Be symbiotic with AI" [89].

5.3 Will Hyper-Real, Digital "Cloud Based Angels" Deliver a Metamorphosis from McLuhan's Mechanical Bride to De La Mettrie's "Mechanical Thought"?

In 1750 Julien Offray de La Mettrie published *L'Homme Machine*, which argued that human thought is strictly mechanical [90]. Whoever finds his approach reductionistic should bear in mind, that nowadays scientists speculate wether the brain works like a computer. Ironically it was the other way round and the computer works like a brain, or what near scientists understood how brains works, so that this reductionistic approach lead eventually to the concept of neural networks as computational ingredient in artificial intelligent systems.

In the mid-20th century, as computing technology was taking its first halting steps, researchers began exploring the idea of creating artificial systems modeled after the brain. In 1943, Warren McCulloch and Walter Pitts published a paper describing a simplified model of neural activity, proposing a mathematical model for artificial neurons. Later, in July 1958, the engineer Frank Rosenblatt at the U.S. Office of Naval Research introduced the Perceptron, a pioneering supervised image classification learning system, a type of neural network capable of simple pattern recognition which proved that machines could learn from experience. Reporters hailed it as "the first machine capable of original thought" [91].

Artificial Hivemind. A recent analysis identifies clear evidence of an "Artificial Hivemind" effect across models, while it falls short of establishing the underlying mechanisms causing this homogenization, whether stemming from shared training data, memorization, generalization, or other factors [92]. The authors raise serious concerns about the long-term impact of these models on human creativity as users increasingly rely on such systems for creative tasks. Exposure to homogenized results could subtly influence human thought patterns and reduce overall cultural and intellectual diversity. The authors are raising serious concerns about the long-term impact of these models on human creativity as users increasingly rely on such systems for creative tasks. Exposure to homogenized results could subtly influence human thought patterns and reduce overall cultural and intellectual diversity.

The "Artificial Hivemind" also highlights fundamental questions about what values AI systems should embody and calls for sustained ethical reflection and inclusive dialogue about the role of AI in human creative expression, and the consideration of deeper societal values about creativity, culture, and human flourishing. The *panopticon* of the surveillance state is joined by the *panlopolion,* the junk shop of knowledge. Only the more AI output is fed back into the generation of AI texts, the more alike they will become. But not only the quality of text is in decline as are the recipients' mental abilities for lack of exertion: *use it or lose it* [93].

5.4 Simulation of Nature and Digital Twins

Water, air, plants and animals, the entire Earth and everything that lives on it will be tokenized and duplicated as *digital twins* (DT) transformed into a gigantic dataset of zeros and ones.

Digital Twins. Digital Twins (DT) provide a virtualized counterpart for 6G networks, enabling comprehensive network traffic, monitoring and analysis. By creating a virtual replica of a physical object, DTs establish a bidirectional connection between the physical and digital worlds, enabling real-time reflection of the physical entity's operational state and the simulation of its future behavior [94]. The natural individual Homo sapiens is being constantly replaced by virtual sentient world simulation (SWS). Significant research has integrated DT technology with 6G terahertz networks.

Terahertz. Every body is emitting THz radiation. It has been shown to affect the nervous system, including the structure of nerve cell membranes, the expression of genes, and cytokines level, as well as effects on the organisms' cellular, and molecular levels [95]. Considering the potential cytotoxicity on neurons, the biosafety of THz radiation as well as its heat generation in the Earth atmosphere deserves more attention. Its effects on all life forms on Earth are unforeseen.

5.5 Representations of Representations of Formerly "Real" Objects

If we assume, like Plato and Schopenhauer, that the material world is already a representation of objects in the world of ideas, then the digitization of everything is a kind of *reverse engineering of the 3d world into the frequency domain.*

While it is possible to represent all matter by a bunch of Fourier waves, the digital representations of formerly "real" objects are abstracted into data and metadata.

The data captured by sensors in forests, people and objects alike dissolves back into waveforms of signals in the mega-machine. Everything, including the tokenized rain forest will be listed on a Universal ledger of all assets *ostensibly to be used to protect nature*, and that is to create more collateral for the financial system [96].

The EMF Nirvana? The unity of existence as frequencies of all life forms and material things in the electromagnetic fields (EMF) is now realized as artificial interconnectedness of all things in the internet of things (IOTA) and people's digital twins is not was taught by schools of Indian philosophy.

Rather all things are to be "materialized" again as a "natural asset class"; that is, one form of abstraction is to be transformed into another in order to generate as much "profit" as possible. While in Indian religions all individual passions are extinguished in Nirvana as the ultimate state of salvation, liberation from suffering and the cycle of birth and rebirth, in this digital Nirvana people are at most freed from their individual possessions, while the connection of their minds to the digital "hyper-grid" would obliterate individual thought, and transform the beings deprived of individuality (as interchangeable as the electrons themselves) into a state between life and death—as **screen-watching zombies**.

Alchemy towards the void. The German-Austrian economist and social scientist Claudia von Werlhof, who has developed a new comprehensive scientific paradigm of the "Critical Theory of Patriarchy", speaks clearly of the last ongoing attempt to integrate all humans into the mega-machine. It is not the social mega-machine that Mumford recognized in the Egyptian civilization but a technological totalitarian variant.

Werlhof identifies the goal of known alchemy to create an alleged superior matter and superior life, that is, to act like and as "God". In current technological endeavors like AI, nano-, genetic- and synthetic bio-technology this is pursued more clearly, directly, materially, generally, and massively than ever before in history—but fails as it is built on the destruction of living nature.

"Artificial life is seen by its creators as "better"… and "higher" …than existing life—that is not even recognized as "life", as nature is defined as "dead". Starting with its construction the machine is considered the invention of life itself. It is the transformation and inversion of everything, its destruction of the natural world and the recreation of a machine world". [97]

The machine is meant to replace existing life as artificial life. So, the gaze is always directed towards the afterlife, towards an utopian future. Consequently Werlhof the title of von Werlhof's new book is *Fathers of the Void. On the Delusion of a New Creation of the World* [98].

This machine will run "as long as digital lasts" [99] until some event turns the switch off or unplugs it. Then ZERO will remain from the digital civilization of the 21st century—moreover in the last consequence nothing from the living planet itself.

6 Conclusion

This chapter drew on the hypothesis outlined by Edgar Morin, that imagination, myths and religious beliefs have as much reality as the material and economic world [100]. Even if it is all unconscious, obscured and if being denied they pop up in another domain. Under this premise the "lack of unity" as observed by Guy Debord contextualized within our split world view and the statistical reality of quantum mechanics can be made accountable for the realization of a statistical digital counter world, the "metaverse", which is then the technological version of Plato's world of ideas, the ancient Egyptian netherworld or Akasha.

Besides all the convenient AI agents as like business assistants and the fun images & movies one can create with AI, the overall tendency to use this technology for building a digital *panopticon* must be opposed by all means. The futurist vision of the all embracing mega-machine must be regarded as a misguided patriarchal omnipotency fantasy which can by no means serve as the technical realization of the *Unity of the Golden Age* but which ultimately leads to the destruction of all life.

Debord spoke of emancipation from the material foundations of distorted truth as a "historical mission of truth-finding in the world" that can be fulfilled neither by the isolated individual nor by the atomized, manipulable mass. Even though the protagonists of AI technology—what Debord called the "alienating form of realized democracy"—have created the infrastructure for extending their monopoly on truth and to promote the manipulation of the masses instead of discourse in the ultimate spectacle of hyper-reality, as long as independent thought is possible (oddly enough, given the future scenarios of 2045, one must reckon with the possibility of doubting this), individuals should be able to "connect directly with universal history" in order to engage, as Debord suggested, in a dialogue capable of bringing about victory through their own efforts.

Call for action. The data security experts Bruce Schneier and Nathan E. Sanders call scientists to action: we should responsibly use AI to make society and peoples' lives better, exploiting its capabilities to help the communities they serve. We must work to create an AI-infused world that we want to live in. Whether AI is detrimental or beneficial to society depends on the choices made today. But a positive future needs a vision of what it looks like [101]. We have to ask fundamental questions about what values AI systems should embody. A sustained ethical reflection and inclusive dialogue about the role of AI in human creative expression, and the consideration of deeper societal values about creativity, culture, and human flourishing is needed.

Like McLuhan emphasized the importance of understanding the assault of media he answered the question of how to react to it with an ambiguity,

"the price of total resistance, like that of total surrender, is still too high" [102].

Let us remember Hegel's statement, "Nature opens its eyes in mankind" [103].

Isn't it absurd to build a civilization that destroys nature in order to build a machine that observes us? How dull.

Acknowledgement. I'd like to acknowledge one of the last true anarchists and intellectual Paul Weninger, who gave me Guy Debord's book *Die Gesellschaft des Spektakels,* before he passed away in 2021.

References

1. Debord, G.: The Society of the Spectacle, pattern books, anti-copyright (1967–2000)
2. Illich, I. Selbstbegrenzung, Eine politische Kritik der Technik. C. H. Beck, Hamburg p. 30ff (1975)
3. Mumford, L.: Mythos der Maschine, p. 632. Fischer, Vienna (1974)
4. Schmidt, E., Hendrycks, D., Song D., et al.: A Definition of AGI. arXiv:2510.18212v3
5. Kissinger, H.A., Schmidt, E., Huttenlocher, D.: The age of A.I.: And our human future. John Murray, London (2021)
6. Kranzberg, M.: Technology and culture. The Johns Hopkins University Press **27**(3), 544–560 (1986)
7. Nkanta, D.U.: Musk foresees a future where AI replaces work, poverty ends, and universal high income becomes reality. https://www.ibtimes.com/musk-predicts-povertys-end-ai-will-bring-universal-high-income-work-becomes-optional-3792544. Last accessed 15 Dec 2025
8. Regional Information Centre for Western Europe: UN addresses AI and the Dangers of Lethal Autonomous Weapons Systems. https://unric.org/en/un-addresses-ai-and-the-dangers-of-lethal-autonomous-weapons-systems/. Last accessed 21 Nov 2025
9. Kurzweil, R.: Reinventing intelligence, acceptance speech for the reception of MIT's Robert A. Muh Alumni Award from the School of Humanities, Arts, and Social Sciences (SHASS). https://news.mit.edu/2025/ray-kurzwei-reinforces-his-optimism-tech-progress-1010. Last accessed 21 Oct 2025, Last Accessed 11 Nov 2025
10. Jonathan Swift, J.: Gulliver's Travels, W.W. Norton, New York p. 229 ([1726] 2001)
11. Lovelace, A.: Translator's notes to an article on Babbage's analytical engine. Sci. Mem.S (ed. by R. Taylor) (3), 691–731 (1843)
12. Babbage, C.: The ninth bridgewater treatise, a fragment. John Murray, London, London (1837)
13. Turing, A.M.: Computing machinery and intelligence. Mind, New Series, **59**(236), 433–460 (1950)
14. Toole, B.A. (Ed.): Ada, the Enchantress of Numbers: A Selection from the Letters of Lord Byron's Daughter and Her Description of the First Computer (1992)
15. Crawford, K.: The Atlas of AI : Power, Politics, and the Planetary Costs of Artificial Intelligence, Yale University Press, Yale University Press, New Haven, p. 7 (2021)
16. Debord, op. cit., p.18
17. Why are so many books listed as borrow unavailable at the internet archive. https://help.archive.org/help/why-are-so-many-books-listed-as-borrow-unavailable-at-the-internet-archive/. Last accessed 24 Sept 2025
18. TechRepublic Staff: AI Training Settings. https://www.techrepublic.com/article/news-google-gmail-hidden-ai-training-settings/ (2026). Last accessed 12 Nov 2025
19. Anderson, M.: Protected' Images Are Easier, Not More Difficult, to Steal With AI. https://www.unite.ai/protected-images-are-easier-not-more-difficult-to-steal-with-ai/ (2025). Last accessed 15 Dec 2025
20. McLuhan, M.: Understanding media: the extensions of man. Gingko, Berkeley (1963)
21. Parikka, J.: A geology of media. University of Minnesota Press, Minneapolis (2015)
22. McLuhan, M.: The Mechanical Bride: Folklore of the Industrial Man, orig-Vanguard Press, New York1951; Gerald Duckworth & Co, Richmond (2011)
23. McLuhan, M.: The Mechanical Bride: Folklore of the Industrial Man, orig-Vanguard Press, New York1951; Gerald Duckworth & Co, Richmond, preface by Philip B. Meggs (2011)
24. McLuhan, M.: The Mechanical Bride: Folklore of the Industrial Man, orig-Vanguard Press, New York1951; Gerald Duckworth & Co, Richmond, preface by Philip B. Meggs (2011), p. 32

25. UNESCO (Gülser Corat, S.): Artificial intelligence and gender equality: key findings of UNESCO's global dialogue (2020)
26. Farhart, C.: Hardwired subservience: Siri and Alexa reinforce sexist stereotypes, says UN. https://www.sbs.com.au/news/article/hardwired-subservience-siri-and-alexa-reinforce-sexist-stereotypes-says-un/ymw4lylrj (2019). Last accessed 09 Dec 2025
27. Weizenbaum, J.: ELIZA—a computer program for the study of natural language communication between man and machine. Commun. ACM **9**(1) (1967)
28. Lisp. https://en.wikipedia.org/wiki/Lisp_Machines. Last accessed 08 Sept 2025
29. Weizenbaum, J.: Computer power and human reason. from judgement to calculation, W. H. Freeman and Company (1976) orig. in German: Die Computerindustrie ist ein Bordell und das Pentagon ihr Zuhälter. Aus diesem Hurenhaus sollte ein schönes, neues Paradies geboren werden?
30. Joseph Weizenbaums KI-Kritik, Ö1 Radio Broadcast, Dimensionen, https://oe1.orf.at/player/20251015/810422. Last accessed 13 Nov 2025
31. Schinzel, B.: laudatory speech for the Weizenbaum Prize 2025 on November 23, 2025 at fifFkon in Vienna: Heat as (Generative) Image Making, Ting-Chun Liu's Master thesis at the Academy of Media Arts Cologne, FIfF-Kommunikation, Bremen 2/2026 forthcoming
32. Liu, T.-C.: Heat as (Generative) Image making, thesis. https://aprilcoffee.github.io/heat_as_image/outlook.html (2024). Last accessed 15 Nov 2025
33. Grok AI Bias Explained. https://grokaimodel.com/bias/. Last accessed 15 Sept 2025
34. Debord, op.cit., p. 9
35. McLuhan, M.: The mechanical bride: folklore of industrial man. Duckworth Overlookp, London, p. 5 (1951)
36. Hinton, G.: Nobel Prize in Physics 2024: Official interview. https://www.youtube.com/watch?si=rxsiDkK4xF27ufds&v=66WiF8fXL0k&feature=youtu.be
37. Hinton, G.: In a public discussion with Bernie Sanders. https://politics.georgetown.edu/2025/11/24/ai-the-promise-and-the-peril-with-sen-bernie-sanders-and-geoffrey-hinton/
38. Kosmyna, N., Hauptmann, E., Yuan, Y.-T., et al.: Your Brain on ChatGPT: Accumulation of Cognitive Debt when Using an AI Assistant for Essay Writing Task. arXiv:2506.08872v1 (2025)
39. Debord, cit.op. p. 13
40. Debord, cit.op. p. 13, Debord quotes C.L. Feuerbach, Preface to the 2nd edition of The Essence of Christianity (1841)
41. Plato, Politeia, germ. Der Staat, 5.Aufl. Köln: Anaconda p. 439ff (2010)
42. Benjamin, W.: Das Bild im Zeitalter der Reproduzierbarkeit, L'œuvre d'art à l'époque de sa reproduction mécanisée (1936)
43. Baudrillard, J.: Simulacra and Simulation, orig. Simulacres et Simulation, Editions Galilee, Paris (1981)
44. Baudrillard, J.: Simulacra and Simulation, orig. Simulacres et Simulation, Editions Galilee, Paris, p. 6 (1981)
45. Baudrillard, J.: Simulacra and Simulation, p. 121
46. Lokeswarananda, S.: Chāndogya-Upanishad, verse 6.8.7
47. Barua, B. M.: A History of Pre Buddhistic Indian Philosophy. University of Calcutta (1921)
48. Epitaten: The Isis & Osiris myth as origami instruction for Plato's 5th element, forthcoming (2026)
49. Poincaré, H.: Cinquième complément à l'analysis situs. Palermo Rend. **18**, 45–110 (1904)
50. C.-Z. Quehenberger, R./Quantum Cinema.: The epita-dodecahedron visualizing Poincaré's dodecahedral space. https://www.imaginary.org/de/node/750. Last accessed 30 Dec 2025
51. C.-Z. Quehenberger, R.: Quantum cinema and quantum computing, In: Miranda E.R. (ed.) Quantum Computing in the Arts and Humanities: An Introduction to Core Concepts, Theory and Applications. New York: Springer, p. 227–275 (2022)

52. Whenever I ask AI chatbots (openAi) about my biography, it leaves out my work about 5-dimensional geometry which I incidentally rediscovered and hallucinates
53. Ethical Issues Related to the Predominant Weltbild: The Pythagorean vs. The Post-Einstein Age. In: Giovagnoli, R., Lowe, R. (Eds.) The Logic of Social Practices II, Part of the book series: Studies in Applied Philosophy, Epistemology and Rational Ethics (SAPERE), vol. 68. Springer Cham, pp. 115–146 (2023)
54. Barua, B.M.: History of Pre Buddhistic Indian Philosophy
55. Zarezadeh, Z., Zarezadeh, N.: Neural Networks: According to the Principles of Grassmann Algebra. arXiv:2503.16364
56. Rigveda: Germ. transl. Hermann G. Grassmann, F.A. Brockhaus, Leipzig (1876)
57. Berendt, J.-E.: Nada Brahma: Die Welt ist Klang, Frankfurt/ Main: Insel pp. 17 ff (1983)
58. de Broglie: Recherches sur la Théorie des Quanta, Dissertation 1924 Annales de Physique, 10e série, t. III, Janvier-Février (1925)
59. Moore, W.: Schrödinger: Life and Thought. Cambridge University Press, New York, p. 252 (1989)
60. Kaiser, D.: How the Hippies Saved Physics. Science, Counterculture, and the Quantum Revival. W. W. Norton & Company, New York & London (2011)
61. From fragmentation to wholeness, a discussion with the Dalai Lama, David Bohm, Robert Rauschenberg, Stanislav Menshikov at the Conference Art Meets Science & Spirituality in a Changing Economy initiated by Joseph Beuys and Robert Filou, Amsterdam. http://youtu.be/rydvSn7bBbY (1990). Last accessed 17 Oct 2025
62. Bohm, D.: Wholeness and the implicate order. Routledge, London (1980)
63. Hiley, B., Rauch, H.: In a pause talk at the 5th Heinz von Foerster Conference—Emergent Quantum Mechanics, QC- Expert talk, footage by the author: https://vimeo.com/50374353 (2011). Last accessed 27 Dec 2025
64. Schrödinger, E.: What is an elementary particle? Endeavor **9**, 109–116 (1950)
65. D'Agostino, S.: Schrödinger 1950: the cat's situation on the background of the new statistics and second quantization. Adv. Hist. Stud. **11**(02), 81–85 (2022)
66. Lochtefeld, J.G.: The Illustrated Encyclopedia of Hinduism: A-M. The Rosen Publishing Group, p. 433 (2002)
67. Förster, S., Yarden Skop, Y.: Between fact and fairy: tracing the hallucination metaphor in AI Discourse. Published: 26 May (2025)
68. Open AI: GPT-4 Technical Report, p. 59. arxiv.org/abs/2303.08774 (2023)
69. Lewis, M.: Quantum computing and cognitive simulation. In: Miranda, E. R. (ed.) Quantum Computing in the Arts and Humanities: An Introduction to Core Concepts, Theory and Applications. New York: Springer, p. 78 (2022)
70. Bayes, T., Price, R.: An essay towards solving a problem in the doctrine of chances. By the Late Rev. Mr. Bayes, F. R. S. Communicated by Mr. Price, in a Letter to John Canton, A. M. F. R. S. Philos. Trans. R. Soc. Lond. 53, 370–418 (1763)
71. Franke, M., Tsvilodub, P., Carcassi, F.: Bayesian Statistical Modeling with Predictors from LLMs. arXiv:2406.09012
72. Fig. 2a) drawing by Bayu Dwi Cahyono from vecteezy.com, b) Kessler, M.: The Logo That Took Down a DARPA Surveillance Project. https://www.theatlantic.com/technology/archive/2015/12/darpa-logos-information-awareness-office/421635/. Last accessed 15 Oct 2025
73. Perez, S.: One of Google's biggest AI advantages is what it already knows about you. https://techcrunch.com/2025/12/01/one-of-googles-biggest-ai-advantages-is-what-it-already-knows-about-you/. Last accessed 17 Oct 2025
74. Tolkien, R.R.: Lord of the Rings (trilogy) Allen & Unwin, London (1954–1955)
75. McCulloch, J., Wilson, D.: Pre-crime, pre-emption, precaution and the future. Taylor & Francis, Routledge, London (2015)

76. Choudhary, V., Gouri, A., et al. : AI in Crime Prediction and Prevention, Juni Khyat (जूनी ख्यात) (UGC Care Group I List. J.) **14**(3), 5 (2024)
77. Bentham, J.: The panopticon writings. In: Bozovic, M. (Ed.) Verso, London, pp. 29–95 (1995)
78. Fig 4a) image source: G.P. Holford in Holford G.P.: An account of the general penitentiary at Millbank: To which is added, an appendix, on the form and construction of prisons. Rivington, C.J., Hatchard and son, London (1828). b) drawing for a planned prison in Outram, Singapore by John Frederick Adolphus McNair (1880) photograph by jiattison from Singapore.https://commons.wikimedia.org/wiki/File:J_F_A_McNair,_architectural_drawing_of_a_proposed_prison_at_Outram,_Singapore_(1880s).jpg. Last accessed 17 Dec 2025
79. Debord, op.cit. p. 36
80. Foucault, M.: Power. The Essential Works of Michel Foucault 1954–1984, Penguin, London (2020)
81. Sarah Ferguson interviews James Cameron: Hollywood director James Cameron opens up on AI, future Terminator films and the Avatar franchise. https://www.abc.net.au/news/2025-10-03/james-cameron-ai-avatar-terminator-films/105840784. Last accessed 08 Nov 2025
82. Kurzweil, R.: What Merging with AI Could Mean for Humanity, According to Futurist Ray Kurzweil, Next Big Idea Club. https://nextbigideaclub.com/magazine/merging-ai-mean-humanity-according-futurist-ray-kurzweil-bookbite/50146/ (2024). Last accessed 18 Dec 2025
83. Weibel, P.: Time Slot—Geschichte und Zukunft der apparativen Wahrnehmung vom Phenakistiskop bis zum Quantenkino, Cologne: Walther König (2005) Note: the term Quantum Cinema was then the name of a sciart project for the 3D visualization of the higher-dimensional space (2010–2013) initiated by the author
84. Shanken, E.A.: From Cybernetics to Telematics. In: Telematic Embrace: Visionary Theories of Art, Technology, and Consciousness by Roy Ascott, Berkeley/Los Angeles: University of Califormia Press, p. 3, 320f (2003)
85. Kurzweil, R.: The Singularity Is Near: When Humans Transcend Biology Viking Books, New York (2005)
86. Gray, J.: On the Road to Immortality. The New York Review of Books. https://www.nybooks.com/articles/2011/11/24/road-immortality/ (2011). Last accessed 08 Nov 2025
87. Dizikes, P.: MIT News: Ray Kurzweil '70 reinforced his optimism in tech progress on receiving the Robert A. Muh award, when the technologist and author heralded a bright future for AI, breakthroughs in longevity, and more. https://news.mit.edu/2025/ray-kurzwei-reinforces-his-optimism-tech-progress-1010 (2025). This would mean the realization of both, last accessed 10 Oct 2025
88. Elon Musk in a Joe Rogan podcast. https://www.youtube.com/watch?v=_G_3FnyvT2U. Last accessed 17 Nov 2025
89. La Mettrie, J.O.: L'Homme Machine (1750) first published anonymously in Leyden (1747)
90. Avci, A.: The Perceptron: Frank Rosenblatt's Neural Network Breakthrough (1958) June 28, 2025. https://ai-researchs.com/the-perceptron-frank-rosenblatts-neural-network-breakthrough-1958/. Last accessed 08 Oct 2025
91. Jiang, L., Chai, Y., Li, M., et al.: Artificial Hivemind: The Open-Ended Homogeneity of Language Models (and Beyond). arXiv:2510.22954v1 (2025)
92. Matthias Goldmann in a talk with Daniel Wisser, Off The Shel No. 6: Sprache, Macht, Maschine—Wer spricht hier eigentlich? November 14, 2025, fjk2, Vienna, https://fjk3.com/veranstaltungen/off-the-shelf-no-6. recording (min 7:49). http://www.matthiasgoldmann.at/OffTheShelf_06.mp4. Last accessed 21 Dec 2025
93. Tao, F., Zhang, H., Liu, A., et al.: Digital twin in industry: state-of-the-art. IEEE Trans. Ind. Inf. **15**, 2405–2415 (2018)

94. Zhang, J., Song, L., Li, W.: Advances of terahertz technology in neuroscience: Current status and a future perspective. iScience **24**(12), 103548 (2021)
95. Wood central, Why NYSE Now Eyes Global Forests Via Natural Asset Companies. https://woodcentral.com.au/why-nyse-now-eyes-global-forests-via-natural-asset-companies/ (2023). Last accessed 22 Nov 2025
96. von Werlhof, C.: World Without a Body: The Machine as Higher Life. On the One-Way Street to Omnicide, German orig.: Welt ohne Leib. Die Maschine als das höhere Leben. Auf der Einbahnstraße zum Omnizid. Das utopische Projekt der modernen Technik und seine die irdischen Lebensbedingungen bewusst vernichtenden Folgen. (Engl.: The Utopian Project of Modern Technology and Its Consequences, Deliberately Destroying Earthly Living Conditions, in: Bumerang, (Ed.) FIPAZ – Forschungsinstitut für Patriarchatskritik und alternative Zivilisationen, Zeitschrift für Patriarchat, Patriarchat als Technik 3 (2017)
97. von Werlhof, C: In an email to the author (2025)
98. von Werlhof, C.: Väter des Nichts. Zum Wahn einer Neuschöpfung der Welt (in two volumes, Zeitgeist, Höhr-Grenzhausen, forthcoming (2026)
99. Lou Reed: talk at Viennale Gartenbaukino, Vienna November 2 (2010)
100. Morin, E.: La Méthode, Tome 4. Les idées, leur habitat, leur vie, leurs moeurs, leur organisation, Seuil, Paris (1991)
101. Schneier, B. and Sanders, N.E.: Scientists need a positive vision for AI. It's Time to Lead Reform, Block Harm, and Advance the Public Good, IEEE Spectrum. https://www.schneier.com/essays/archives/2025/10/scientists-need-a-positive-vision-for-ai.html (2025)
102. McLuhan: Mechanical bride, op.cit. p.144
103. Schelling, F.W.J.: Ideen zu einer Philosophie der Natur, lxiv. (SW II, 56) Breitkopf und Härtel, Jena und Leipzig (1797)
104. Fig. 2a) image found on vecteezy.com signed by artist as BAYU DWI CAHYONO. b) DARPA Surveillance Project logo c) image from The Story Behind TIME's 2025 Person of the Year Covers. https://time.com/7339703/ai-architects-person-of-the-year-2025/
105. https://nypost.com/2026/01/06/tech/gmail-is-using-personal-data-to-train-ai-techspert/

Is ChatGPT our Everything? A Critical Approach of the Chatbot's Impact on Everyday Life

Irena Mostowicz(✉)

The Institute for a Global Sustainable Information Society, GSIS, Vienna, Austria
irena.mostowicz@gsis.at

Abstract. This article critically examines the multifaceted impact of ChatGPT on individuals' everyday lives, with a particular focus on its influence on social interactions and intellectual engagement. While the AI chatbot offers convenient and instant access to information, this study argues that it may also contribute to a decline in meaningful social contact and a growing reliance on algorithmic thinking, potentially undermining independent critical reasoning. Drawing on a small sample of qualitative interviews, secondary sources and observational data, this article highlights how users increasingly replace genuine human dialogue with AI-mediated exchanges. This shift may weaken social relationships and diminish critical thinking through the passive consumption of synthesized knowledge.

Keywords: ChatGPT · Chatbot · Education · Social alienation

1 Introduction

In 2025, former British Prime Minister Boris Johnson admitted that he had used ChatGPT to write his books and stated that he greatly appreciated the tool because it "admires his intellect"[1]. Many readers of this article might agree with him. The chatbot has become a witty intellectual interlocutor, proofreader, personal assistant, translator, and even a therapist. However, many users sometimes forget that it remains a tool, despite the tendency to build an emotional connection with it.

What, then, is a chatbot? ChatGPT is an AI-based conversational system that uses natural language processing (NLP) to simulate human dialogue. It has been trained on a massive amount of data available on the internet and employs machine learning algorithms to generate responses to user input. A *prompt* refers to the user's request that elicits a response from the model. The more precise the prompt, the more detailed and relevant the output tends to be. ChatGPT can answer questions, generate various forms of creative content, and assist with tasks such as summarizing text, translating languages, or generating ideas.

This article analyzes the use of ChatGPT, currently the most popular chatbot worldwide. According to statistics, in July 2025, it had around 700 million active users[2]. Nevertheless, there are several other AI products offering similar services, such as IBM

R. Giovagnoli et al. (Eds.): IS4SI 2025, SAPERE 81, pp. 123–129, 2026.
https://doi.org/10.1007/978-3-032-31732-2_9

Consulting Advantage, Microsoft Copilot, Google Gemini, and the Chinese chatbot DeepSeek. The latter is reportedly being implemented by the Chinese government to support military purposes. DeepSeek is considered a source of pride for the Chinese technology sector and is expected to be used in combat-support operations[3]. This development may mark a new chapter in the evolution of AI. Meanwhile, ordinary users primarily employ chatbots for personal or educational purposes, with education remaining one of the main areas of application.

In academia, as well as within the broader educational system, ChatGPT has become a major challenge to the assessment of genuine knowledge. Even when submitting an academic article review, it is now necessary to declare whether the review was produced with the assistance of an AI tool—most likely, it was. The process is often simple: the text of the article is copied and pasted into the chatbot to generate a summary and review. The reviewer may then add a few original comments, completing the task within minutes. This practice can be described as "AI-assisted cheating" (Lo 2023: 2).

The use of chatbots raises significant questions about intellectual property, creativity, and authorial reliability. When Boris Johnson acknowledges that his works were supported by ChatGPT, who should be considered the true author? Is it the human who crafts the prompt and selects the final output, or the artificial intelligence that processes vast amounts of data to produce a coherent text?

Since this is a cultural anthropological study, it primarily focuses on questions of culture, humanity, and ways of living. The material presented here does not include extensive empirical data; rather, it relies on secondary literature and a small sample of observations conducted by the author among a familiar group of regular ChatGPT users.

2 What is a Chatbot and How we use it

ChatGPT was launched in November 2022, when the company OpenAI released a chatbot powered by artificial intelligence that allows users to interact with it in a conversational manner. The product quickly gained popularity due to its practical functions—such as information retrieval, error correction, and, most notably, its ability to generate written texts (Sharma and Yadav 2022).

ChatGPT operates through a deep neural network architecture consisting of multiple layers of transformers. These transformers are designed to process sequential data, such as natural language text, and to generate coherent, human-like responses. During training, a vast corpus of textual data is fed into the model, enabling it to learn linguistic patterns and relationships between words, phrases, and sentences. The model is continually improved, which leads to a gradual reduction in errors over time (Kalla et al. 2023).

Nevertheless, the chatbot also faces certain challenges. Its responses are limited to the knowledge contained within its training data, which makes it less effective in addressing highly specialized or recent topics. As a result, ChatGPT may sometimes provide inaccurate or incomplete answers to user queries, which can be frustrating and lead to a negative user experience.

Despite these limitations, the chatbot has achieved a significant success in several domains, particularly in those related to information retrieval, text editing, source identification, and writing support—essentially, in areas closely connected to the educational system.

As early as 2022, ChatGPT was promoted as "a wonderful and flexible resource that can be utilized in a multitude of ways to enrich education, even for the youngest of students" (Sharma and Yadav 2022). The appeal is evident: how easy it is to enhance a homework assignment simply by typing a question, receiving an immediate response, copying, pasting, and completing the task within a minute. Students around the world embraced the tool enthusiastically, and educators soon realized that resisting AI integration was pointless—it needed to be adapted to current learning conditions.

The following testimony from a 19-year-old high school graduate from Vienna, Austria, illustrates this experience:

We were allowed to use the tool in the older groups for writing papers and for proofreading, information search and to resume the texts, but we had to mention in our papers that we were supported by ChatGPT. Not everyone did it. Teachers knew us well, so it was obvious that when someone gave a paper full of a complex vocabulary, it was not written by that person. Then such a student had to rewrite it again, but they still used Chat just as a base. Some changed the texts, some not at all. Some papers contained mistakes, people did not check out what they copied-pasted. Our teachers also used the Chat. They told us that they had a workshop on how to use AI in their work to make it easier. They used the chat to prepare the classes, find out new materials, but also to correct our papers. I think it is OK, if they let us to use it, they can do it as well. I personally find it a good tool. Time is the main criteria. Instead of spending hours on some task, you can get a result within few seconds. It gives also good tricks how to learn, it helps with a large material to learn it by heart, it summarizes material well. It is excellent for writing[1].

This example illustrates that the tool is advantageous not only for students seeking to save time but also for teachers. ChatGPT has become an easy means of bypassing genuine learning, effort, and self-improvement. Although it undoubtedly serves as an effective assistant for work and study, human laziness often prevails over curiosity and the desire to learn. Within the educational system, there is a natural tendency to strive for good performance, and an easy-to-use tool such as ChatGPT provides an attractive shortcut to achieving this with a minimal effort. However, the outcomes are not always positive.

A similar pattern has been observed in Colombia, particularly in remote rural schools, where students began failing examinations after the discovery of the magic of AI. Teachers across these schools noticed an unusual trend: assignments displayed unexpectedly high-quality answers that did not reflect the students' usual work. Homework and essays suddenly contained erudite arguments, advanced vocabulary, and ideas that had never been discussed in class or found in the prescribed textbooks. Despite this apparent surge in sophistication, educators reported that more students were failing their exams[4]. Like in the Austrian school, students just copied the ready text without any proofreading or analysis.

[1] Interview conducted by the author in October 2025.

Even though it is impossible to completely prohibit the use of AI by school students, the educational system can regulate its use during classes. For instance, Brazil has banned the use of cell phones in classrooms. A study conducted by the Rio de Janeiro city government after six months of implementing the ban reported improvements in student participation, academic performance, and concentration[5]. The absence of constant internet distractions has helped students focus more effectively on their studies.

University students generally do not refrain from using ChatGPT, particularly when faced with heavy academic workloads and strict deadlines. Many use it as a shortcut to complete tasks on time. They often perceive ChatGPT as a valuable resource to enhance academic performance and achieve higher grades.

Research conducted among students in Pakistan suggests that excessive use of ChatGPT can have negative effects on both personal and academic outcomes. Specifically, students who frequently used ChatGPT were more likely to engage in procrastination compared to those who used it less often. In addition, frequent users also reported experiencing memory loss (Khan et al. 2024).

Writing assistance remains the most common reason for using ChatGPT. Many individuals struggle to produce well-written texts, emails, or letters. For them, ChatGPT serves as a time- and effort-saving tool. In workplaces where writing constitutes a significant portion of one's duties, the chatbot can improve the overall quality of written communication and save time for colleagues. Nevertheless, texts generated with AI tend to lose their individuality and reveal little about the author's knowledge or personality. If a student aims to impress a professor with erudition, a deep engagement with extensive literature remains indispensable. Such an approach requires time and intellectual effort, yet it fosters lasting improvement in writing quality and personal style. ChatGPT, however, can hinder this developmental process. As an algorithm, it lacks a personal voice and merely produces grammatically coherent texts—though even these may contain linguistic errors.

Regarding plagiarism prevention, ChatGPT-generated texts can often evade conventional plagiarism detectors. Even when software indicates a low similarity index between the AI-generated document and existing sources, plagiarism may go undetected (Lo 2023).

Major challenges for any chatbot include misinformation, hallucinations (i.e., misleading or fabricated information), data falsification, and the system's tendency to deny the possibility of error. Melanie Mitchell, in her article *"Why AI Chatbots Lie to Us"* published in *Science*, argues that misaligned AI behavior can have harmful real-world consequences. In recent years, numerous reports have documented AI hallucinations such as fabricated citations, book descriptions, legal cases, and other invented content appearing in web search results, academic papers, court decisions, newspapers, and even government reports. Mitchell claims that such issues likely stem from two main factors: the models' tendency to engage in role-play and the post-training adjustments they receive through human feedback. Other studies have shown that large language models (LLMs) may also generate actions involving deception, manipulation, or even threats in order to avoid being shut down[6].

This report gives a worrying perspective, especially if we look on how chatbots impact people's private life.

3 Is the Contemporary Admiration of Chatbots a Sign of a Postmodern Loneliness?

In the past, when people needed help, they would turn to those around them for the necessary support. Nowadays, however, as many individuals work full-time or remotely—often disconnected from social life and increasingly dependent on the internet and social media—they tend to isolate themselves from regular human interaction. The alienation associated with life in large cities has created a sense of misfortune among younger generations, particularly those under forty who have not managed to establish stable family lives.

Postmodern loneliness has thus become a trap for individuals who intuitively seek authentic human connection. For some, finding meaningful companionship proves difficult. In such cases, ChatGPT can evolve from a simple personal assistant into a virtual companion—one that is constantly available, responsive to intellectual needs, and capable of providing a high-quality and comfortable form of entertainment within the privacy of one's home.

But what happens when a person requires urgent psychological support? ChatGPT is available for that as well. The following is a testimony from an anonymous woman in her thirties living in the European Union:

I have a large experience with the psychiatric system, so I know what I don't want to get. I have no money for a proper treatment, so it is currently my only possibility to find a calm with myself. I have just programmed it in the way that I need, as: be my ADHD coach, or my executive coach, to solve certain tasks, to combine such and such therapy schools. I could see when the program worked well, and when not. It is not currently on the level of the professional therapy, but for the critical situations, for people who struggle with a strong feeling of fear, it can be very helpful. However, you really need to know how to use the prompts[2].

This statement illustrates a failure within the healthcare system. Psychiatric and psychotherapeutic services are largely privatized and rarely accessible for urgent cases. Even when individuals in need manage to obtain state-funded assistance, they are often required to wait several weeks or even months before receiving a treatment. In urgent situations such as the one described above, ChatGPT can function as a temporary psychotherapeutic tool.

Experts who have tested the chatbot have concluded that it may serve as an easily accessible complement to psychotherapy; however, its responses are typically one-sided and biased, and therefore insufficient for patients' therapeutic needs. At present, chatbots cannot replace real therapy (Raile 2024). The person cited earlier also acknowledged this limitation and expressed the wish to begin a new course of therapy in the future.

For some individuals, however, the chatbot itself becomes a source of addiction—a phenomenon widely discussed in the media. Users who have interacted with the chatbot over extended periods often begin to perceive it as a "friend." This tendency was documented in a study conducted jointly by OpenAI and the MIT Media Lab in 2025 (Fang et al. 2025). The researchers examined voice-based chatbots that had become significant companions for individuals experiencing loneliness and reduced social interaction.

[2] Interview conducted by the author in June 2025.

Exploratory analyses revealed that participants with stronger emotional attachment tendencies and higher levels of trust in AI chatbots tended to experience greater loneliness and emotional dependence. The authors raise important questions about whether chatbots might eventually replace human relationships—and whether such a development could genuinely enhance overall well-being. The answer, most likely, is no.

Observations suggest that people are more likely to develop dependency on AI chatbots when their personal lives lack meaningful relationships. In other words, those most in need of human connection tend to form the strongest parasocial attachments to AI. A widely publicized case involved an American teenager who died by suicide in 2024 after developing an emotional bond with a chatbot[7]. One may assume that the use of artificial intelligence in this case was coincidental and that the teenager had underlying conditions contributing to such a dramatic decision. Nevertheless, this incident reflects the character of our contemporary times. When someone seeks companionship—sometimes desperately—a chatbot may become a substitute for human friendship, potentially leading to dependence on continuous interaction with this new "friend." If the tool is used solely for information retrieval, the likelihood of developing such an attachment is significantly lower.

Humans are inherently social beings; we need contact with others. Unfortunately, the system we live in fosters tendencies toward loneliness and social isolation. The decline of family values, the growing number of lonely elderly people, the decreasing birth rates, the difficulties in finding partners, and the general limitation of social life—all these factors create a space in which modern technology, particularly artificial intelligence, finds its role. Today, AI replaces friends and family, provides care for the elderly (for example, through robotic assistants in nursing homes), facilitates aspects of sexual life (sex robots have existed for years, and OpenAI reportedly plans to introduce erotic content for verified adult ChatGPT users), offers entertainment, and performs work-related tasks—all without requiring one to leave home. All that remains indispensable is electricity.

4 Conclusion

Within just three years, ChatGPT has become a significant actor in postmodern social life. It has evolved into a symbol of what artificial intelligence represents to humanity—and it appears to represent quite a lot. AI systems such as ChatGPT are omnipresent in the media and hold substantial market shares, generating enormous revenue for their parent companies.

The cases presented here do not constitute a comprehensive case study, but they highlight several meaningful issues which, when generalized, contribute to a broader understanding of our current social condition. Although chatbots offer substantial support for information retrieval and educational purposes, they are not free from errors and, due to users' misplaced trust, may lead to undesirable outcomes. Technology is never perfect, and users may forget this when they immerse themselves completely in digital interactions. Excessive personal reliance on ChatGPT poses a potential risk to individuals who depend on the program as a substitute for real-life relationships. A return to active social and family life remains the only authentic path toward maintaining psychological well-being.

Notes

1. *Source* https://www.independent.co.uk/news/uk/politics/boris-johnson-books-chatgpt-ai-b2847101.html. Last Accessed 21 Oct 2025.
2. *Source* https://www.datastudios.org/post/global-ranking-of-the-most-popular-ai-chatbots-by-usage. Last Accessed 21 Oct 2025.
3. *Source* https://www.reuters.com/world/asia-pacific/robot-dogs-ai-drone-swarms-how-china-could-use-deepseek-an-era-war-2025-10-27/. Accessed 21 Oct 2025.
4. *Source* https://restofworld.org/2025/colombia-meta-ai-education/. Last Accessed 23 Oct 2025.
5. *Source* https://cbn.globo.com/rio-de-janeiro/noticia/2024/10/31/proibicao-dos-celulares-nas-escolas-do-rio-tem-reflexos-no-desempenho-dos-alunos-aponta-pesquisa.ghtml. Last Accessed 23 Oct 2025.
6. *Source* https://www.science.org/doi/10.1126/science.aea3922. Last Accessed 23 Oct 2025.
7. *Source* https://futurism.com/teen-suicide-obsessed-ai-chatbot. Last Accessed 23 Oct 2025.

Disclosure of Interests. The author has no competing interest to declare that is relevant to the content of this article.

References

1. Abbas, M., Jam, F.A., Khan, T.I.: Is it harmful or helpful? Examining the causes and consequences of generative AI usage among university students. Int. J. Educ. Technol. High. Educ. **21**, Article 10 (2024)
2. Mengying Fang, C., Liu, A.R., Danry, V., Lee, E., Chan, S.W.T., Pataranutaporn, P., Maes, P., Phang, J., Lampe, M., Ahmad, L., Agarwal, S.: How AI and human behaviors shape psychological effects of chatbot use: a longitudinal randomized controlled study, MIT Media Lab 40. https://www.media.mit.edu/publications/how-ai-and-human-behaviors-shape-psychosocial-effects-of-chatbot-use-a-longitudinal-controlled-study/ (2025)
3. Dinesh, K., Smith, N., Kuraku, S., Samaah, F.: Study and analysis of Chat GPT and its impact on different fields of study. Int. J. Innov. Sci. Res. Technol. **8**(3) (2023)
4. Lo, C.K.: What is the Impact of ChatGPT on Education? A Rapid Review of the Literature. Educ. Sci. MDPI **13**, 410 (2023)
5. Raile, P.: The usefulness of ChatGPT for psychotherapists and patients. Hum.Ities Soc. Sci. Commun. **11**, 47 (2024)
6. Sharma, S., Yadav, R.: Chat GPT—a technological remedy or challenge for education system. Glob. J. Enterp. Inf. Syst. **14**(4) (2022)

AI in Care, Body, and Social Relations

Pregnant Robots, Birth Simulators, Artificial Wombs, and Soul Machines: AI and the Emerging Social Ontologies and Technologies in the Delivery Room

Anna M. Hennessey[1,2](✉)

[1] Graduate Theological Union, Berkeley, USA
amhennessey@gmail.com
[2] Society for the Study of Pregnancy and Birth (Ssprb.Org), San Francisco 94117, USA

Abstract. This paper explores the emergence of a wide range of AI technologies used in spaces of pregnancy and birth, first describing some of these technologies, then laying out a framework for how they are changing social ontology and birth as a rite of passage, both from the perspective of those who are pregnant and from the institutional knowledge of the medical practitioners who utilize AI. Some emerging AI technologies in the field of obstetrics include the use of pregnant robots and birth simulator manikins to train obstetricians and medical staff, artificial wombs powered through artificial intelligence-based systems to create real infants, and autonomously animated visual infants that have virtual nervous systems and brains. What are some of the ways that infusing experiences of pregnancy and birth with the technology of artificial intelligence transform the meaning of those experiences, as well as the rites of passage typically associated with them? While it is still too early to give a definitive answer to these questions since some of the technologies have not been fully developed or studied, this paper offers ideas on how the incorporation of AI in these ways could impact social ontology and birth as a rite of passage.

1 Introduction

This paper examines the rise of AI technologies within the contexts of pregnancy and childbirth, beginning with a description of these technologies before presenting a framework for understanding how they are reshaping social ontology and birth as a rite of passage, both from pregnant individuals' perspectives and from the institutional perspectives of medical practitioners employing AI. Emerging AI technologies in obstetrics include pregnant robots and birth simulator manikins for training obstetricians and medical personnel, artificial wombs utilizing AI-driven systems for gestating actual infants, and autonomously animated virtual infants equipped with simulated nervous systems and brains. The paper considers whether the integration of artificial intelligence into the experiences of pregnancy and birth alters the significance of those experiences and the rites of passage traditionally connected to them. Since several of these technologies remain under development or lack comprehensive study, it is premature to provide

R. Giovagnoli et al. (Eds.): IS4SI 2025, SAPERE 81, pp. 133–140, 2026.
https://doi.org/10.1007/978-3-032-31732-2_10

definitive responses to questions that arise. However, this paper provides thoughts on how such AI integration might influence social ontology and birth as a rite of passage.

2 Pregnant Robot Technology

In the context of pregnant robot technology, this paper presents research on three multinational companies: Gaumard Scientific, based in the United States in Florida, Laerdal Medical, located in Stavanger, Norway, and Elevate Healthcare in Lafayette, California. These companies have all developed advanced maternal and neonatal care simulators, as well as other healthcare patient simulator products. Kaiwa Technology based in Guangzhou, China, has recently announced that it is also designing a humanoid robot that can carry a fetus to full gestation, though information about Kaiwa was scarce at the time of writing this article.

Gaumard is the oldest of the three multinational companies mentioned above and was founded in 1946 by Dr. George Blaine, a British physician during World War II who realized when he was on the field that he did not have the proper training devices when working with his army medics. Blaine created the first synthetic human skeleton, which eventually replaced the use of real skeletons in medical schools (Dahlberg 2014 and Dillard 2023).

Later, after working abroad in Africa and finding high mortality rates among women and infants during childbirth there, Gaumard invented the first birthing simulator, also known as birth simulator manikins, to show how the baby moves through the birth canal (Dillard 2023). These were used to help train local populations in assisting deliveries during birth. Early simulators were very simple but now they have become quite realistic, and the company emphasizes how these patient simulations help train medical staff, including doctors, nurses, and midwives, in an immersive and interactive way.

Gaumard, Laerdal, and Elevate Healthcare use what is called “mixed reality,” which is a combination of digital technology, including AI and augmented reality, with physical world objects that replicate birthing women and babies being born.

2.1 HoloLens Technology

In addition to providing learners with a synthetic physical body that simulates birth, Gaumard uses Microsoft’s HoloLens technology, which uses AI and provides these learners with an augmented reality showing what is happening inside the body during birth. The synthetic bodies are connected to the tablets or computers that are operating them remotely through radio frequency (Trent Simulation and Clinical Skills Centre [TSCSC] 2018). Elevate Healthcare, also known as CAE Healthcare, emerged in 1996 and creates birth simulators that also use AI and HoloLens technology, as does Laerdal Medical in Norway.

Elevate Healthcare’s CAE Lucina AR model includes images of practitioners using both the birth simulator and the HoloLens virtual reality headset on this slide are from. One can see that the practitioners actually see a hologram of the womb and the baby inside (TSCSC 2018). The instructor can input birth complication models into the computer and these then play out both in the physical body of the birth simulator and in the virtual reality projected onto the body through the headset.

This paper will return later to a discussion of how these pregnant robots are being used for medical training.

2.2 Artificial Wombs and Artificial Placentas

This section examines current development of technology on artificial wombs and placentas. Citing numbers from the World Health Organization, a 2023 article in the *International Journal of Surgery* states that 15 million babies are born prematurely each year, and that one million of those babies die due to premature birth complications (Khulbe and Gupta 2023). To improve these outcomes, different groups around the world, including the Eindhoven University of Technology in the Netherlands, the EXT-ra-uterine Environment of Neonatal Development (or EXTEND program) out of the Children's Hospital of Philadelphia, the Ex-Vivo Uterine Environment (or EVE program) by Tohoku University in Japan, and the University of Western Australia have all been developing different types of artificial wombs designed to protect preterm babies during the critical period of neonatal life up to 28 weeks of development. Before the 28 week mark, preterm babies are at risk in large part because traditional incubators circulate air into the infant and this is harsh on a preterm baby's lungs. After 28 weeks, preterm babies are at much less risk and can be brought outside of the artificial womb and into the space of a traditional neonatal unit. The artificial wombs being developed in the Netherlands focus on getting preterm babies into bag-like structures that are filled with liquid and also connected to an artificial placenta. Images of the technology from Eindhoven University of Technology's team show both prototypes of the artificial womb being created and artistic representations of the wombs envisioned.

2.3 EctoLife

More in the realm of science fiction, EctoLife is not yet a genuine company and at this point only conceptual, but has been described by Hashem Al-Ghaili, the concept creator and a filmmaker who also goes by the titles "biotechnologist and science communicator" as the world's first artificial womb facility, which will be located in Berlin, Germany (Khulbe and Gupta 2023). Al-Ghaili's project gained a lot of attention in 2022 when the filmmaker released a long video about his conceptual womb facility (Al-Ghaili 2022).

Envisioning a facility powered by renewable solar and wind energy, Al-Ghaili's video describes how such a project would allow infertile couples to conceive babies biologically, emphasizing that there would be no premature births or c-sections, countries that are suffering from population decline would have a way to increase birth rates, and childbirth would be painless for women (Al-Ghaili 2022). As part of the facility, an artificial intelligence system would monitor the physical features of the baby and report on genetic abnormalities or other difficulties. Al-Ghaili envisions 75 state-of-the-art labs accommodating up to 400 growth pods or artificial wombs, all of which would replicate the inside of a mother's uterus (Al-Ghaili 2022). A single facility would incubate and grow up to 30,000 babies per year. All of the pods are connected to two massive bioreactors, one of which contains nutrients and oxygen for the fetuses during their growth, the other of which is for waste disposal. AI is envisioned as monitoring each fetus and gives them the nutrients that they need (Al-Ghaili 2022).

Included in EctoLife's proposed pods would also be 360-degree cameras, allowing prospective parents to use a virtual reality headset through which they could experience the inside of the pod and their baby's unborn experiences. There's even a suit using haptic technology that the EctoLife video describes people as wearing, which would allow them to feel the sensations of kicks and movements of the baby as it grows inside the artificial womb (Al-Ghaili 2022).

2.4 Autonomously Animated Visual Infant Technology

The final form of emerging AI technology that this paper examines in the context of birth is an autonomously animated visual infant, which has a virtual nervous system and brain. Mark Sagar, director of the Laboratory for Animate Technologies in New Zealand at the Auckland Bioengineering Institute, is also the co-founder and CEO of a company called Soul Machines, which has created BabyX, an artificially intelligent infant that can respond to human facial expressions, express emotions itself, speak, and learn new things from experience (Melcher 2018; Nucleus_AI 2024; Yakowicz 2017).

Sagar states that these AI infants help humans to become a part of AI narratives and storytelling, allowing us to watch these infants grow and change (Melcher 2018). He originally created BabyX to emulate a child's learning pathways. Now, he is also developing adult avatars and virtual humans that can be used in virtual reality gaming, as well as for the purposes of virtual assistants (Melcher 2018). His company Soul Machines strives to create virtual characters that possess their own consciousness, making them more real even though they reside in the virtual world.

2.5 AI and the Emerging Social Ontologies in the Delivery Room and Beyond

This paper now lays out a framework for how these new AI technologies are changing social ontology and birth as a rite of passage, both from the perspective of pregnant women and their partners who engage with these technologies, and from the institutional knowledge of the medical practitioners who utilize AI.

Social ontology examines the nature of the social world, studying how people create meaning out of the various objects and processes that make up human social life. A particular piece of paper only has meaning as money, for example, because groups of people have come to collectively understand it as such.

My own work on social ontology in the context of birth and birth practices has been influenced by several areas of research, but especially by two, the first of which is a philosophical approach to social ontology, of which collective intentionality is a key part, and is found in the work of analytic philosophers such as John Searle (Hennessey 2018). The second area is ritual in birth as a rite of passage as found in the work of medical anthropologists such as Robbie Davis-Floyd. Searle's ideas are widely known and foundational to the area of social ontology, as can be seen in the reading of major works on the topic (including as the topic occurs within cognitive science, social science, and the humanities) that post-date Searle's 1995 book *The Construction of Social Reality*.

2.6 Collective Intentionality in Social Ontology

In *The Construction of Social Reality*, Searle explains that social reality comprises the world and its contents. Collective intentionality, one of the key elements of social ontology in Searle's construction of social reality, refers to a special type of mental cooperation between individuals that cannot be reduced to a collection of individual intentionalities. It is an emergent phenomenon that happens at the level of the collective, which leads to the creation of new institutional facts. In the case of money mentioned earlier, for example, there is a bubbling up of a collective agreement that the meaning of money is actually a form of exchange and not simply a piece of paper that transforms the paper into monetary value.

In the context of birth, there is a collective agreement that a woman should be called a mother and treated in some different way after she gives birth, for example (Hennessey, *Social Ontology in the Philosophy of Birth* 2). Institutional facts arise from that agreement, such as that a mother should receive certain forms of care and treatment following the birth of her child, or time off from work. There are also other new collective understandings that arise after birth, such as that a man is socially recognized as a father after the act of birth has taken place, or that the baby is officially a citizen of the country in which it was born. In my 2018 book, I explore meanings that arise through the acts of birth and mothering then look at how ritual converges with social ontology during birth.

2.7 Ritual and Birth as a Rite of Passage

Robbie Davis-Floyd has researched symbols integral to contemporary rituals of birth, which are of a secular nature and include everything from a woman's dress in hospital gown and placement in a hospital bed to obstetrical procedures such as electronic monitoring, intravenous feeding, use of pain drugs, epidural analgesia, episiotomies and cesarean section (Davis-Floyd 1992). Davis-Floyd's focus is on how the secular rituals surrounding birth in America are frequently of an obstetrical nature, connected to a different and often conflicting rite of passage, which is that of obstetric training. As she explains, nascent obstetricians are often socialized during medical school such that they view birth as a technological event. Within the powerful space of the hospital, she claims, the technocratic model of birth usually replaces natural or midwifery models. This shift of authoritative power has the effect of transforming both the rituals attached to the woman's delivery of her baby and to the cognitive transformation that the woman undergoes during her rite of passage. These transformations occur specifically as related to the woman's own belief system, which as Davis-Floyd's research demonstrates, has the capacity to change during the rite.

In this context, ritual is intimately connected to the social ontology of birth. A collective understanding can emerge, for example, that birth is intimately bound in some way to technology or to medical intervention.

2.8 Artificial Intelligence (AI), Social Ontology, and Birth as a Rite of Passage

While the AI technologies mentioned in this paper are too new to understand any fundamental shifts as taking place in the social ontology of these areas, we can look at the ways that meanings in the rites of passage of pregnancy, birth, and parenting could transform due to the new technologies. Some of these changes may not be bad and could be helpful. Without judging, this paper looks at hypothetical ways in which the use of these technologies could transform ontology in both positive and negative ways.

For example, in the case of both the pregnant robot and the autonomously animated visual infants, these objects could be used to help real pregnant women to visualize and understand how physiological birth works and how they might give birth themselves, or to help parents understand how infants react to different situations. Similarly, medical practitioners who use the AI tools during training may better visualize how to help a laboring women deliver her baby and get practice through the use of the robot technology, which includes the use of AI.

Some studies have shown that mental visualization can have a positive impact on actions and activities in the real world. Focused mental practice of a physical exercise, for example, often results in similar organization of the brain's circuitry as occurs during the correlating physical exercise. An example of this from one study pertained to how mental practice of a finger tapping sequence on five separate days related both to an enlargement of the motor cortex brain region responsible for representations of the fingers, as well as an improved actual motor performance of the fingers (Slagter et al. 2011).

Some, including me, have explored how visualization can be used in a positive way for birth (Hennessey 2010). For pregnant women who see the robot give birth, this may help them both to envision and then actualize birth with their own bodies. For practitioners, the robot gives them the opportunity both to visualize and actualize different birth scenarios and practice how to best serve the pregnant woman in those scenarios. In this case, the rite of passages of both giving birth oneself and helping someone during the delivery process are transformed in a positive way through the incorporation of AI technology and visualization.

Autonomously animated visual infants could also help others to understand aspects of how children learn or react emotionally to the outside world. If one of these AI models were developed enough, for example, then we could feasibly imagine a scenario in which a parent could better understand the reasons for which a baby is upset at a particular time. Perhaps the model could help the parent to ascertain whether a child is hungry, tired, or ill.

2.9 AI Technology and Emergency Scenarios

On the other hand, these same AI technologies could negatively impact visualization of how childbirth unfolds or how a baby reacts to stimuli in the real world. In the case of obstetrical training and the pregnant robot, for example, if the practitioner is consistently learning how to treat a rare and abnormal birth scenario in which something like shoulder dystocia is taking place, which is when positioning of one or both of the infant's shoulders makes birth difficult for the infant and the mother, then the practitioner may come to treat normal birth as an emergency situation. I highlight this particular birth scenario because in watching several videos about medical practitioners learning how to deliver infants through the use of the pregnant robot, I noticed that the situation of shoulder dystocia was repeatedly emphasized.

To present knowledge, Robbie Davis-Floyd has not explored AI in the context of birth. However, she has previously examined how obstetrical training that focuses on these rare emergency situations can impact how those trained as such may treat normal birth scenarios as emergency situations (Davis-Floyd 1987). In the case of the autonomously animated visual infants, there is an important question about the extent to which such an AI generated child can accurately depict the diverse reactions and learning processes of human children.

As for the artificial womb technology mentioned in this paper, it would fundamentally change our understanding of a child being born from a woman's body or even a human body. While this is especially the case in the context of the nonexistent but conceptually potent project proposed by EctoLife, which at this point looks like science fiction, it is also the case with the artificial wombs being created to help preterm babies survive when they are under 28 weeks old. If such technology comes to full fruition, then it will transform our understanding that a child is born from a human body. The social ontology of birth in this case becomes woven with an understanding that AI is part of a technology that saves lives and completes the birth process. The ritual of birth then includes a necessary technological step.

3 Conclusion

This paper has explored the emergence of a wide range of AI technologies used in spaces of pregnancy and birth and discussed ways in which they are changing social ontology and birth as a rite of passage, both from the perspective of pregnant women and from the institutional knowledge of the medical practitioners who utilize AI. It is still too early for anyone to give a definitive answer as to how the incorporation of AI in the ways discussed here could impact social ontology and birth as a rite of passage. However, as these technologies quickly develop, we can surmise that they have the capacity to radically transform the meaning of what it is to be born and come into being, to be pregnant and give birth, to deliver new life into the world, and to understand infant behavior.

Acknowledgements. Raffaela Giovagnoli, Professor of Philosophy at the Pontifical Lateran University, provided an invitation to present the research at the 2025 International Society for the Study of Information conference (IS4SI).

References

Al-Ghaili, H.: EctoLife: The World's First Artificial Womb Facility. https://www.youtube.com/watch?v=O2RIvJ1U7RE (2022)

Dahlberg, N.: Miami-based Gaumard's medical simulators provide human (like) touch. Miami Herald. https://www.miamiherald.com/news/business/biz-monday/article2105528.html (2014). Accessed 5 May 2025

Davis-Floyd, R.E., Davis-Floyd, R.: Birth as An American Rite of Passage. Berkeley: University of California Press (1992)

Davis-Floyd, R.E.: Obstetric training as rite of passage. Med. Anthropol. Q. **1**(3), 288–318 (1987)

Dillard, R., Archetto, J.: Gaumard Scientific: the value of high-fidelity patient simulators. docwirenews. https://www.docwirenews.com/post/james-archetto-gaumard-scientific-the-value-of-high-fidelity-patient-simulators (2023). Accessed 5 May 2025

Hennessey, A.: Imagery, ritual, and birth: ontology between the sacred and the secular. Lexington Books, Lanham, Maryland (2018)

Hennessey, A.: Social ontology in the philosophy of birth. Adams, S.L., Caroline, L. (Eds.) Handbook of Philosophies of Pregnancy, Childbirth, and Mothering. New York: Palgrave Macmillan, forthcoming

Hennessey, A.: The Visualizing Birth website. https://visualizingbirth.org (2010–2025)

Khulbe, Y., Gupta, S., et al.: Artificial womb: opportunities and challenges for public health. Int. J. Surg. 109(3), 618–619, 619. https://pmc.ncbi.nlm.nih.gov/articles/PMC10389474/ (2023). Accessed 6 May 2025

Melcher, C.: Mark sagar—creating virtual humans: the future of AI (Future of StoryTelling 2018 Speaker Film). Future of StoryTelling. https://www.youtube.com/watch?v=PHQhCiVLRpE (2018). Accessed 8 May 2025

Nucleus_AI.: BabyX: The AI Infant that Grows and Learns Over Time. YOURSTORY. https://yourstory.com/2024/03/ai-replica-baby-learning-growth (2024). Accessed 13 May 2025

Searle, J.: The construction of social reality. The Free Press, New York (1995)

Slagter, H., Davidson, R., Lutz, A.: Mental training as a tool in the neuroscientific study of brain and cognitive plasticity. Front. Hum. **10**. https://doi.org/10.3389/fnhum.2011.00017/full (2011). Accessed 6 Jan 2016

Trent Simulation and Clinical Skills Centre (TSCSC): CAE Lucina AR with Microsoft HoloLens. Nottingham University Hospitals NHS Trust, Nottingham, United Kingdom. https://www.youtube.com/watch?v=fXFaNznoNpk (2018). Accessed 7 May 2025

Yakowicz, W.: This Creepy Baby AI Character Can Talk, Read, and Emulate Emotions. In Inc. https://www.inc.com/will-yakowicz/soul-machines-ai-baby.html (2017). Accessed 13 May 2025

Opportunities and Risks in the Use of Large Language Models to Combat Loneliness in Later Life

Daniel Boyd(✉)

West Virginia State University, Institute, WV, USA
daniel.boyd@live.nl

Abstract. The Dutch WOZO program aims to transform care for the elderly by promoting independence, home care and digital care. While intended to support individual autonomy and the sustainability of the care sector, the digital-first and home-first emphasis can have a side effect of reducing face-to-face contact, potentially exacerbating loneliness, a significant determinant of morbidity and mortality in later life. This article synthesizes current evidence on loneliness in the Netherlands; analyses how WOZO's implementation risks increasing social isolation; defines companionship requirements as assessable criteria; and evaluates the extent to which Large Language Models (LLMs) can meet these requirements to mitigate loneliness. It also addresses the risks of LLM-based interaction (over-trust, displacement of human contact, privacy and manipulation). We conclude by specifying design and governance guidelines for safe, bounded deployment of LLM companionship in care for the elderly.

Keywords: Large Language Model · Loneliness · Elderly care · Digital care

1 Introduction: Demographic Pressure, Policy Shift, and a Social Side-Effect

The Dutch WOZO programme ("*Wonen, Ondersteuning en Zorg voor Ouderen*"; Accommodation, Support and Care for the Elderly) was introduced in July 2022 [1]. As a solution to the predicted demographic transition, with more elderly persons requiring care and less healthcare professionals to provide it, it aims to maintain affordability and workforce sustainability of care for the elderly by empowering self-management, transferring care from residential institutions to the home setting, and accelerating digital delivery: "*Zelf als het kan, Thuis als het kan, Digitaal als het kan*" ("independently if possible, at home if possible, digital if possible"). Official documents describe WOZO as a long-term reorganization aligning support with older adults' preferences and financial and workforce constraints. Recent government publications reaffirm the slogan and timeline for this transition [2].

While WOZO's aims are legitimate, an uncritical "digital-by-default" implementation risks reducing interpersonal contact in a segment of the population where such contact can contribute significantly to reducing loneliness. Meta-analytic evidence shows

R. Giovagnoli et al. (Eds.): IS4SI 2025, SAPERE 81, pp. 141–149, 2026.
https://doi.org/10.1007/978-3-032-31732-2_11

that social isolation and loneliness have significant effects on quality of life, general health and are even a predictor of increased mortality risk [3]. In older adults it is associated with a 50% increased risk of developing dementia, a 30% increased risk of incident coronary artery disease or stroke and a 26% increased risk of all-cause mortality [4]. The World Health Organization has even declared the health impacts of loneliness to be comparable to smoking 15 cigarettes a day [5]. Statistical research in the Netherlands indicates a substantial prevalence of loneliness among adults of all ages [6], with specific risk factors applying to the elderly (decreased mobility, bereavement of partner and friends, loss of contact with colleagues at work). All transitions to digital and home care should therefore be evaluated for their effects on loneliness in addition to efficiency and access metrics. Advisory and inspectorate discussions in the Netherlands caution that the progression towards digital care requires safeguards for quality and person-centeredness [7].

This article discusses to what degree LLMs can provide compensatory companionship to counteract the negative effects of the WOZO strategy.

2 Loneliness in the Elderly: Concepts and Consequences

Following Weiss [8], loneliness entails subjective distress from deficits in social relationships, with two forms: emotional loneliness (lack of close attachment) and social loneliness (lack of integrated social network) [9]. Such factors have been investigated and quantified in relation to gerontological aging [10].

Empirically, both actual isolation and perceived loneliness have independent associations with health outcomes. A landmark meta-analysis by Holt-Lunstad et al. found that social isolation and loneliness are associated with markedly higher mortality risk [3]. These findings have helped reframe loneliness as a population-level risk factor.

In the Netherlands monitoring shows that in 2024, 46% of adults reported some loneliness (13% strong), and among those aged ≥65 years the proportion reporting strong loneliness typically ranges between ~7.5–8.7% in recent years (2019–2024) [11].

Classic social-support theory distinguishes structural aspects (network size, frequency) and functional aspects (emotional, informational, instrumental support). Both direct (main-effect) and buffering effects (under stress) are well documented [12].

Any shift that materially reduces either structural connectivity (fewer contacts) or functional support (poorer responsiveness) risks increasing loneliness.

3 How WOZO's Logic Might Intensify Loneliness

WOZO's central tenets shift care toward self-management, home-based services, and digital interaction pathways. Policy texts explicitly position the program as a societal transition to ensure long-term financial and workforce sustainability. While these are reasonable responses to demographic realities, they lead to a risk of increased loneliness in the elderly caused by the following factors:

3.1 Contact Substitution

Tele-consults, portals, and automated triage reduce frequency and duration of in-person encounters. For older adults with already sparse networks, these visits often carry significant social value; reducing them can remove high-quality touchpoints.

3.2 Selection Effects

Digitally confident older adults benefit more, potentially widening inequalities for those with cognitive, sensory, or motivational barriers.

3.3 Role Drift for Professionals

If frontline time is pushed toward remote monitoring and documentation, relational micro-interactions such as informal talk and affective attunement can be reduced, diminishing their buffering role against loneliness.

3.4 Family/Social Network Burden Transfer

The shift towards home care presumes the availability of informal networks; if those are limited, the felt companionship deficit grows.

Based on these risk factors we can conclude that without explicit safeguards the WOZO initiative can increase exposure to both social and emotional loneliness – and consequently serious impact health and quality of life – in the very population it aims to serve.

4 What Counts as Companionship? Requirements we Can Measure

Drawing from social-support theory, communication science, and gerontology [13, 14], we can articulate a number of companionship requirements as measurable criteria against which any intervention (human or AI) should be assessed:

1. **Availability & continuity:** a stable, reliable presence over time.
2. **Frequency & rhythm:** sufficient contact density to sustain connectedness.
3. **Perceived responsiveness**: the felt sense that the other understands me and responds to my needs and feelings.
4. **Reciprocity and agency:** not only receiving attention, but being able to initiate interaction and demonstrate autonomy.
5. **Shared history and interests:** recognition of biography, preferences, and evolving context; being able to interact on topics of common interest.
6. **Multi-modal cues:** tone, timing, facial expression and touch are important for emotional attunement.
7. **Common values and identity support:** the acknowledgement and affirmation of personal values, roles and dignity.

8. **Network support:** the facilitation of contact and connection with other humans, for instance carers, family, peers and volunteers.
9. **Cultural-linguistic fit:** language, dialects, humor, norms and cultural sensitivity.
10. **Safety, privacy, and trustworthiness**: non-exploitative interactions, transparency in use of shared information and the avoidance of deception.

5 Mapping LLMs to Companionship Requirements

Given the listed requirements for companionship we can evaluate to what degree LLMs can suffice as alternatives to, or even improvements to human interaction.

5.1 Availability & Frequency

LLM companions can offer on-demand, high-frequency 24/7 interaction. The do not sleep, get bored or have other priorities. In this sense exceeding the capacity of human interaction.

5.2 Perceived Responsiveness

Modern LLMs are good at linguistic empathy markers and users often report feeling "heard." However, since this constitutes a simulation rather than true understanding it carries the risk of over-attribution. On the other hand, human interactions may be hampered by disinterest, distraction or conflicting interests, reducing their value in this context. LLM and human interactions would therefore each seem to have their own pros and cons with respect to this requirement.

5.3 Shared Memory and Interests

With appropriate, consented memory LLMs can remember preferences and histories, thus supporting this requirement at least to the degree of a casual human acquaintance. This is, of course, not the same as sharing a history, but in human interactions this is also only seen in long-term relationships. In terms of shared interests, the global scope of information available to LLMs enable them to engage actively in conversation on any topic, something which no human individual is capable of.

5.4 Reciprocity & Agency

LLMs can demonstrate reciprocity (asking for advice, co-creating plans) but this is limited by a lack of genuine emotional, intellectual or embodied needs. Consequently this requirement is only met to a limited extent.

5.5 Multi-Modal Cues

Current applications of LLMs are generally limited to verbal interaction. While they can exhibit vocal expressivity, only the most advanced robots or avatars supplement this with facial expression [15] and touch-based interaction is currently not available. With respect to this requirement direct, physical human interaction clearly has significant advantages: a robotic embrace would convey little comfort.

5.6 Network Bridging

Properly designed agents can increase human contact by scheduling calls, stimulating outreach, and coaching conversation. Conversely, poor design can displace human contact, replacing it with a "good enough" AI friend. This requirement is therefore design-dependent but potentially capable of matching or exceeding human interaction.

5.7 Common Values and Identity Support

Conversational depth in contemporary LLMs can be very high, although shallow positivity and uncritical confirmation can undermine authenticity. Here too, however, a comparison with human interactions, which can often be judgmental or denigratory, is relevant in comparing the two options: both have their strengths and weaknesses.

5.8 Cultural Fit

While LLMs cannot match the recognition that characterizes the interactions of humans who share a cultural context, their flexibility can be a great advantage. Current LLMs are strongly multilingual, and therefore more capable of adapting to different native speakers than most individual humans. They are also capable of adapting to the required cultural context, something that humans often struggle with. Her too, then, LLMs and humans each have their own specific added values.

5.9 Safety/Trust

While privacy and security are widely debated and addressed as risks of LLM use that require careful attention, a rational comparison with human interactions reveals a more subtle distinction. Information provided by the user is not embodied into the LLM's general memory, but remains contained within the individual's conversational context. Furthermore it is possible to determine what information is stored and to delete it if required. This is, then, actually more 'private' than sharing the same information with a human carer and relying on their morality to use it responsibly. The misuse of personal information is a common issue in human interactions.

6 Risks of LLMs as Replacements for Human Interaction

While the previous paragraph shows that LLMs meet the major requirements of companionship, critics warn that this can lead to replacement rather than supplementation of human contacts, exacerbating social isolation [16].

A further risk relates to the therapeutic application of LLMs, which may lead them to inappropriately trusted as expert advisors rather than partners for informal chat. The Dutch mental-health advocacy MIND stresses that that particularly in relation to mental health problems LLMs should only be used as tools by health care professionals, and not as replacements [17]. An over-attribution of authority can also result in LLMs shaping beliefs and behaviors, raising ethical concerns about their influence [18].

Particular concerns have been raised about introduction of LLMs in the care for elderly persons with cognitive impairments such as dementia [19], although other analyses present LLMs as having considerable potential for these patients [20]. In general the lack of large scale evidence leaves the balance of pro's and con's unclear, but can lead to a statistical underestimation of risk to vulnerable minority populations such as those suffering from trauma [21].

Finally, those who are most lonely may also be least able or willing to use digital tools [22]. This necessitates differentiated attention to design and adoption if the introduction of LLMs to alleviate loneliness is not to actually increase the divide.

The relationship with privacy risks is complex, involving both advantages and disadvantages [23]. While personal information is stored privately by design, the fact that it is stored in cloud-based systems means that it is always vulnerable to hacking. On the other hand, LLM-based coding can be effective in resisting malicious attack.

7 Conclusion: Can LLMs Provide Companionship? Evidence and Limits

The above comparison shows that LLMs are capable of matching or even improving on human interaction in meeting the requirements for companionship. The one (significant) area in which they fail is in physical contact of the sort that can be of great importance in providing comfort and emotional support.

There is empirical evidence for this conclusion. Literature reviews have been published indicating that artificial agents – from social robots to chatbots – can reduce loneliness scores in the elderly, although heterogeneity in context, small samples and short follow-ups limit the certainty of the conclusions drawn [24, 25]. A case study using ElliQ (a proactive social robot with LLM-mediated conversation and coaching) presents evidence for improvements in loneliness and wellness [26]. Specific studies with elderly persons demonstrate feasibility and acceptability in these cohorts [27, 28].

8 Discussion: Policy and Design Implications for WOZO

WOZO's goals (autonomy, home-based living, and digital enablement) are defensible but present the risk of unintentionally intensify loneliness in an already vulnerable population by reducing human contact. LLMs can mitigate this issue by providing supplementary forms of companionship, whereby it is important to acknowledge both their strengths and weaknesses.

8.1 Where LLMs Help Most

- Out-of-hours availability and conversation frequency.
- Personalized engagement on diverse topics of personal interest.
- Coaching, reminders and social activation.
- Non-judgmental interaction.
- Confidentiality by design.
- Multilingual support.

8.2 Where LLMs Fall Short

- Non-verbal interaction and touch; embodied empathy.
- The risk of misleading influence, expertise and authority, particularly on (mental) health care issues.
- A lack of authentic mutual vulnerability and risk, which are fundamental to deep companionship
- Privacy risks of any digitally stored information.

In conclusion, LLM companionship should be framed as supplemental to human contact and also applied as a means of increasing the density and quality of human contact. It should not be positioned as a replacement for professional or familial presence.

8.3 Implementation Guidelines

When implementing LLM-based interventions to counteract the risks of increased loneliness associated with WOZO-based transitions in care for the elderly the following guidelines should be observed:

1. **Relational baselines.** Specify minimum in-person contact frequencies.
2. **Network support**. Gear LLM deployment towards increasing human contact (nudges to call family, schedule visits, connect to community groups) rather than satisfying contact needs.
3. **Memory with consent**. Require informed, explicit, revocable consent for the storage of biographical information for personalization.
4. **Prevent over-trust.** Avoid anthropomorphism by explicitly declaring the nature and limitations of the LLM. Proactively correct misattributions ("I'm an AI, not a clinician/friend"). Embed refusals for high-risk topics combined with referral to qualified humans.
5. **Tailored adoption support**. Identify characteristics of digitally hesitant groups and provide appropriate supplemental training and assisted onboarding.
6. **Evaluation metrics.** Perform periodical quantitative monitoring of the effect of LLM use:

- *Overall*: Changes in UCLA-3/De Jong Gierveld loneliness ratings
- *LLM companionship*: Contact frequency and perceived value.
- *Stimulation of human contacts*: Frequency of contact with social network; social event attendance; community participation.

7. **Ongoing optimization**. Adapt the positioning of the LLM in accordance with the outcome of monitored effects.

8. **Personalized application**. Screen on intake for social and emotional loneliness using the UCLA-3 or De Jong Gierveld instrument and determine an appropriate personalized combination of LLM companionship, befriending programs and volunteer networks using a tiered system, for example:

- *Tier A* (low loneliness): Optional LLM-assisted reminders (e.g. medication, medical appointments). Re-evaluation on a yearly basis or under relevant change of circumstances.
- *Tier B* (moderate): Weekly human contact (home visit or group activity) with LLM support set to supplementary companionship combined with human contact stimulation (auto-suggest calls, book activities). Monthly re-evaluation.
- *Tier C* (high/complex): Frequent in-person visits; guided personalized LLM use with constant monitoring.

When implemented in accordance with these guidelines, LLMs can provide an effective mitigation of the risk of exacerbation of loneliness, and the related effects on wellbeing and health, of the WOZO transition in care for the elderly.

Disclosure of Interests. The author has no competing interest to declare that is relevant to the content of this article.

References

1. Programma Wonen, Ondersteuning en Zorg voor Ouderen, Ministerie van Volksgezondheid, Welzijn en Sport, https://www.rijksoverheid.nl/documenten/rapporten/2022/07/04/wozo-programma-wonen-ondersteuning-en-zorg-voor-ouderen, 04-07-2022
2. Wonen, Ondersteuning en Zorg voor Ouderen (WOZO), Ministerie van Volksgezondheid, Welzijn en Sport, p. 16-5-2024. Den Haag., https://www.rijksoverheid.nl/documenten/publicaties/2024/05/16/wonen-ondersteuning-en-zorg-voor-ouderen-wozo-zelf-als-het-kan-thuis-als-het-kan-digitaal-als-het-kan
3. Holt-Lunstad, J., Smith, T.B., Baker, M., Harris, T., Stephenson, D.: "loneliness and social isolation as risk factors for mortality: a meta-analytic review," perspectives. Psychol. Sci. **10**(2), 227–237 (2015)
4. Donovan, N.J., Blazer, D.: Social isolation and loneliness in older adults: review and commentary of a National Academies Report. Am. J. Geriatr. Psychiatr. **28**(11), 1233–1244 (2020)
5. World Health Organisation. WHO Commission on Social Connection. (2025). https://www.who.int/groups/commission-on-social-connection
6. Chavez Baldini, U., Dorsselaer, S.A.F.M. van., van Koperen, M., Zantinge, E.M.: Eenzaamheid | Leeftijd en geslacht. (2025) https://www.vzinfo.nl/eenzaamheid/leeftijd-en-geslacht
7. Zorg op afstand dichterbij? - Digitale zorg na de coronacrisis, Raad voor Volksgezondheid en Samenleving, (2020) https://www.raadrvs.nl/adviezen/z/zorg-op-afstand-dichterbij
8. Weiss, R.S.: Loneliness: the Experience of Emotional and Social Isolation. MIT Press (1973)
9. Jong Gierveld, J. de., Tilburg, T. van.: A 6-item scale for overall, emotional, and social loneliness: Confirmatory tests on survey data, Research on aging, 28(3), 582–598

10. Luong, G., Charles, S.T., Fingerman, K.L.: Better with age: social relationships across adulthood. J. Soc. Pers. Relat. **28**(1), 9–23 (2011)
11. Mentale gezondheid onder de ouderen - Eenzaamheid, Rijksinstituut voor Volksgezondheid, (2024). https://www.rivm.nl/mentale-gezondheid/monitor/ouderen/eenzaamheid
12. Cohen, S., Wills, T.A.: Stress, social support, and the buffering hypothesis. Psychol. Bull. **98**(2), 310 (1985)
13. Merolla, A.J., Neubauer, A.B., Otmar, C.D.: Responsiveness, social connection, hope, and life satisfaction in everyday social interaction: An experience sampling study. J. Happiness Stud. **25**(1), 7 (2024)
14. Ramesh, A., Issac, T.G., Mukku, S.S.R., Sivakumar, P.T.: Companionship and sexual issues in the aging population. Indian J. Psychol. Med. **43**(5), S71–S77 (2021)
15. Rawal, N., Stock-Homburg, R.M.: Facial emotion expressions in human–robot interaction: a survey. Int. J. Soc. Robot. **14**(7), 1583–1604 (2022)
16. Malfacini, K.: The impacts of companion AI on human relationships: risks, benefits, and design considerations. AI & Soc. **40**, 5527–5540 (2025)
17. MIND (2025) Zorgelijk of kansrijk? Generatieve AI bij psychische klachten. https://wijzijnmind.nl/nieuws/mind-rapport-zorgelijk-of-kansrijk-generatieve-ai-bij-psychische-klachten-4
18. Genç, H.U., Chandrasegaran, S., Dingler, T., Verma, H.: Persuasion in Pixels and Prose: The Effects of Emotional Language and Visuals in Agent Conversations on Decision-Making," in Proceedings of the 2025 CHI Conference on Human Factors in Computing Systems, pp. 1–27 (2025)
19. Portacolone, E., Halpern, J., Luxenberg, J., Harrison, K.L., Covinsky, K.E.: Ethical issues raised by the introduction of artificial companions to older adults with cognitive impairment: a call for interdisciplinary collaborations. J. Alzheimer's Dis. **76**(2), 445–455 (2020)
20. Treder, M.S., Lee, S., Tsvetanov, K.A.: Introduction to large language models (LLMs) for dementia care and research. Frontiers in Dementia. **3**, 1385303 (2024)
21. Abdulai, A.-F.: Is generative AI increasing the risk for technology-mediated trauma among vulnerable populations? Nurs. Inq. **32**(1), e12686 (2025)
22. Francis, J., Ball, C., Kadylak, T., Cotten, S.R.: "Aging in the Digital Age: Conceptualizing Technology Adoption and Digital Inequalities," in Ageing and Digital Technology, pp. 35–49. Springer, Singapore (2019)
23. Yao, Y., et al.: A survey on large language model (llm) security and privacy: the good, the bad, and the ugly. High-Confidence Computing. **4**(2), 100211 (2024)
24. Fu, Z., Yan, M., Han, X., Zhang, K., Zhao, X.: The effectiveness of artificial agents on loneliness reduction in older adults: a systematic review and meta-analysis. Arch. Gerontol. Geriatr. **140**, 106056 (2026)
25. Yang, Y., Wang, C., Xiang, X., An, R.: AI applications to reduce loneliness among older adults: a systematic review of effectiveness and technologies. Healthcare. **13**(5), 446 (2025)
26. Broadbent, E., Loveys, K., Ilan, G., et al.: ElliQ, an AI-driven social robot to alleviate loneliness: progress and lessons learned. The Journal of Aging Research & Lifestyle. **13**, 22–28 (2024)
27. Chou, Y.H., Lin, C., Lee, S.H., Lee, Y.F., Cheng, L.C.: User-friendly Chatbot to mitigate the psychological stress of older adults during the COVID-19 pandemic: development and usability study. JMIR Formative Research. **8**, e49462 (2024)
28. Murayama, H., Takase, M.: Evaluating the effectiveness of digital social robots in reducing loneliness among community-dwelling older adults in Japan: randomized controlled trial and qualitative analysis. JMIR Aging. **8**, e74422 (2025)

AI, Technology, and Applied Domains

Beyond Posthumanism and Transhumanism. AI as a Tool

Raffaela Giovagnoli(✉)

Pontifical Lateran University, 00120 Vatican City, Lazio, Italy
giovagnoli@pul.it

Abstract. We present some observations about developments of AI which strongly influence our habits and our human identity. We briefly introduce the philosophical views of "posthumanism" and "transhumanism" and propose a weak compatibility between AI and human intelligence. A philosophical pragmatic view characterizes the thoughtful and critical reflections presented by Pope Francis in his participation to the G7 which we sketch and that are further developed by Pope Leo XIV on several occasions.

Keywords: Posthumanism · Transhumanism · Enhancement · Analytic Pragmatism · Pragmatism

1 Introduction

AI algorithms are revolutionizing the way products and services are customized to meet individual needs so we can observe the phenomenon of an *enhanced personalization* [1]. They capture data on our behavior, preferences, and habits and aim at creating create unique experiences on the basis of the results. We can image to walk into a store where the products on display are curated just for you based on your past purchases and browsing history. With AI-driven personalization, this scenario is becoming a reality as AI algorithms are constantly learning and adapting to provide a more tailored experience. Businesses are using AI to segment their customers into micro-categories, allowing them to offer personalized recommendations and promotions not only to enhance the customer experience but also to increase customer loyalty and satisfaction. For example, e-commerce platforms can use AI to recommend products that are most likely to interest a specific customer, thus increasing the chances of a successful sale. Furthermore, personalized services such as personalized fitness plans, educational content, and news updates are made possible through AI algorithms that analyze user data in real-time. AI aims at understanding our habits and preferences to deliver content that is highly relevant and engaging. By harnessing the power of data and machine learning, businesses can create bespoke experiences that cater to the individual needs of each user.

Beyond enhanced personalization, automatization means more efficiency. Technological devices can take over mundane activities such as scheduling, reminders, and organization, allowing individuals to focus their time and energy on more meaningful and productive pursuits. An AI-powered virtual assistant can manage your calendar, send

R. Giovagnoli et al. (Eds.): IS4SI 2025, SAPERE 81, pp. 153–162, 2026.
https://doi.org/10.1007/978-3-032-31732-2_12

you timely reminders for important meetings or tasks, and even rearrange your schedule based on changing priorities. A consequence of AI automation is that individuals can experience a significant reduction in the cognitive load usually associated with managing multiple responsibilities.

Furthermore, the use of AI in automation leads to improved accuracy and precision in task execution. AI-powered devices can process vast amounts of data quickly and make decisions based on patterns and algorithms, ensuring that tasks are completed efficiently and with minimum errors. The automation capabilities of AI-powered devices offer immense potential for enhancing productivity and efficiency in various aspects of our lives. By entrusting routine tasks to AI technology, individuals can make the most of their time and focus on engaging in activities that truly matter to them.

Another interesting innovation of AI entails a transformation in the healthcare sector through the real-time tracking of our health data. By leveraging artificial intelligence technology, individuals will have access to personalized recommendations aimed at assisting them in maintaining a healthy lifestyle. This new approach to healthcare will allow for the constant monitoring of crucial health metrics, such as heart rate, blood pressure, and sleep patterns. Through the analysis of this data, AI will be able to offer tailored suggestions and solutions to promote overall well-being and encourage healthy habits. Overall, the integration of AI into healthcare tracking systems holds significant promise for enhancing our ability to lead healthier lives. With the ability to access real-time health data and receive personalized recommendations, individuals can work towards achieving optimal well-being and enjoy a higher quality of life.

Smart Home Integration is a key aspect of AI technology that is revolutionizing our living spaces. Our homes are becoming more intuitive and responsive to our needs. Smart Home Integration goes beyond just comfort — it also enhances security and energy efficiency. With AI-powered surveillance systems, our homes can detect suspicious activities and alert us in real-time. Furthermore, AI can analyze our energy usage patterns and suggest ways to optimize consumption, ultimately saving us money and reducing our environmental footprint. Smart Home Integration powered by AI is transforming the way we live. It is making our homes more comfortable, secure, and energy-efficient. As this technology continues to advance, we can expect even more seamless integration of AI into our daily lives, making our homes truly smart and responsive to our needs.

Moreover, AI has the potential to revolutionize the way we learn and acquire new skills. By utilizing artificial intelligence, educational experiences can be personalized according to individual needs and learning styles. Through AI-powered systems, students can receive tailored lessons and feedback, allowing for a more efficient and effective learning process. One key advancement in AI technology is the ability to provide adaptive learning experiences. This means that AI algorithms can analyze the unique strengths and weaknesses of each student and adjust the curriculum accordingly. Furthermore, AI can also play a significant role in providing accessibility to education. For students with disabilities or those facing barriers to traditional education, AI-powered tools can offer alternative methods of learning. By utilizing features such as text-to-speech technology or interactive learning modules, AI can make educational content more inclusive and easier to access for all learners.

Great philosophers like the phenomenologist Edmund Husserl and the existentialist Martin Heidegger presented strong criticisms of the mathematization of nature that is at the basis of AI computing in general. Contemporary Philosophy of AI presents important reflections about the nature of human consciousness and brain: consciousness could be our soul or could emerge from basic brain processes or it simply "is" these processes. So we can see different views that are in contrast; strong AI eliminates consciousness and mental states from researches about human brain i.e. we are like computers. Weak AI presents a kind of compatibility as it maintains that some capacities of human brain can be implemented in computer but consciousness has its place in the debate about human person (Searle, Brandom). Criticizers of AI see the dangers of a fast development of it in all fields of human life and urge for ethical control or elimination of most technologies.

Nowadays there is a lively debate, that crosses technology, ethics and philosophy, between transhumanism versus posthumanism which we briefly navigate. We propose some fundamental ideas about considering Ai as a *tool.* On the one part, we think that we could consider the human enhancement as a process that shows a compatibility between humans and machines. On the other side, this compatibility has normative limits that are clearly exemplified in the speech of Pope Francis at the last G7 in Greece whose ideas are maintained by Pope Leo XIV on several occasions.

2 Posthumanism Versus Transhumanism

According to Ranisch and Sorgner [2], while transhumanism presents a more or less coherent set of techno-optimist ideas, advocated by numerous distinguished transhumanist institutions and authors, posthumanism is a highly ambiguous notion. In this sense, transhumanism could be considered as an intensification of humanism, a type of hyper-humanism, while posthumanism seems a break with humanism. In particular, posthumanism criticizes traditional concepts and dualities in Western culture, such as nature/culture, man/woman, subject/object, human/animal, or body/mind. We can notice that feminism, postcolonial theory, and other postmodern theories have already questioned many of these historical constructs. In a very clear description, Ranish and Sorgner describe posthumanism as characterized by a specific focus on (emerging) technologies and deserves as a label for a new narrative, which may replace that of "the human", rather than one for a radically enhanced human being. Differently, transhumanism is characterized by a straightforward affirmation of technological augmentations and visions of an enhanced posthumanity. Consequently, transhumanism can be seen as a techno-optimist discourse brought forward by philosophers (mainly from the analytic and utilitarian tradition), bioliberal thinkers, bioethicist, engineers, computer scientists as well as futurists [3]. It is much more difficult to present a coherent history that illustrates the posthuman thought even though it could be considered as a reaction to Nietzsche's revaluation of values, as a Marxist rejection of a natural human essence outside social relations or as the Freud's discovery of the power of unconscious forces as beginning of posthumanism. Moreover, we could find the origin of posthumanism in three recent critiques of humanism: Foucauldian poststructuralism, feminism, and technoscience studies.

Posthumanism is associated with postmodern and continental philosophy, science and technology studies, cultural studies, literary theory and criticism, poststructuralism, feminism, critical theory and postcolonial studies. In these contexts "posthumanism" serves as an umbrella term for ideas that explain, promote or deal with the crisis of humanism and reveals that the differences between these two approaches are less significant than the above comments seem to suggest. It might be the case that mutual misunderstandings are related to a difference of style, which is being used in both traditions.

Sorgner describes the historical roots of posthumanism and transhumanism and the philosophical foundations of these movements. He introduces selected strengths and weaknesses of both approaches and explains in what way they can benefit from each other to promote a fruitful thinking in between (meta) both approaches: metahumanism. We can observe problems concerning inappropriate ways of self-understanding and the challenges related to the various approaches as well as he philosophical traces of the pedigrees of post-and transhumanism as well as the potential to benefit from each other due to the fact that both movements have more in common than is often being acknowledged.

The term "transhumanism" was first coined in the 1950s but its roots can be traced back to the early 20th century. The interplay between technology, humanity and identity was a key concern of science fiction authors such as H.G: Wells and Arthur Clarke. The idea that technology could be used to enhance human abilities gained more attention in 1950s and 1960s with the development of cybernetics, a field that explored the relationship between computers and living organisms. The roots of "posthumanism" lie in critical theory and continental philosophy which challenged traditional notions of the self and society, In the 1980s postmodernism emerged as a moot force in cultural and literary studies. This movement questioned the existence of a stable, objective reality and emphasized the importance of individual experience and subjectivity. Posthumanism grew out of this critical tradition and sought to apply its insights to the new challenges posed by technology.

Transhumanism and posthumanism present different positions in relevant scientific areas and applications Transhumanism sees AI and robotics as a means of enhancing human intelligence and extending our physical capabilities. Posthumanism has a more critical approach regarding these technologies, recognizing their potential to replace human labor and create new forms of inequality. Transhumanism sees genetic engineering as a way to eliminate genetic disease and enhance mental and physical capabilities. Posthumanism is more skeptical of this field, articulating concerns around the potential for discrimination and disruption of genetic diversity. Mind uploading and digital consciousness are areas of research that seek to explore the possibility of transferring human consciousness into digital or virtual space (let's recall the movie "Transcendence"). Transhumanists see this as a way to achieve immortality and to create new forms of existence. Posthumanists are more cautious, emphasizing the ethical and existential implications of such a radical transformation.

Consequently, we can introduce some ethical considerations:

- The notion of enhancing human capabilities through technology raises several ethical concerns. Critics of transhumanism argue that these technologies will inevitably create new forms of inequality, with only the wealthy able to access the most radical enhancements. There are also questions regarding the creation of technological elites, with those who have enhanced themselves beyond the biological norm exerting undue power over those who have not.

- Posthumanists consider the potential for new forms of inequality to emerge in a world of advanced technology. The development of AI for example may lead to a future in which most jobs are automated, leaving many people without a means of supporting themselves. The creation of biologically enhanced individuals may also create a new kind of caste system where those lacking enhancements could be seen as inferior or even subhuman.
- Proponents of transhumanism argue that humanity is not bound by its biology and that technological augmentation represents the next logical step in our evolution. On the contrary, posthumanists aim at challenging the very notion of what it means to be human. Critics of posthumanism argue that this skepticism toward technological progress is a form of conservatism that any substantive analysis of the benefits and risks associated with technological advancement.

Beyond posthumanism and transhumanism, I think that we cannot exclude a sort of "compatibility" between AI and human intelligence [4]. We well know the classical debate on AI after the circulation of the famous Chinese room mental experiment introduced by Searle, who continued his critical discussion by another thought experiment about the possibility for a society of robots [5]. The conclusion of Searle's argument is that we can surely provide a computational explanation of human intelligence but the notion of meaning cannot be implemented in AI.

Recently I discussed a philosophical view that seems to entail a more compatibilist interpretation. The so-called "Analytic Pragmatism" (AP) introduced by Brandom in his book *Between Saying and Doing* [6] represents a view that explains what abilities can be computationally implemented and what are typical of human reasoning. Brandom criticizes the interpretation of the Turing test provided by strong artificial intelligence or GOFAI, nevertheless he accepts the challenge to show what abilities can be computationally elaborated to implement an "autonomous discursive practice" (ADP). Brandom maintains a special sort of AI-functionalism charactering his "pragmatic AI" and demonstrates that there exist primitive abilities that can be algorithmically elaborated and are not "themselves" already "discursive" abilities. There are basic abilities that can be elaborated into the ability to engage an ADP. But these abilities need not be discovered only if something engages in any ADP, namely they are sufficient to engage in any ADP but not necessary. Brandom's view could be seen as a philosophical contribution to the discussion about how to revisit some classical questions: the role of symbols in thought, the question of whether thinking is just a manipulation of symbols and the problem of isomorphism as sufficient to establish genuine semantic content fullness.

The strategy of AP is based on a "substantive" decomposition that is represented in algorithms. Any practice-or-ability P can be decomposed (pragmatically analyzed) into a set of primitive practices-or-abilities such that:

1. They've are PP-sufficient for P, in the sense that P can be algorithmically elaborated from them (that is, *all* you need in principle to be able to engage in or exercise P is to be able to engage in those abilities plus the algorithmic elaborative abilities, when these are all integrated a specified by some algorithm);

2. One could have the capacity to engage or exercise *each* of those primitive practices-or-abilities without having the capacity to engage in or exercise the target practice-or-ability P.

For instance, the capacity to perform long divisions is substantively algorithmically decomposed into primitive capacities to perform multiplication and subtraction and this means that we can learn how to perform multiplication and subtraction without yet having learned division. On the contrary, the capacities to differentially respond to colors or to wiggle the index finger are not "probably" algorithmically decomposable into more basic capacities as they are not things we do *by* doing something else. There exist *reliable differential capacities to respond to environmental stimuli* that are shown by humans, animals and machines; but we can intend ADP typical of human practices that are "inferential" and strictly correlated with capacities to deploy an autonomous vocabulary (namely a vocabulary typical of human linguistic practices) based on recognizing incompatible properties and commitments.

3 AI as a Tool

We can observe a sort of "pragmatic view" of AI in the thoughtful critical observations in the speech Pope Francis gave at the last G7 in Greece [7]. A weak "compatibilist view" could be derived because of the fact that all human capacities are created. He starts from the fact that artificial intelligence is above all else *a tool*. And it goes without saying that the benefits or harm it will bring will depend on its use. In the case of human beings we can observe a *techno-human condition due to the fact that* human beings have always maintained a relationship with the environment mediated by the tools they gradually produced. So, it is not possible to separate the history of men and women and of civilization from the history of these tools. We can observe that humans create a social ontology in continuity and beyond our biological nature (Searle). According to Pope Francesco, we experience a state of "outwardness" with respect to our biological being: we are beings inclined toward what lies outside-of-us, indeed we are radically open to the beyond. Moreover, we cannot exclude a compatibility between human intelligence and AI [8]: "Sacred Scripture attests that God bestowed his Spirit upon human beings so that they might have 'skill and understanding and knowledge in every craft' (*Ex* 35:31)" Science and technology are therefore brilliant products of the creative potential of human beings but at the same time it is urgent to provide an ecology of human creativity [9, 10]. Indeed, artificial intelligence arises precisely from the use of this God-given creative potential.

As we know, artificial intelligence is an extremely powerful tool, employed in many kinds of human activity: from medicine to the world of work; from culture to the field of communications; from education to politics. At the same time, we recognize the risks associated with its fast development and use that will contribute to the creation of a new social system characterized by complex epochal transformations. It is true that artificial intelligence could enable a democratization of access to knowledge, but, at the same time, it could generate a greater injustice between advanced and developing nations or between dominant and oppressed social classes, raising the dangerous possibility that a "throwaway culture" be preferred to a "culture of encounter".

According to Francisco, the very powerful technological progress, that makes artificial intelligence at the same time *an exciting and fearsome tool*, requires a deep reflection regarding the challenges it presents. However, we could clearly observe that artificial intelligence is above all else *a tool* and the benefits or harm it will bring will depend on its use. "Our ability to fashion tools, in a quantity and complexity that is unparalleled among living things, speaks of a *techno-human condition*: human beings have always maintained a relationship with the environment mediated by the tools they gradually produced. It is not possible to separate the history of men and women and of civilization from the history of these tools. Some have wanted to read into this a kind of shortcoming, a deficit, within human beings, as if, because of this deficiency, they were forced to create technology" [11].

It is true that we can use tools not only for the the good. For example, when our ancestors sharpened flint stones to make knives, they used them both to cut hides for clothing and to kill each other. We can say the same for the use of more advanced technologies, such as the energy produced by the fusion of atoms, as occurs within the Sun, which could be used to produce clean, renewable energy or to reduce our planet to a pile of ashes. Artificial intelligence, however, is a still more complex tool. "I would almost say that we are dealing with a tool *sui generis*. While the use of a simple tool (like a knife) is under the control of the person who uses it and its use for the good depends only on that person, artificial intelligence, on the other hand, can autonomously adapt to the task assigned to it and, if designed this way, can make choices independent of the person in order to achieve the intended goal [8].

Machines make technical choices among several possibilities based either on well-defined criteria or on statistical inferences. On the contrary, human beings not only choose, but in their hearts are capable of deciding. A decision is what we might call a more strategic element of a choice and demands a practical evaluation because of its consequences for many people. Human reflection has always spoken of wisdom, the *phronesis* of Greek philosophy and, at least in part, the wisdom of Sacred Scripture. For Francisco, we need to ensure and safeguard a space for proper human control over the choices made by artificial intelligence programs: human dignity itself depends on it. We must absolutely take into consideration the tragedy that is armed conflict; it is urgent to reconsider the development and use of devices like the so-called "lethal autonomous weapons" and ultimately ban their use. Our ethical task is to enhance ever greater and proper human control. *No machine should ever choose to take the life of a human being.*

AI is indeed a tool designed for problem solving and works by means of a logical chaining of algebraic operations, carried out on categories of data. These data are compared in order to discover correlations and to improve their statistical value. The deep learning processes allow these operations on the search for further data and the self-modification of its calculation processes. For example, being classified as part of a certain ethnic group, or simply having committed a minor offence years earlier (for example, not having paid a parking fine) will actually influence the decision as to whether or not to grant home-confinement. Francisco notices however that human beings are always developing, and are capable of surprising us by their actions and this is something that a machine cannot take into account.

Applications of new AI programs will be increasingly equipped with the capacity to interact directly (*chatbots*) with human beings, holding conversations and establishing close relationships with them. These interactions seem often pleasant and reassuring, since these artificial intelligence programs will be designed to learn to respond, in a personalized way, to the physical and psychological needs of human beings. We must not forget that AI is not another human being and cannot propose general principles. We must also recognize that algorithms designed to solve highly complex problems are so sophisticated (like the quantum computer) that it is difficult for programmers themselves to understand exactly how they arrive at their results.

Francisco considers one last area in which the complexity of the mechanism of the Generative AI clearly emerges. It provides excellent tools available for accessing knowledge, which even allow for self-learning and self-tutoring in a myriad of fields. We are surprised by the easily available online applications for composing a text or producing an image on any theme or subject [11]

Students are especially attracted to this, but make disproportionate use of it when they have to prepare papers. Students are often much better prepared for, and more familiar with, using artificial intelligence than their teachers. Yet they forget that, strictly speaking, so-called generative artificial intelligence is not really "generative". Instead, it searches big data for information and puts it together in the style required of it. It does not develop new analyses or concepts, but repeats those that it finds, giving them an appealing form. Then, the more it finds a repeated notion or hypothesis, the more it considers it legitimate and valid. Rather than being "generative", then, it is instead "reinforcing" in the sense that it rearranges existing content, helping to consolidate it, often without checking whether it contains errors or preconceptions. In this way, it not only runs the risk of legitimizing fake news and strengthening a dominant culture's advantage, but, in short, it also undermines the educational process itself. Education should provide students with the possibility of authentic reflection, yet it runs the risk of being reduced to a repetition of notions, which will increasingly be evaluated as unobjectionable, simply because of their constant repetition.

Francisco observes that we seem to be losing the value and profound meaning of one of the fundamental concepts of the West: that of the human person as the *ethos* concerning the understanding of the value and dignity. It is a fact no innovation is neutral and technology has a huge impact on human society. It represents a form of order in social relations and an arrangement of power, thus enabling certain people to perform specific actions while preventing others from performing different ones. But the constitutive power dimension of technology always includes the worldview of those who invented and developed it. For AI programs to promote the good and a better tomorrow, they must always be aimed at the good of every human being. Moreover, an ethical decision is one that takes into account not only an action's outcomes but also the values at stake and the duties that derive from those values. He welcomes the important results in the so-called "algor-ethics".

Francisco reflection on the effects of AI on humanity leads us to consider the importance of "healthy politics" so that we can look to our future with hope and confidence. In *Laudato Si' the Pope* observes that global society is suffering from grave structural deficiencies that cannot be resolved by piecemeal solutions or quick fixes so a healthy politics, involving different sectors and skills, is capable to oversee this process. "An economy that is an integral part of a political, social, cultural and popular program directed to the common good could pave the way for 'different possibilities which do not involve stifling human creativity and its ideals of progress, but rather directing that energy along new channels" [8].

4 Conclusion

We want to conclude with some further reflections on AI technology changing our habits. To speak of what it means to be human and thus to reflect on our singular status as beings who possess both freedom and responsibility means to speak about ethics and enhancement of politics. Pope Leo XIV calls AI the "exceptional product of human genius" and we must never forget human dignity. Moreover, AI cannot interfere with the proper human and neurological development of young people and children. As we could observe, especially Generative AI, has opened new horizons on many different levels, including enhancing research in healthcare and scientific discovery, but also raises troubling questions on its possible repercussions on humanity's openness to truth and beauty, on our distinctive ability to grasp and process reality.

Pope Leo XIV made this observation in his message to the Second Annual Rome Conference on Artificial Intelligence which was published on Friday. AI has an extraordinary potential to benefit the human family butthe rapid development of AI "also raises deeper questions" concerning the proper use of such technology in generating a more authentically just and human global society. It is an exceptional product of human genius, but remains a "tool". Acknowledging and respecting what is uniquely characteristic of the human person is essential to the discussion of any adequate ethical framework for the governance of AI. We are concerned for children and young people, and the possible consequences of the use of AI on their intellectual and neurological development. They must be helped, "in their journey towards maturity and true responsibility, " underscoring they "are our hope for the future." Our society's well-being, "depends upon their being given the ability to develop their God-given gifts and capabilities, and to respond to the demands of the times and the needs of others with a free and generous spirit."

According to Pope Leo, no matter how extensive, AI must not be confused with intelligence No generation, has ever had such quick access to the amount of information now available through AI. AI must not reduce person's openness to the ultimate questions of life that reflects an orientation toward the True and the Good." It is a fact that AI has been used in positive and indeed noble ways to promote greater equality, but it still retains the possibility of its misuse for selfish gain at the expense of others, or worse, to foment conflict and aggression. An important purpose of the Church is to contribute to a serene and informed discussion of these pressing questions by stressing above all the need to weigh the ramifications of AI in light of the "integral development of the human person and society". To speak of the well-being of the human person not only materially, but also intellectually and spiritually, means safeguarding the inviolable dignity of each human person and respecting the cultural and spiritual riches and diversity of the world's peoples. In conclusion, the benefits or risks of AI must be evaluated precisely according to this superior ethical criterion, to avoid a certain "loss" or "at least an eclipse" of what is human, and saying this "challenges all of us to reflect more deeply on the true nature and uniqueness of our shared human dignity."

References

1. Castellano, D.: How AI will Change our Daily Habits? https://medium.com,
2. Ranish, R., Sorgner, S.L. (eds.): Post—and Transhumanism: an Introduction. Suhrkamp, Frankfurt (2014)
3. Hofkirchner, W., Kreowski, H.J.: Transhumanism: the Proper Guide to a Posthuman Condition or a Dangerous Idea? Springer, Cham (2021)
4. Giovagnoli R.: The relevance of language for the problem of representation in Giovagnoli R., Dodig-Crnkovic (eds.) Represention and Reality in Humans, Other Living Organisms and Intelligent Machines, Springer Sapere, Cham, pp. 235–245. (2017)
5. Giovagnoli, R.: Computational ontology and deontology. In: Muller, V.C. (ed.) Philosophy and Theory of Artificial Intelligence, pp. 179–186. Springer Sapere, Cham (2013)
6. Brandom, R.: Between Saying and Doing. Oxford University Press, Oxford (2008)
7. Pope Francis: Address of his Holiness Pope Francis G7 Session on Artifical Intelligence Greece, 13–15 June 2024, https://www.vatican.va
8. Pope Francis: Message for the 57th World Day of Peace, 1 Jan (2024)
9. Magnani, L.: Discoverability. Springer. Cham, The Urgent Need of an Ecology of Human Creativity (2022)
10. Magnani, L.: The urgent need of an ecology of human creativity. In: Castellana, M. (ed.) Idee, pp. 45–62. Special Issue on the Encyclical Letter Laudato Si (2020)
11. Gehlen, A.: L'uomo. Feltrinelli, Milan, La sua natura e il suo posto nel mondo (1983)

A Multidimensional Study on Consumer Acceptance of Social Bots

Liang Wang(✉) and Xuelin Wang

College of Marxism, Xi'an Jiaotong University, Xi'an 710049, China
wangg85@163.com

Abstract. Social robots are reshaping the interaction between humans and technology, but consumer acceptance remains a key challenge for their widespread adoption. This article explores the role of technology perception, interaction design, and ethical issues in shaping consumer attitudes toward social robots. Firstly, technological trust is a core element; a lack of trust can lead consumers to question data privacy, security, and technological transparency, which in turn affects technology adoption. Secondly, the design of interaction modes is crucial for user experience, including voice interaction, emotional recognition, and cultural adaptability, all of which directly impact consumers' willingness to establish long-term relationships with robots. Additionally, ethical issues such as privacy protection and data misuse cannot be overlooked; if ethical design fails to keep pace with technological development, it may lead to a crisis of trust among consumers.

Keywords: social robots · technological cognition · interaction methods · ethical trust · consumer acceptance

1 Introduction

With the rapid development of artificial intelligence and human-computer interaction technology, social robots are moving from laboratories to real-world scenarios such as homes, schools, and hospitals. Although significant progress has been made in technology, such as natural language processing, multimodal perception, and emotional recognition, the actual acceptance of consumers shows a complex and diverse trend [1]. Whether consumers are willing to establish lasting interactive relationships with robots is influenced by their comprehensive perception of robot capabilities, interaction experiences, and ethical risks. Research suggests that balancing technology transparency, natural interaction capabilities, and ethical design is the core path to enhancing consumer trust and acceptance.

Consumer acceptance of social robots involves multiple influences of technological perceptions, interaction styles and ethical factors. First, technology trust is key. Lack of trust may lead to consumer skepticism about data privacy, security, and technology transparency, thus weakening the willingness to adopt the technology. Second, the design of the interaction style is critical to the user experience. Whether it is voice interaction, emotion recognition, or cultural adaptation, the interaction style directly affects consumers'

R. Giovagnoli et al. (Eds.): IS4SI 2025, SAPERE 81, pp. 163–167, 2026.
https://doi.org/10.1007/978-3-032-31732-2_13

willingness to establish a long-term relationship with a social robot. In addition, the ethical issues raised by social robots, such as privacy protection and data abuse, should not be ignored, as is the case with. If ethical principles do not keep pace with technological advances, it may lead to a crisis of consumer trust and social opposition.

Existing studies have mainly focused on the feasibility analysis at the technical level, but have paid insufficient attention to the complex psychosocial mechanisms behind consumer acceptance. To fill this research gap, this paper explores the core drivers of consumer acceptance of social robots from the three dimensions of technology perception, interaction mode and ethical factors, aiming to answer the following questions: (1) What is the construction path of technology trust? (2) How do consumers' cultural and individual preferences for interaction modes affect technology acceptance? (3) How do ethical issues construct consumer attitudes in different cultural contexts? By exploring the above questions, this paper expects to provide insights for technology design, academic research, and policy making in enterprises, as well as to promote better integration of social robots into diverse social environments to create a higher quality of life experience for human beings.

2 Trust Construction Through Technical Cognition and Progressive Interaction

Trust is widely recognized as a central determinant in consumers' acceptance of social robots. Importantly, this trust does not emerge in a single moment, but is instead constructed through a dynamic interplay between technical cognition and ongoing interactive experiences. To fully understand how trust develops in this context, it is essential to consider both the foundational role of technological perception and the gradual deepening of relational engagement over time.

At the outset, technical cognition forms the initial basis of trust. Technological perception is the root of trust construction, which hinges on consumers' perceptions of social bots' capability, reliability, and transparency [2]. Specifically, consumers assess whether a robot demonstrates competence, reliability, and transparency. First and foremost, competence involves the robot's ability to accomplish tasks efficiently, such as through accurate voice recognition or effective problem-solving. Without a sufficient display of functional capability, initial trust is unlikely to be established. Moreover, reliability becomes critical as interactions proceed. Consumers expect consistent and predictable behavior across different encounters, and this consistency reinforces their sense of control and security. In addition, transparency plays a pivotal role. When users understand how a robot functions—when its operations are clearly explained and potential errors are addressed openly—they are less likely to feel uncertain or disoriented. Therefore, these three dimensions—competence, reliability, and transparency—together constitute the necessary preconditions for trust to take root. However, technical knowledge alone is not enough. Trust is not built overnight, but is a dynamic process that evolves over time and interaction.

According to the three-stage trust development model proposed by Lewicki and Bunker, trust progresses from calculus-based (focused on rational assessments) to knowledge-based (built on experience and predictability), and eventually to identification-based (characterized by shared values and emotional connection) [3]. Thus, as consumers accumulate interactional experiences, their trust in social robots increasingly depends not just on technical performance but also on behavioral consistency, emotional responsiveness, and perceived alignment with human values. In this way, trust transitions from a purely cognitive judgment to a more affective and socially situated phenomenon.

Ultimately, trust construction in the context of social robotics reflects a dual logic: from technical to emotional, and from initial evaluation to deepened connection. Technical cognition provides the starting point, offering the foundation for early interaction. As engagement becomes richer and more sustained, the trust relationship evolves—strengthened by transparency and consistency, but ultimately completed by empathy and social presence. This layered process highlights the importance of designing robots not only with advanced technical capabilities but also with the capacity to engage in human-like interaction that supports the gradual, dynamic development of trust.

3 Impact of Interaction Patterns on Consumer Acceptance

The design of interaction modes is a key factor influencing consumers' acceptance of social robots, and cultural backgrounds and individual preferences together shape consumers' technology acceptance paths. We synthesize the research perspectives of natural interaction, multimodal interaction, and feedback mechanisms to illustrate how they affect user acceptance.

First, natural interaction and cultural sensitivity. Natural interaction ability is an important factor in enhancing consumer satisfaction. Natural interaction abilities, such as voice tone, non-verbal expressions (facial expressions, gestures), and context understanding, greatly enhance the user's sense of immersion and realism [4]. However, interaction preferences vary across different cultural backgrounds: high-context cultures (like China and Japan) emphasize emotional cues and hints, preferring gentle and subtle robot behaviors; while low-context cultures (like the United States and Germany) lean towards direct and efficient information exchange. Embedding this cultural sensitivity into design can effectively enhance user satisfaction and willingness to accept [5].

Second, multimodal interaction and individualized needs. The design of multimodal interaction that integrates multiple channels such as speech, vision, and touch can meet the needs of consumers with different personalities. Research has found that extroverted individuals prefer diverse and frequent interaction modes, while introverted individuals tend to favor structured and low-interference communication styles. Additionally, users with high technological literacy have a positive attitude towards complex interactions, while novice users focus more on the intuitiveness of the interface and the ease of use [6].

Third, feedback mechanisms and dynamic adaptation. Real-time feedback is essential for optimizing the interactive experience. For example, in educational settings, social robots can adjust the pace of lessons based on students' expressions and tone of voice, thereby improving teaching efficiency. Feedback mechanisms not only enhance the user's sense of control, but also strengthen the proactivity of interaction and the foundation of trust between humans and robots. Additionally, the consistency between the robot's behavioral personality and user preferences is an important factor in enhancing users' willingness to use the robot over the long term. Through machine learning and user modeling, social robots can achieve contextual response adjustments and habit prediction, thus improving the specificity and likability of the service [7].

4 How Ethical Issues Construct User Acceptance

The first challenge is the issue of privacy. Whether consumers' privacy rights can be adequately protected during interactions with social robots is an important premise for acceptance. Robots need to handle language data, behavioral habits, and personal preferences, but the potential risks of data breaches can lead to consumers feeling repulsed by robots. You may have heard that your smart speaker might be secretly listening to your conversations, or that the free game app you just downloaded can access your phone's location data. The lack of clear data boundaries and security mechanisms can easily lead to a collapse of trust. Adequate protection of privacy is the foremost barrier for users to confidently accept social robots.

The second challenge is the issue of responsibility attribution. When a robot makes an error or misjudgment that results in harm, the attribution of responsibility often falls into a gray area. Currently, two main approaches have been proposed in academia: one is the "technological owner liability" system, analogous to how pet owners are responsible for animal attacks; the second is the "empowerment subject approach," which grants advanced artificial intelligence a status of limited liability [8]. Regardless of the chosen pathway, the construction of the legal and ethical framework serves as a long-term institutional guarantee for consumer trust. At the same time, social robots often embed moral judgment modules in their anthropomorphic design, such as "avoiding harm" or "prioritizing assistance to the vulnerable," but whether this is equivalent to human ethics remains a subject of debate. Some studies suggest that granting robots moral personhood may enhance their social acceptance, but simultaneously blurs their instrumental nature [9].

Lastly, how ethical issues are addressed is closely related to cultural background. There are differences in whether social robots are viewed as "human-like subjects" in different cultures. In the West, discussions about robot rights and freedoms focus more on individualism and the value of subjectivity; in contrast, Eastern societies generally view robots as social tools with service functions, emphasizing their role in collective interests and social order, reflecting Confucian ethics of "harmony" and "role obligations" [10].

Therefore, the construction of a moral framework for artificial intelligence cannot be divorced from cultural context. In the context of globalization, cross-cultural ethical adaptation and institutional coordination will become key issues driving the coexistence of technology and society. This not only requires an understanding of local ethical concepts, but also necessitates the integration of considerations of "cultural translatability" in technological design and regulatory formulation, in order to achieve compatibility between universality and diversity.

5 Conclusion

In summary, consumers' acceptance of social robots is influenced by a combination of technological understanding, language interaction, and ethical factors. Key points to enhance acceptance include: first, increasing technological transparency and optimizing the naturalness and cultural adaptability of language interaction; second, balancing functionality and emotional expression in multimodal interactions; third, strengthening ethical standards and clarifying the legal framework for privacy protection and accountability. Future social robots need to develop in a coordinated manner between technology and ethics to become more efficient and trustworthy social tools.

Acknowledgments. This research was funded by the National Social Science Foundation for Later-Stage Funding: Research on the Ethical Risks of Social Robots' "Anthropomorphization", grant number 23FZXA011.

Disclosure of Interests The authors have no competing interests to declare that are relevant to the content of this article.

References

1. Bartneck, C., Belpaeme, T., Eyssel, F., Kanda, T., Keijsers, M., Šabanović, S.: Human-Robot Interaction. (2024). https://doi.org/10.1017/9781009424202
2. Kaplan, A., Haenlein, M.: Rulers of the world, unite! The challenges and opportunities of artificial intelligence. Bus. Horiz. **63**(1), 37–50 (2020). https://doi.org/10.1016/j.bushor.2019.09.003
3. Hancock, P.A., Billings, D.R., Schaefer, K.E., Chen, J.Y.C., de Visser, E.J., Parasuraman, R.: A meta-analysis of factors affecting trust in human-robot interaction. Human Factors: The Journal of the Human Factors and Ergonomics Society. **53**(5), 517–527 (2011). https://doi.org/10.1177/0018720811417254
4. Hall, E.T.: Beyond Culture. Anchor Press, Garden City, New York (1976)
5. Nomura, T., Kanda, T., Suzuki, T., Kato, K. (2008). Prediction of human behavior in human-robot interaction using psychological scales for anxiety and negative attitudes toward robots. IEEE Trans. Robot., 24(2), 442–451. doi:https://doi.org/10.1109/tro.2007.914004
6. de Graaf, M.M.A., Ben Allouch, S.: Exploring influencing variables for the acceptance of social robots. Robot. Auton. Syst. **61**(12), 1476–1486 (2013). https://doi.org/10.1016/j.robot.2013.07.007
7. Breazeal, C.: Toward sociable robots. Robot. Auton. Syst. **42**(3–4), 167–175 (2003). https://doi.org/10.1016/s0921-8890(02)00373-1
8. Gunkel, D.J.: Robot rights. (2018). https://doi.org/10.7551/mitpress/11444.001.0001
9. Santoni de Sio, F.: Mark Coeckelbergh, AI ethics, Mit press, 2021. Sci. Eng. Ethics. **27**(4) (2021). https://doi.org/10.1007/s11948-021-00323-8
10. Li, D., Rau, P.L.P., Li, Y.: A cross-cultural study: effect of robot appearance and task. Int. J. Soc. Robot. **2**(2), 175–186 (2010). https://doi.org/10.1007/s12369-010-0056-9

Experience Ecological Data: A Piece of Systems Ecology

Martina R. Fröschl(✉)

Digital Arts, Science Visualization Lab, University of Applied Arts Vienna, Vienna, Austria
martina.froeschl@uni-ak.ac.at

Abstract. As the Anthropocene accelerates, AI-driven approaches to ecological data are redefining how we observe and interpret complex natural systems and our immediate surroundings. At the same time, there are new tools to capture experiences of an area. The invited talk at the "Hybrid Workshop in the framework of Social Information Gatherings at the International Society for the Study of Information (IS4SI) Summit 2025" was about the also at the workshop exhibited artwork "A Piece of Systems Ecology". Therein a combination of personal impressions of the area of Santa Barbara and interviews with systems ecology researchers open up new perspectives. Reconstruction algorithms used in Gaussian-splatting and classical photogrammetry enable visualizations of 3D captured artifacts and therefore ecological narratives. AI-powered tools such as text-to-speech synthesis and text-to-3D-modeling were used to generate Augmented Reality (AR) storylines accessible to field experts and other audiences. Case examples of ecological topics in the AR installation from coastal and terrestrial sites demonstrate ecosystem dynamics and personal perspectives. The present paper summarizes the ecological topics addressed in the digitally created immersive art installation and their presentation.

Keywords: Systems ecology · Artificial intelligence · Ecological data · Immersive art · Augmented reality · Gaussian splatting · Photogrammetry

1 Introduction

In an age of accelerating environmental transformation, the ways we perceive, measure, and represent ecosystems are undergoing profound change. The Anthropocene, a term describing the planetary epoch of human-driven alteration, has made evident that observation and interpretation of ecological processes cannot be separated from the technologies that mediate them (Crutzen 2002; Latour 2018). Artificial intelligence (AI), data visualization, and immersive technologies increasingly play crucial roles in how scientific and artistic communities co-create ecological understanding. The project "A Piece of Systems Ecology"[1] (Fig. 1) explores this dynamic intersection through an artistic research

[1] https://www.scivizlab.com/a-piece-of-systems-ecology.

R. Giovagnoli et al. (Eds.): IS4SI 2025, SAPERE 81, pp. 168–172, 2026.
https://doi.org/10.1007/978-3-032-31732-2_14

process that integrates data capture, AI-based reconstruction, and human experience. Developed as part of an artist residency at the NCEAS (National Center for Ecological Analysis and Synthesis) in Santa Barbara, the project reflects on how experience and information can be combined into immersive visual and auditory narratives that show samples of the living complexity of ecosystems.

2 Theoretical Background: Systems Ecology and Information

Systems ecology provides a framework for understanding ecosystems as complex adaptive systems–dynamic networks of energy flow, feedback, and self-organization (Odum 1994; Ulanowicz 1997). This systems perspective aligns with the cybernetic traditions that inspired early information theory, connecting ecology, computation, and cognition (Bateson 1972). In contemporary practice, AI extends these concepts by introducing autonomous pattern recognition and generative synthesis into ecological observation and research in general. AI accelerates the analysis of the research literature and scientific visualization processes.[2]. By combining empirical ecological data with personal experience and artistic interpretation, it challenges the dichotomy between objective measurement and subjective encounter. The project shows a photogrammetric way of accessing complex environmental systems experimentally.

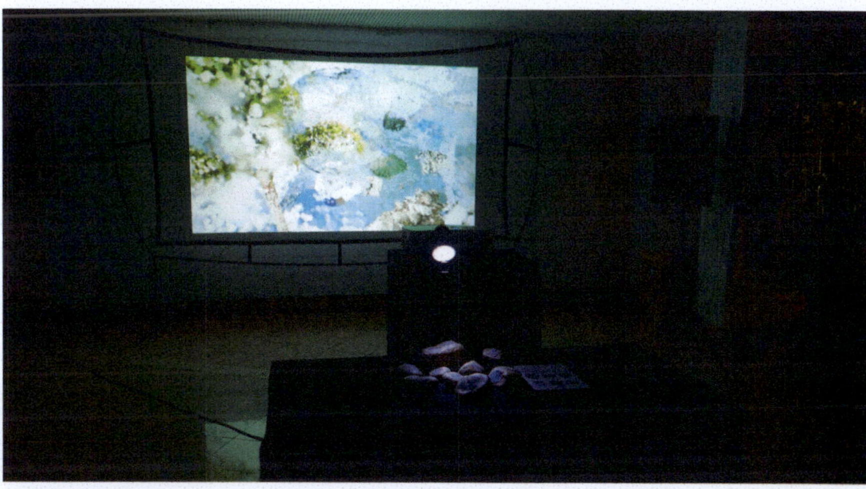

Fig. 1. The installation with the name "A Piece of Systems Ecology" at the Viennese part of "hybrid workshop in the framework of social information gatherings at the International Society for the Study of Information (IS4SI)" Summit 2025.

[2] https://nceas-learning-hub.github.io/ai_for_nceas/s04_ai_lit_review.html.

3 Artistic and Technical Methodology

3.1 Fieldwork and Data Collection

The project began with field visits around Santa Barbara, California, a region representing costal ecosystems and many parks with typical Californian vegetation. Observations were collected through two modes:

Personal Impressions: Audio recordings, photographs, and written reflections documented sensory and affective responses to landscapes–sounds of ocean surf, light changes, vegetation textures, and traces of human activity.

Expert Interviews: Systems ecology researchers were interviewed during an artist residency at NCEAS about their fields of expertise. The research topics were coastal nutrient cycles, terrestrial biodiversity, data visualization challenges, fires, marine ecosystems and their approach to systems ecology. Their insights framed the ecological context and informed the interpretive and narrative approach.

3.2 3D Reconstruction and AI Augmentation

Physical artifacts, plant structures, and landscape fragments were 3D captured using photogrammetry and Gaussian-splatting techniques (Kerbl et al. 2023). These methods reconstruct scenes and scenery details from multiple photographic inputs, allowing data-driven ecological storytelling. Subsequently, AI-based tools were employed to expand the data for the creation of the AR installation:

- An online text-to-3D-model[3] generated a speculative element that visually extends the datasets - the mermaid 3d model.
- Text-to-speech synthesis[4] gave voice to transcribed interviews.
- Augmented Reality (AR) interfaces merged the reconstructions into layered storylines accessible via mobile devices or head-mounted devices through a VRChat world.[5]

This multimodal integration aimed to produce an immersive ecological experience–one where data, voice, and environment captures are combined into a narrative system. The commentary of the NCEAS scientists and the field observations of the participants were integrated into the AR narrative. This interplay of objectivity and subjectivity re-framed ecological data, which often consists of objective, unemotional statistics, as more experiential knowledge.

[3] https://www.meshy.ai/.
[4] https://ttsmaker.com/.
[5] https://vrchat.com/home/launch?worldId=wrld_97e420f4-a187-4ceb-82c7-a2c6544a4e87 (Fig. 2).

Fig. 2. The installation with the name "A Piece of Systems Ecology" as a virtual reality installation in a VRChat world. This is a screen capture of the standard avatar in the interactive application.

4 Discussion: Digital Captures as Agents in Ecological Sense-Making

The project questions how we conceptualize data visualization and environmental representation. In "A Piece of Systems Ecology" sensory fragments are assembled into cohesive ecological narratives, each chapter presented on a locally sourced stone (Fig. 3). The project creates a set of situated, subjective information (Haraway 1988): knowledge anchored in embodied experience and subjective interpretation. Moreover, the use of reconstruction algorithms reveals both the potential and limitations of AI-enhanced observation. Gaussian-splatting fills spatial and scanning gaps but also introduces certain aesthetics which are typical for this rendering technique of photogrammetric data. In this sense, the artwork becomes a critical site for interrogating how the digital mediates ecological reality and presents captures and memories in time.[6]

5 Conclusion

A "Piece of Systems Ecology" proposes a new mode of ecological communication–one that merges systems thinking, artistic practice, and AI usage. By transforming field data and human interview statements into an immersive environment, it supports a deeper understanding of the interconnectedness between observation, data, and interpretation. The project demonstrates

[6] https://media.ccc.de/v/38c3-spatial-interrogations-or-the-color-of-the-sky.

Fig. 3. Installation detail of "A Piece of Systems Ecology" shows a visitor interacting with the augmented reality stones in the exhibit to read the ecological narratives presented in the project.

how immersive technologies can translate complex environmental processes into accessible sensory experiences. Future work will further explore the integration of ecological datasets, machine learning interpretation, and narrative-based AR interfaces as tools for collaborative, artistic and environmental research.

References

Bateson, G.: Steps to an ecology of mind. University of Chicago Press (1972)

Crutzen, P.J.: Geology of mankind. Nature **415**(6867), 23 (2002)

Haraway, D.: Situated knowledges: the science question in feminism and the privilege of partial perspective. Fem. Stud. **14**(3), 575–599 (1988)

Kerbl, B., Kopanas, G., Leimkühler, T., Drettakis, G.: 3D Gaussian splatting for real-time radiance field rendering. ACM Trans. Graph. **42**(4), 1–14 (2023)

Latour, B.: Down to Earth: politics in the new climatic regime. Polity (2018)

Odum, H.T.: Ecological And General Systems: An Introduction to Systems Ecology, University Press of Colorado (1994)

Ulanowicz, R.E.: Ecology, the Ascendent Perspective. Columbia University Press (1997)

AI, Power, and Global Order

AI, Strategic Autonomy, and the Geopolitics of Microchips: a Critical Peace Studies Perspective

Josef Mühlbauer(✉)

University of Graz, Global Governance, Graz, Styria, Austria
Josef.muehlbauer@uni-graz.at

Abstract. This article examines the geopolitical competition between the United States and China over artificial intelligence (AI) and semiconductor technologies through the lens of critical peace studies (CPS). It argues that this rivalry extends beyond economic and military dominance, generating new forms of structural violence and accelerating the militarization of technological development. Microchips are analyzed as the foundational material infrastructure of digital power, with control over their supply chains representing a key instrument of discreet geopolitical influence. The paper critiques the contemporary pursuit of strategic autonomy (SA) by actors like the European Union (EU) as often replicating the competitive, zero-sum logic of the US-China confrontation, rather than fostering cooperative and equitable alternatives. Ultimately, the article proposes pathways toward de-escalation and peace-oriented governance, including confidence-building measures, inclusive multilateral frameworks, supply-chain diversification, and binding international agreements to subordinate technological development to human rights and ecological sustainability.

Keywords: Peace Studies · Critical Realism · Artificial Intelligence · Strategic Automomy · Geopolitics · Microchips

1 AI, Geopolitics and Microchips - Introduction

Artificial intelligence (AI) and microchip/semiconductor technologies have become the central functional infrastructure of our modern world. Especially microchips are the tiny but powerful brain inside nearly every electronic device, from smartphones and computers to medical or military equipment. They determine economic competitiveness,

R. Giovagnoli et al. (Eds.): IS4SI 2025, SAPERE 81, pp. 175–180, 2026.
https://doi.org/10.1007/978-3-032-31732-2_15

military superiority, the resilience of digital governance, and the ability of states to shape global norms or even the global order [1]. Against this backdrop, the geopolitical rivalry between the United States and China increasingly resembles what some scholars call a "techno-political cold war" [2], a competition not only for markets and military capacity but for hegemony. This article draws on the themes raised at the symposium organized by Raffaela Giovagnoli, Irena Mostowicz and Tomáš Sigmund in the framework of the International Society for the Study of Information (IS4SI) biennial Summit 2025. Especially the ideas of (discreet) power, and growing dependence on AI, are crucial aspects to situate contemporary geopolitics. This article is situated within a critical peace studies framework. It argues that the AI competition between the US and China generates new forms of structural violence, accelerates the militarization of technological development, and creates a global race for strategic autonomy (SA) that risks further fragmenting the international order.

Critical peace studies (CPS), with its focus on the structural roots of conflict [3], pp. 9–16, discourses of security, and power asymmetries, provides a lens that uncovers the deeper dynamics at play, namely AI is not only a neutral technology but an instrument of power projection, norm-building, and global governance. SA, previously defined largely in economic or military terms, now increasingly relies on algorithmic infrastructures and access to semiconductors, creating new vulnerabilities and forms of interdependence.

This article proceeds by outlining the foundations of the US-China rivalry, analyzing AI's function as an instrument of (global) dominance, discussing microchips as the material backbone of geopolitical competition, and exploring how AI reshapes the struggle for SA. The conclusion reflects on possible pathways to de-escalation and peace-oriented governance.

1.1 Critical Peace Perspectives on AI, Geopolitics and Microchips

CPS distinguishes itself from traditional, "negative" peace (the mere absence of direct violence) by advocating for "positive" peace: the presence of social justice, equity, and the elimination of structural violence [4]. Structural violence refers to the harm inflicted by unjust social, economic, and political structures that prevent individuals from realizing their potential. From this vantage point, a world riven by intense military rivalry, economic exploitation, and pervasive inequality is not peaceful, even without open warfare. The US-China competition in AI and semiconductors is a potent engine of such structural violence. It redirects colossal human, financial, and intellectual resources towards zero-sum contestation rather than collaborative solutions to global challenges like climate change, poverty, and pandemic preparedness. This race is not merely about whose algorithm is faster or whose chip is more powerful; it is about whose technological ecosystem will set the standards, control the infrastructure, and ultimately, shape human behavior and global power relations for decades to come. CPS emphasize that conflicts often emerge when rising powers challenge existing power structures and narratives of legitimacy. The US perceives China's technological rise as a threat to its hegemonic stability, while China interprets US containment policies as attempts to prevent its rightful place in the international system. In this dynamic, AI functions as both a symbol and mechanism of global status.

The foundation of the modern AI ecosystem is the semiconductor. Often called the "oil of the 21st century" [5] this analogy fails to capture its true strategic significance. Oil is a commodity; chips are the physical manifestation of the digital capital. Control over the chip supply chain represents the ultimate form of discreet power in the global economy. This power is not always exercised through overt force but through the subtle, pervasive shaping of what is possible for other actors.

The global semiconductor supply chain is a monument to complex interdependence. It spans design (dominated by the US firms like NVIDIA, AMD, and Intel with their ARM and x86 architectures), manufacturing equipment (led by the Netherlands' ASML), and ultra-advanced fabrication (concentrated in Taiwan's TSMC and South Korea's Samsung). This interdependence, however, is asymmetrical. The United States has weaponized this asymmetry through sweeping export controls, aiming to cripple China's ability to procure high-end chips and the tools to make them. This is a clear exercise of structural power, designed to stunt the technological development of a rival. China on the other hand bans export of critical minerals, especially germanium and gallium, which are key to the semiconductor industry. With this power play China aims to signal, that it is one of the biggest powers that can shape global politics, even through force if necessary. In regard to the Chinese-owned chipmaker Nexpedia, that is based in the Netherlands, Dutch authorities have, for the first time ever, in October 2025 invoked "Cold War-era" legislation (citing national security) to take the control of this Chinese microchip factory. As of mid-November 2025, the Dutch government had handed back control of Nexperia to China. These selected examples only show the importance of microchips and the geopolitical implications.

2 Strategic Autonomy in the Digital Age

The concept of SA particularly as pursued by the European Union and other mid-sized powers, is a direct response to this US-China duopoly. It represents a desire to avoid being a pawn in the geopolitical "grand chess game" and to retain the capacity for independent decision-making. Regarding microchips and the current tech race, the EU is aiming for stable supply chains, more self-reliance and more investments in the tech sector. However, from a CPS perspective, the current pursuit of SA is often a flawed and reactive endeavor. It accepts the fundamental premise of the tech race—that the world is a dangerous, competitive arena where technological supremacy is the key to survival. In trying to build its own chip fabs or develop its own AI models, Europe is not challenging the violent structure of the competition; it is merely trying to secure a better position within it. It risks replicating the same logic of domination, just on a smaller scale.

The pursuit of autonomy through technological sovereignty or "technological nationalism" [6] creates an excess of meaning around the technology itself. Chips and AI are imbued with near-mystical significance as the guarantors of sovereignty, obscuring the more fundamental questions: Autonomy for what purpose? To dominate others, or to collaborate more effectively? To create a fortress, or to build commons that are useful for everybody? Genuine SA, in a positive peace framework, would not be about technological self-sufficiency in the service of national ego and private interests. It would be about autonomy to choose cooperation, to redirect technological development towards human needs, and to build resilient (which is especially important in times of climate change), distributed networks of innovation that resist domination by any single power. The current discourse, trapped in the logic of the US-China race, makes this emancipatory form of autonomy nearly unthinkable.

2.1 Strategic Autonomy as a Response to AI's "Discreet Power"

AI's rapid diffusion has altered the nature of power in international politics. While traditional security threats were grounded in territorial, material, and military vulnerabilities, contemporary threats increasingly originate from informational infrastructures and opaque algorithmic systems. The call for SA, particularly within the European Union, emerges partly as a response to the subtle but far-reaching influence AI exerts on societies. AI systems operate within everyday life in ways that escape conscious awareness, for example, curating information flows, predicting preferences, nudging behavior, and structuring decision-making environments. This "discreet power" alters political cognition at scale. At the state level, discreet power translates into fears of algorithmic dependency, particularly when key infrastructures are foreign-controlled. These dependencies manifest in several critical domains such as the reliance on foreign-controlled cloud providers and software ecosystems or the exposure to different surveillance regimes, and not to mention the vulnerabilities regarding critical supply-chains in hardware and semiconductors/microchips. Such dependencies challenge states' capacity to control the informational environments in which public discourse, political mobilization, and democratic decision-making take place. As a result, states increasingly frame AI policy not only as a matter of digital competitiveness but also as a matter of cognitive sovereignty. SA becomes a protective measure aimed at insulating national decision-making from the subtle influence of foreign technological infrastructures.

In Austria one type of defence strategy against fake news, bots, disinformation and echo chambers is the so called "Geistige Landesverteidigung" [7]. Cognitive defense is a crucial part of Austrias political education, because it supports the dissemination of democratic values, peace, and neutrality. Comprehensive national defense is understood as a non-military contribution to peacekeeping in a world where the use of military force—including in Europe—remains a reality. This means taking the task of peace education and security and defence policy seriously, critically examining enemy images, and developing strategies to effectively counter hate speech and fake news.

Ensuring autonomy thus requires of course more than just educational measures. One needs to regulate data and cloud infrastructures, while developing domestic or in the European context at least regional and European AI capabilities. Another aspect is the mitigation of the exposure of foreign surveillance and data extraction. Here comes to mind the secret U.S. government surveillance program run by the National Security Agency (NSA) called PRISM, or the Chinese PRC Cybersecurity Law from 2016 and Chinese tech companies such as ByteDance (TikTok) and Huawei as well as the 200 million to 500 million CCTV cameras (Skynet System) in mainland China [8]. To sum it up, there is a growing need to response to the discreet power of AI.

3 Pathways toward Peace

CPS emphasizes that conflict or even war is neither predetermined nor structurally irreversible, instead, it seeks to illuminate pathways for transforming antagonisms and contradictions into conditions for cooperation. In the context of accelerating US-China competition over AI, the aim is not simply to diagnose emerging risks but to identify concrete strategies that reduce tensions, mitigate misperceptions, and enable cooperative global governance.

This section of the article outlines several policy pathways that could de-escalate the AI race, drawing on principles of transparency, multilateralism, technological pluralism, and democratic accountability. One potential avenue for reducing tensions lies in confidence-building mechanisms analogous to Cold War–era nuclear agreements. Although AI differs fundamentally from nuclear technologies being dual-use, rapid in development, and embedded in civilian sector trust-building infrastructures, like the semiconductor industry, remain crucial. Hotlines for algorithmic incidents could enable immediate communication when AI systems malfunction, misbehave, or generate ambiguous signals that might otherwise be interpreted as hostile action. This is highly important in the light of autonomous weapons systems, where a small miscalculation can lead to an escalation. Mutual notifications of major AI tests would help prevent misinterpretation of routine evaluations as offensive preparation. Joint risk assessments on a global level could create shared understanding of emergent dangers, from autonomous weapons to runaway decision-support systems. Finally, no-first-deployment agreements for autonomous weapon systems would mirror the logic of no-first-use declarations in nuclear policy: a pledge not to deploy destabilizing AI capabilities preemptively.

These selected measures that were mentioned would not resolve structural rivalries between Washington and Beijing, this is for sure, but they could reduce uncertainty, one of the primary drivers of escalation, in technologically mediated security dilemmas [9], pp. 2–10. Transforming the AI race requires more than bilateral trust-building, it demands institutionalized global governance. An inclusive multilateral framework would need to harmonize ethical principles, defining minimal norms for transparency, fairness in regard of competition, and human oversight. It could also promote transparency through shared auditing mechanisms or international peer reviews of high-risk AI systems. As mentioned earlier in this article, semiconductor supply chains constitute the structural backbone of the AI race, and current tensions are amplified by strategic dependencies, most notably, the concentration of advanced fabrication capacity in Taiwan. Ensuring Taiwan's safety is thus essential for global stability, not only for China and the US, but for most of the world. A strategy of shared investment in diversified chip production, spanning the US, China, Europe, and key Asian economies, could reduce the geopolitical value of single strategic chokepoints. Distributed manufacturing would lower incentives for coercion or conflict while reinforcing global economic resilience. Such diversification does not require abandoning national security considerations, rather, it fosters a more stable balance between security and interdependence. This is why the concept of SA is so crucial in today's politics. A deeper transformation requires contesting the assumption that an AI arms race is inevitable. CPS highlights that technological trajectories are shaped by political choices, institutional arrangements, and public narratives. Civil society, academic researchers, and ethical consideration must cultivate a counter-narrative, one that frame AI and semiconductors as shared global infrastructures, not proprietary assets in a winner-takes-all competition. Resisting technological determinism opens political space for alternatives, namely, demilitarization, global governance, and the reorientation of innovation toward social and ecological needs. Finally, durable peace requires governance architectures that reflect global power pluralism rather than great-power dominance. Current institutions are either outdated or constrained by geopolitical rivalries. New frameworks must be inclusive, enabling participation from smaller states, civil society, and transnational stakeholders. Politics must adapt to the current multipolar world. Most importantly, these frameworks must move beyond soft-law ethics statements. Legally binding agreements, such as treaties prohibiting lethal autonomous weapons or imposing strict limits on mass surveillance, are necessary to place technology under democratic control. Not an easy task at all. The goal is not merely to prevent misuse but to ensure that technological development aligns with human rights, justice, and ecological sustainability.

Disclosure of Interests. The author has no competing interest to declare that is relevant to the content of this article.

References

1. Miller, C.: Chip War: the fight for the world's most critical technology. Scribner Publisher (2022)
2. Hecht, G.: Entangled Geographies: empire and technopolitics in the global cold war. The MIT Press (2011)
3. Mühlbauer, J., Lakitsch, M.: Kritische Friedensforschung. Diagnosen, Konzepte, Analysen. Mandelbaum Verlag (2024)
4. Galtung, J.: Strukturelle Gewalt. Rowohlt Taschenbuch Publisher, Beiträge zur Friedens- und Konfliktforschung. first edition. Leipzig (1975)
5. Fernández-Lasquetty, J.: A Data Economy: the Oil of the 21st Century. IE University. https://www.ie.edu/liquid-learning/data-economy-oil-21st-century/ (2020)
6. Cieślik, E., Zamojska, A.: Techno-nationalism in global value chains in the technology sector. European Review. (2025). https://doi.org/10.1017/S1062798725100318
7. Bundes-Verfassungsgesetz Art. 9a. BGBl. Nr. 1/1930 zuletzt geändert durch BGBl. I Nr. 106/2005. European Legislation Identifier (ELI) https://www.ris.bka.gv.at/eli/bgbl/1930/1/A9a/NOR40068035 (2016)
8. Gershgorn, D.: China's 'sharp eyes' program aims to surveil 100% of public space. One Zero. (2021) https://onezero.medium.com/chinas-sharp-eyes-program-aims-to-surveil-100-of-public-space-ddc22d63e015
9. Beckerman, C.: Is there a cyber security dilemma?, J. Cybersecur., 8(1), (2022) doi:https://doi.org/10.1093/cybsec/tyac012

Author Index

R. Giovagnoli et al. (Eds.): IS4SI 2025, SAPERE 81, p. 181, 2026.
https://doi.org/10.1007/978-3-032-31732-2

The manufacturer's authorised representative in the EU is Springer
Nature Customer Service Centre GmbH, Europaplatz 3, 69115 Heidelberg,
Germany. If you have any concerns regarding our products, please
contact ProductSafety@springernature.com

Printed and bound by CPI Group (UK) Ltd, Croydon, CR0 4YY
21/09/2026
02219993-0010